T0248232

Praise for
THE BUSINESS BEHIND THE SONG

"BRICKELL WAS A MENTOR to MercyMe prior to him signing us as a client in the early 2000s, and he has championed us along the entire way. If it weren't for his in-depth knowledge about the music industry, I don't know if I would be doing full-time music. There is no one better to write a book and teach others about the ins and outs of the industry than Scott Brickell."

—**BART MILLARD,** *Lead Singer of the Band MercyMe*

"SCOTT BRICKELL has been my manager since 2015 and a day has not gone by where I have not been thankful for his leadership, his wisdom, and his honesty. Not only does he tell it like it is, he explains to me 'why it is' what 'it is' from a lifetime of hard work and experience. His name and reputation are always met with respect, but his heart outshines his skill sets."

—**MICAH TYLER,** *Singer of "Walking Free" and "I See Grace"*

"I HAVE HAD the privilege of working with Scott Brickell for over fifteen years, and you simply can't put a price tag on the well of wisdom and knowledge that I gained from his friendship and expertise. Not only does he know the ins and outs of this business, but he's trustworthy, which makes him the most qualified to share all he has learned during his years in the industry."

—**PHIL WICKHAM,** *GRAMMY Award-Nominated Artist*

"SCOTT BRICKELL has helped guide the careers of some of our biggest artists. A manager like Brickell touches every aspect of an artist's career from songwriting to making records to touring and even personal finances. He is someone you want to be in the trenches with, loyal and steady. I've enjoyed watching him help his artists make wise decisions while navigating the competitive and volatile music industry."

—**TOBYMAC,** *GRAMMY Award-Winning Christian Artist*

"ABSOLUTE HONESTY and true compassion. These are the traits that have guided Brick as a man—in business and now as an author. He has written a book that should be required reading for anyone considering running away and joining the circus. In writing a what-to-expect letter to his younger self, this book can be taken as a warning about or an invitation to the music business."

—**TRACE ADKINS,** *ACM Award-Winning Artist, and Actor*

"BRICKELL IS A LEGEND! Scott's knowledge and wisdom and his generosity with both have been invaluable to me throughout my entire career. It is no surprise he'd pull the curtain back so we can all benefit from his expertise and experience and get to see the passion and heart behind it all."

—**DAVID CROWDER,** *Lead Singer of the Band Crowder*

"AS AN ARTIST, I'm thankful for the practical management philosophies Brickhouse Entertainment passed on to me. As an academic, I'm thankful this book can help provide clarity in an obscure industry. As a friend, I'm thankful that Scott Brickell has courageously shared his expertise, questions, and heart in these pages."

—**MORIAH SMALLBONE,** *Artist, Actress, and Producer*

"IN THESE PAGES, Scott gives away his secret playbook in an effort to see others succeed. Page after page, Scott lays out a holistic strategy that can garner the best results. *The Business Behind the Song* is a must-read for anyone in the music industry, and I recommend it wholeheartedly."

—**DAVID NASSER,** *Author, Speaker, and President of For Others*

"RARELY DO YOU FIND a music industry veteran with more experience, tenacity, and passion. I've walked with Brickell for decades and his commitment to navigate, serve, and protect his artists is incomparable. No one lives out "the business behind the song" better."

—**MARK STUART,** *Lead Singer for Audio Adrenaline,*
Speaker, and Founder of the Hands and Feet Project

THE BUSINESS
BEHIND THE SONG

NAVIGATING A CAREER
IN THE MUSIC INDUSTRY

SCOTT BRICKELL

WITH ROBERT NOLAND

Forefront
BOOKS

Published by Forefront Books.
Distributed by Simon & Schuster.

Library of Congress Control Number: 203901149

Print ISBN: 978-1-63763-097-6
E-book ISBN: 978-1-63763-098-3

Cover Design by Jake Brickell
Interior Design by Mary Susan Oleson, Blu Design Concepts

This book is dedicated to my family: My wife, Dr. Stacy, who I love with all of my heart, whose tenacity is endless, and who has always supported me, loved me, and encouraged me to follow my crazy ideas; my kids, Jake and his wife, Emily, Sara, Mary-Clair, and Ruthie, whose love is my strength; my dad, Jay "Pop-pop," for teaching me work ethic, and my mom, Ruth Ann "Bubba," I miss you. I love you. Thank you for being my motivation to actually complete this book, knowing you were never able to finish yours . . . but I don't miss the horrendous six years of piano you forced me to take, even though I gained an appreciation for music from it; and my older sister Geri for being the best sister a younger brother could ask for.

Finally, I want to dedicate this book to the younger version of me who wished he had a resource like this that would save ten years of having to figure out the music business.

So, to all of you who are new to music, here's your fast track.

Enjoy!

CONTENTS

*Any word included in the Glossary of Terms is marked the first time by an asterisk.

BEFORE YOU BEGIN

For the Novice:

If you know nothing about the music business but think you may want to be an artist or are interested in some other aspect of the industry, I wrote this book with you in mind. My team and I worked very hard to make no assumptions that you might know a term or understand a very common concept in the music business. That's why I defined words and gave you a glossary. My 101 approach in this book is very intentional and will help you build a wide base of knowledge about this crazy business, where I have made my home for three decades.

For the Newbie:

Maybe you're already in Nashville, L.A., New York, or even London, and are a year or three into trying to get a break in music. Even though you may have learned some things the hard way, I hope taking a comprehensive look at the industry with me can help you, and maybe even accelerate you in your career. I want you to have several moments throughout the book where you say to yourself, "Oh! That makes so much sense now." Or, better yet, "I can do that! I get it. I'll get to work on that."

For the novice and the newbie, I want these pages to offer both offensive and defensive strategies by encouraging you to be proactive in new ways, while also helping you see how you can protect yourself from the traps and pitfalls that happen to so many.

For the Pro:

Even if you know a lot of the info I have offered here and might even disagree with my approach on a few things, I hope you can get your money's worth out of something you find of value here. As I state in the book, the industry is a big, dysfunctional family and, as your older and uglier brother, I hope I can encourage you to keep pressing on in your own career.

To everyone:

Another major goal I have for this book is to encourage young people to become managers, agents, producers, engineers, tour managers, public relations reps, and so on. Very few who start out hoping to become artists get to experience that dream. Within the ocean of jobs available in the music industry, there are so many great careers that can actually make for a better life than some artists have. You can have more of a nine-to-five gig, while still being a part of great art and making a difference through music.

That's exactly why, following each chapter, I have included a list of jobs that are associated with the industry role you will have just read about. These span from very specific to loosely associated. You may start this book thinking you want to be an artist or a producer, but once you dive into the actual nuts and bolts of what they do, you could realize that's not really your thing. At the same time, you could be drawn to some other area of the music business that gets your motor running. It's far better to spend time figuring out what we love to do and work hard to find the right career that allows us that opportunity. We can all have a more joyful life and be happier people, and in the end, more of a good hang.

I bet that, right now, you can name several people who are always negative, complaining, disgruntled, and frustrated. I would also bet that whoever you named, a major reason for their bad attitude is because they are working a job they don't enjoy. One of the best pieces of advice I give these days is to work really hard to try to make sure that your job lines up with who God created you to be. But too often, people don't spend the time when they are younger to take personality tests, accept internships, take classes, and make sure that the job they end up doing is the job that they were made to do from their core being.

Once any of us start down the path of chasing money, it's hard to shift gears when we realize we don't really enjoy what we do. But by then, you have rent or a mortgage, a car payment, and dating or marriage expenses. You're trying to do all of these things at a job that you don't really enjoy, but life is cranking up, and you're getting caught in the never-ending cycle of "stuff you gotta do." Therefore, you go with what is in front of you, which might be waiting tables, working at your dad's tire shop, working on the family farm like I did, or something else that really isn't you.

To tie a bow around all of this, the lists at the end of each chapter will help give you an idea of the wide range of opportunities and areas where you can find your calling and engage in jobs within the music industry. This could end up being your career that will put a roof over your head, provide a living for your family, put your kids through college, allow you to have a community, enjoy the field in which you work, and most of all, love your life.

Lastly, I want to encourage you to take your time reading the book and make sure you understand each role and responsibility before you move on. It's not a sprint, but a marathon, so press on and find your higher calling.

I think back to a line from one of the major hooks of Audio Adrenaline's hit that was voted Song of the Decade by *CCM Magazine* for the 1990s. Years ago, I discovered there was lots and lots of room in this "big, big house" called the music business. If you decide you want in, I believe there's room for you too. So, come on . . . let's take a tour together and find your place.

CHAPTER ONE

NOTHING'S CHANGED

IF YOU READ this title and thought to yourself, "That's not true! The music business has changed drastically over the last two decades," I am here to tell you it hasn't!

Let me explain:

I have been in the music industry for over thirty years. In that time, I have:

- Traveled across the U.S. and 15 countries on six continents.

- Stood side-stage and watched my artists perform in every historic U.S. venue, from the Hollywood Bowl in Los Angeles to Radio City Music Hall in New York and everywhere in between.

- Sat beside artists I managed as they heard their name called to walk onstage to receive a Grammy, American Music Award, Dove Award, and other industry accolades.

- Had the privilege of meeting cultural icons like Bono, Muhammad Ali, and David Letterman, along with sports heroes such as Ben Roethlisberger and Terry Bradshaw.

- Experienced you-couldn't-write-stuff-this-good events, like Trace Adkins portraying me in the film *I Can Only Imagine*, which brought in $17 million on opening weekend, totaled $85 million at the box office, and grossed over $110 million dollars to date.[1]

Granted, there are certainly some glamorous moments after you reach a certain level of success in the music business. But there are *far* more, shall we say, dues-paying circumstances, especially in the early years. Like the time an artist's van was overheating in the middle of nowhere, and with no water, we had to pour our own urine into the radiator to try and make it to the show. Then there was the time I nearly died from a carbon monoxide leak in another artist's vehicle. (Explains why I slept so well that night.) Then, of course, there have been countless all-night drives with little to no sleep to get to the next show and hit the ground running, the eighteen-hour days of up-to-my-neck admin work that no one else wanted to do, and the being told no or "that will never work" over and over and over again.

I Didn't See *That* Coming

Growing up, I was into sports. *Yeah, I was a jock.* From elementary to high school, I was on the swim team and played football, but my main sport and passion was always basketball. My sophomore year, I was a starter on the varsity team, and I played all the way through junior college. My dad and the junior college coach have always been best friends. In the summers, the coach's son and I would help with the basketball camps he hosted—as many as four weeks of boys' camps and three weeks of girls' camps. His son and I assisted and demonstrated drills.

Following junior college and a transfer to Baylor University in Waco, Texas, I tried to walk on the basketball team, but that didn't work out. Always being up for a new challenge, one day I went over to the Baylor marina on the Brazos River and began learning how to windsurf. I took to it quickly and went on to be twelfth in the nation in collegiate windsurfing in 1991. Becoming proficient at that sport landed me a job working several weeks every summer at Kanakuk Kamps, a Christian sports camp in Branson, Missouri, which is where I met my wife, Stacy.

I'm sharing my sports highlight reel for you to see that a music career was *never* on my radar. My interests and focus were clearly on sports. One time in college, I did try a guitar class, but, well, let's just say I figured out quickly that playing an instrument was not my thing *at all*.

As for my life goals and dreams growing up, assuming the NBA probably wasn't in my future, when I was twelve years old, I felt like I was being called into the ministry and wanted to become a youth pastor. Investing my life in helping change other people's lives just seemed right to me. But then, sometime later in my high school days, the lure of the business world caught my attention. My Plan A morphed into graduating college with a business administration degree and going to work for Texas Instruments, which at the time was a market leader in consumer, industrial, and military electronics.

This next part of my story brings up another key life lesson: you never know when a relationship or connection is going to come into play to alter your course.

In school, there was a guy named Brian Becker, who was five years older than me. Brian and I were always on the swim team, but he was in high school when I was going into middle school. Due to the age difference, we weren't friends, but we knew of each other because we were both top swimmers in our respective divisions.

The summer I was seventeen, the student ministry at our church went to camp in Van Buren, Missouri. On the last night, Brian showed up to perform a concert. Being a talented singer and keyboard player, he had decided to go into Christian music following his graduation from college.

After his show, I wanted to say hi and catch up, but Brian was quickly swarmed by students for autographs and pictures. Always being one to stay busy and seeing he had no one to help him with his gear, I went onstage and started packing up his equipment. I found the cases, matching up what went where. He had a couple of keyboards, stands, speakers, a mic, and some lights—enough to fill up the back of his small box truck.

I had all his gear packed up and saw that he was still talking, so I went over and asked him for his keys. Obviously distracted, he just tossed them to me without thinking. I backed his van up to the pavilion stage and grabbed a couple of the camp guys to help me load out*. Brian had graduated from Mizzou with a computer and electrical engineering degree and was super-organized. He had everything labeled, along with a laminated diagram taped just inside the back of the truck, showing the exact order and placement of how to pack his gear.

As we got the last case in, I realized his merch* was still set up at the back of the pavilion. I went and grabbed an armload of his items, walked up to the group standing around him, and announced, "Hey, folks, we're packing up, so this is last call on Brian's stuff. It's now or never." Over the next few minutes, as he kept visiting with students, I sold a total of $368 worth of merchandise. (A good night of sales for artists back in that day.) I packed up the rest of his merch in the van and went back to give him his keys and a fistful of cash.

After the last person had walked away and it was just Brian and me, he was surprised when he saw what all I had done, and he began to thank me profusely. Realizing who I was from our days at school and the swim team, we caught up and had fun reminiscing. As we were shaking hands to leave, never one to be shy about saying what's on my mind, I offered, "Hey, if you ever need any help on the road, I'd be glad to go out with you to help you drive, set up and tear down your gear, and sell T-shirts . . . for free." I intentionally emphasized the "for free" part. I was already working without pay for my dad on the farm. But Brian's truck had air-conditioning; dad's tractor didn't. If I was going to work for nothing in the blistering heat of summer, I thought I might as well get to see the country, traveling in a vehicle with cold AC.

But here's the ironic part of the story with Brian. I hadn't seen him in a very long time when he came to the camp. But over the next week while he was back home, we randomly bumped into each other on five occasions. Every time, I reminded him that I would love to go out and be his roadie . . . *for free*.

Here's what happened on the fifth and final "coincidence." To get your car tags renewed in our town, the line was always at least two hours long, no matter what day or time you chose to go. Being a young man with a healthy appetite, I swung through the McDonald's Drive-Thru on the way there and picked up two Big Macs, two large fries, two large orange drinks, and, of course, "Yes, ma'am, I *would* like two cherry pies with that! Thanks for asking!"

With my huge McDonald's sack and drink carrier, along with my car-tag paperwork, I got in line to wait it out while scarfing down my two-thousand calorie lunch. Lo and behold, who walks up directly behind me to renew his tags? None other than Brian Becker. When he realized it was me, he grinned and said, "Well, I guess I'm *supposed* to take you on the road, huh?"

Looking to close the deal any way I could, I asked if he was hungry. After all, I had bought two of everything and McDonald's would still be open when I was done, right? Being a typical starving artist, Brian quickly agreed to the free lunch. So, for the next two hours while inching up slowly in the line, we ate and talked nonstop.

As agreed, I began to go out on the road with Brian every chance I could—weekends, holiday breaks, and for some camps in the summer. While he always covered my expenses, I wasn't on his payroll. I kept my end of the deal on the "for free" part.

Fast-forward to my graduation from Baylor. Following my Plan A I told you about earlier, I sent my resume to Texas

Instruments, specifically their Dallas office for the position of Quality Control Manager. But my fast track to success and security went off the rails when, to my surprise, TI passed on me in the *first* interview. The career I had thought was set in stone dropped like a rock. I was suddenly thrown back to square one. And unfortunately, there's no college course to prepare you for *those* moments.

But sometimes the earth-shattering noes are the best things that can happen to us. Then, there are the times that you realize what you have been searching for has been right under your nose all along.

Doing the only thing I knew to do, I decided to move back home to work on the family farm. But I also asked to talk with Brian. We set up a meeting at the local Pizza Hut. (Food was obviously a priority for us both in those days.) During that conversation, I told him that I couldn't sing. I couldn't play an instrument. But then I shared how, after having felt a call to the ministry at twelve years old, for a while thinking I was going to be a youth pastor, and then getting shoved off the first rung of the ladder to corporate success, maybe working in Christian music was somehow my answer. Going out on the road the past few years to help him may have been a divine appointment because I realized I could be involved with both ministry *and* business. (In my experience, I have found that God never wastes anything, and He cares about our dreams.)

At the time, Brian's career was on the rise. He had signed with Benson Records, which was one of a few major Christian labels*. (In 1997, Benson was sold to Provident/Zomba and later to Sony.) Soon after our conversation, Brian brought me on as his paid road manager. From that point, I kept working for my dad on the farm, but was also working for Brian part-time.

Eight months later, while in Nashville, Brian's manager asked if we could talk. He made me an offer to come to work for him during the week, helping all the artists on his roster, then go out with Brian on the weekends as I had been doing. Seeing this as my opportunity to finally go into the music business full-time, I accepted. For the first year, because money was tight, I slept on the manager's couch in his apartment.

Bottom line is the career I thought I was supposed to have never materialized, and a random night at a camp with a fellow athlete I knew from my hometown eventually launched me down the road and led to all the accomplishments I told you in my opening paragraphs. My calling, which I had sensed at twelve, was also connected to this new direction because I would work with artists who reached students. Everything came back around and fit together.

Funny how life works, huh? Like I said, sometimes the noes turn out to be the best things for us because they free us up to say yes to the *right* opportunity. It's also vital to be kind and treat everyone with respect because you never know when someone who is *not* on your radar now could become crucial to the trajectory of your life later. For me, that was Brian Becker.

Mastering Multitasking in Music City

I went to work for Chapel Hill Management in Nashville, Tennessee, a one-owner, one-man company that provided career oversight and navigation for various artists and producers* as well as financial services for select artists. This was no internship where you occasionally got sent out to fetch someone's latte. I was his first hired employee, so he immediately threw me into the deep end with no lessons and no life vest.

I was tasked with what was essentially project management for their producers. My responsibilities were to:

- Book the recording studio*
- Book the engineer(s)*
- Hire the session players*
- Hire the background vocalists* (BGV*)
- Coordinate instrument cartage*
- Be the miscellaneous catchall guy and do anything needed to support the recording project.

Another crucial role I was given early on was the responsibility for overseeing the accounting for an album's budget. Along with the per-project work, I was also doing bookkeeping for two of the top up-and-coming Christian artists at that time—dc Talk and Newsboys. Through this experience, I gained specific business knowledge and expertise in details like handling company start-ups, filing for federal tax ID numbers, getting signature cards signed for banks, and setting up escrow accounts. I became lightning-fast on the popular accounting software QuickBooks, reconciling credit card statements and bank statements, and balancing accounts. A comprehensive on-the-job education, for sure.

Being a fast learner, getting good at taking care of details, and multitasking quickly garnered me a solid and trusted reputation with all those I worked for and with. Since the music business is full of creatives and visionaries, from the heads of record labels* and management companies to songwriters and artists, being meticulous and having a strong work ethic goes a long way. They needed someone like me to connect the dots, cross the T's, and dot the I's. Nothing's changed. They still do!

If a recording session was scheduled to load in* at 8:00 a.m. and begin at 10:00 a.m., I arrived early to hand out checks to everyone slated for that session. Independent hired guns tend to work better when the check is in their pocket. That said, many in the industry, particularly record labels, would require an invoice *after* the session and then often wait sixty to ninety days (or longer) to pay. But a little ignorance on my part, while just trying to do good business, played in my favor. When people got a call from me, they would book the sessions of the producer I represented over someone else's because they knew a check would be waiting for them upon arrival. As they say, money talks.

But I realized my get-paid-when-you-play method was unusual the day that I called Guy Penrod, a well-known artist and sought-after background vocalist, who was late for a session. I caught him right as he was walking into a local theme park with his family. I apologized, thinking I had made a mistake with the scheduling. He assured me I had not, that he would change his plans and head to the studio right away. To which I said, "Hey, it's okay. We can do this one without you." He laughed and responded, "Are you kidding me? I know you'll have a check waiting that will pay for my family's day at the park. I'll be there in fifteen minutes!" His comment made me realize what I didn't know about waiting to pay, yet also showed me I had gained one of the best reputations in town among the production project managers.

Our office for Chapel Hill was in the basement of TobyMac's home. At that time, Toby was in dc Talk, before he became a legendary solo artist. I would work during the day, running all over town to studios, and then at night I would take care of the admin work—all the financial and scheduling details. In 1992, Toby was writing for their *Free at Last* record. He would arrive home from the studio late at night. Pulling into his garage, Toby would have to walk through the basement where I was working to take the stairs up into his home. Many times, he would come in, collapse onto a sofa in the office, and start talking business. I was trying to finish up after an eighteen-hour day, and he was ready to get some answers on their financial state.

To head Toby off and provide him with some numbers to allow myself to finish the day's work, I started leaving out a file folder of items for him to look through. Issue resolved. Client happy. Job done. That's the key to *any* business, really. But as I burned the midnight oil in his basement and was available when he wanted to talk, I was also unknowingly endearing myself to Toby and his team. As they prepared for the tour to support the *Free at Last* album, they offered me the role of tour accountant, and I accepted, leaving Chapel Hill and going to work for True Artist Management.

For a while, Toby and the team had been working on the possibility of bringing me on, but I was unaware of those discussions. The crucial connecting point for this move was that it would introduce me to their opening act on that tour—Audio Adrenaline. That connection was one of the most important moments in my career. The domino effect of commitment and hard work was in play and starting to fall in my favor.

I want to stop here and make a crucial point for you. I hope that while I have been sharing my story with you, some lightbulbs have been going off in your head. I hope you are applying *my past* to *your future*! Was it a different time? Yes. Different generation, even? Yes. Different culture and economy? Yes. But here's where personal value connected to business needs *never* change in the work environment. I'll spell it out for you in three points:

1. **Show a strong work ethic.** Even more so in today's culture, this can automatically put you at the front of the line in the top ten percent, if not five percent, *anywhere* in *any* career.

2. **Be a self-starter.** Successful people, especially visionaries and creatives, don't have the time, or will rarely take the time, to teach you the ropes. If you wait around to be told what to do, and if you won't get busy and make yourself useful, you won't last and certainly won't get promoted.

3. **Learn to multitask.** Yes, some folks are better at this than others because of personality, gifting, and background, but *anyone* can learn how to expand their bandwidth and workflow. Don't say you *can't*. Just go ahead and admit that you *won't*. If you question your ability on this point, see the first bullet above—show a strong work ethic!

Now, if you're thinking, "But Brickell, I want to be the *artist* that all the support people you're talking about are working together to make a success." Okay, well, I've got some game-changing news for you then. The most successful artists I have ever worked with started out with and still show three attributes: strong work ethic, self-starter, and multitasker, especially the ones whose careers have lasted for decades. Nothing's changed. They are all hard workers at their craft! Write the record, record the record, rehearse the tour, tour the record, all while doing press and promotion. Take a break. Do it all again. Year after year. "The life" may look glamorous on the outside, but anyone who has been more than a one-hit wonder will tell you that it can be a hard road and a tough job.

Building the House, Brick by Brick

I worked with Toby and his crew at True Artist Management for the next four years. During that time, I was immersed in the world of live events, touring, festivals, promoters, contracts, attorneys, record labels, booking agencies, and all the necessary logistics of the music business. From my start as a road manager for Brian Becker, traveling together in his box truck, playing churches and conferences, to working with some of the biggest artists of the day, living for months on tour buses, and playing arenas, I had put together a solid resume with a roster of honed skills. By this point, I had a firm grasp on how the industry worked as a whole.

By May of 1995, I was the tour manager for Audio Adrenaline and got married to my sweetheart, Stacy. Three years later, in May 1998, when Stacy and I found out we were expecting our first child, I met with the band to tell them the news and that I was going to need to get a better-paying job where I was home more. But Mark Stuart, the lead singer, had a great idea. He suggested I start my own management company and take the band on as my first artist to represent.

I gave True Artist Management a two-month notice to offer them plenty of time to transition everything I did to someone else. On August 15, 1998, I started my own company that I still run today—BrickHouse Entertainment.

After launching with Audio Adrenaline, I was looking to build my roster. Switchfoot had released their now-classic second album *New Way to be Human*. Mark Nicholas, the son-in-law of legendary producer and songwriter Charlie Peacock, told me the band was looking for management. Charlie had originally signed Switchfoot to his mainstream label, distributed by EMI. Mark helped me arrange a meeting with the band in the label's boardroom. Once I arrived, I realized I was one of many managers* they were interviewing that day.

As always, I was up front, telling them I was weeks away from my first child being born, and that I wasn't certain what my life was going to look like on the other side of starting a family. But if I did become their manager, my goal would be to help them achieve *their* goals and dreams. I asked a few questions, but mostly let them do the talking. I wanted to listen, to hear where they wanted to go as a band.

I enjoyed the time and closed by saying that I would love to work with them. But I also made it clear I would understand if they decided to go with a more seasoned manager. After all, at the time BrickHouse's doors had only been open for five months. Honestly, I left there expecting to never hear from them again. About a week later, to my surprise, they called. But when they told me their deciding factor, that was the real revelation. I was the only manager all day that listened to what *they wanted to do* versus telling them all the things that *they should do*.

I learned a powerful principle from that meeting with Switchfoot that I have utilized my entire career: Listening is both critical and crucial. People want and need to be heard. Working hard to bring one's own idea to reality is often more appealing to artists than doing half the work to bring someone else's idea to fruition.

During my time at True Artist I met a small up-and-coming band called MercyMe. I introduced them to True Artist, but they decided not to sign the band. Once I established my own company, I was free to sign whoever I wanted. So, I was fortunate that my first three artists were Audio Adrenaline, Switchfoot, and MercyMe. I'm proud to say that, to this day, those three bands are some of the most renowned and respected in their genres.

Meeting MercyMe

A story I am asked to tell quite a bit, especially because of the *I Can Only Imagine* movie, is how I first connected with MercyMe. In the fall of 1996, touring with Audio Adrenaline, we were working with the Activities Director on a date to play at Oklahoma Baptist University in Shawnee. When I called to discuss the details to try and lock it down, I told her that since we had a show the night before and the long drive in between, we couldn't arrive until noon. Because we were bringing all our own production, the window to set up and get ready would be tight.

The director told me about a local band who she wanted to open the show. She said they had a strong following in the area and were awesome. As with most artists who have been on the road for a while, local openers can be a touchy subject. We had already been burned by some other people who had assured us that someone was great and then, let's just say, the opposite turned out to be true. Because of the bad experiences, I had learned to ask some questions. Number one—are you married to, are you dating, or are you romantically interested in this person or someone in the band? Number two—are you related to this person or anyone in the band?

After the answers to these questions were a no, I asked her to send me a cassette of their music. Because, yeah, cassettes were the preferred format at the time. She sent it. I got it. I listened to it. Their music was horrible. I called her back and told her I didn't think the band would work for our show. But the lady persisted: "Would you please pray about it?" I agreed. I prayed. I didn't hear anything any different. I called her back and told her no again. But she wouldn't relent.

Finally, I asked her, "If I don't let this band open, are you going to cancel Audio Adrenaline?" Politely, she answered, "Well, I didn't want to have to say that." The handwriting was on the proverbial wall. I had to agree to her "offer." I told her, "We won't arrive until noon. We need six hours to set up and do sound check. The doors have to open at 6:00 p.m. Your band can play through our sound system but can't use our racks and stacks. They need to have all their instruments set up and ready to move onto the stage in between our sound check and doors being opened, but they can't move any of our equipment. They have to quickly get their instruments onstage in front of ours to get ready to play. Then when their set is over, they have to strike everything immediately."

On the day of the show, when MercyMe showed up, they were all great guys and fully cooperated with the plan. Audio Adrenaline finished sound check at about 5:30 or 5:45 p.m., and I told them I would open the doors to let the fans in at 6:00 p.m. The guys hustled to get their instruments onto the stage and get a fast sound check. I left the auditorium to go eat dinner backstage.

When I heard MercyMe start their set, I finished my meal and went in to listen. I walked up and stood beside the Activities Director. In all honesty, I was fully prepared to give her the classic "I told you so" . . . but I couldn't. Because she was right. The band was great. They did an incredible job of interacting with the crowd. (He was Bart.) I could tell that they had played together for quite a while, because they played like a band that had gelled. One impressive factor was that at one point Bart changed the set list, and the guys followed him and adjusted like pros.

After the show, I met with the guys. When we said goodbye, I gave Bart my business card and also gave him my cell and home phone numbers. I told him, "I know you guys can't afford a manager right now, but if you have any questions or I can help you, call me." For the next year, he called me about once a month. The second year, he began calling once a week. By the third year, he was calling almost every day. Finally, in 1999, everything came together. He wrote "I Can Only Imagine" and then Amy Grant came into the picture. For MercyMe, that's when the plane left the runway.

One Big Family

The following February our oldest child and only son Jake was born. Two years later we had Sara. Mary-Clair followed two years after that. At this point, my wife and I agreed that we were done having children. However, several years later we reevaluated that decision and knew our family wouldn't be complete without one more. And we were right. Our Ruthie arrived in May 2010, named after my mom. We're so grateful they were able to get to know each other before Mom passed away at the end of that year in December.

Thriving in Music City, I loved figuring out who industry professionals were, what they did, and how everything pieced together. From day one to today, connecting to so many amazing people has helped me understand the flow of the music business. There is a science to the art of music. There is an art to the science of music. Artist management requires understanding and navigating *both*.

In twenty-plus years, BrickHouse has managed:

- Audio Adrenaline
- Switchfoot
- MercyMe
- T-Bone
- Monk & Neagle

- Connersvine
- Phil Wickham
- Addison Road
- Sidewalk Prophets
- Matthew West
- Fee
- Moriah Peters
- Rend Collective
- Luminate
- Revive
- KB
- Citizen Way
- JJ Weeks Band
- Travis Ryan
- Micah Tyler
- Mitchell Lee
- Micah Christopher
- Iveth Luna

We also managed *The Rock and Worship Roadshow* from conception through the first six years until the production was sold to another organization. I've been on the board of the Gospel Music Association (GMA) since 2005. I have served on the Executive Committee for ten-plus years, and from 2019 to 2021, I was chairman of the board.

I have obviously established myself in Nashville, and I am

embedded in the Christian music industry. But, I have never forgotten the lessons I learned growing up on our family farm in Missouri. I learned things like work ethic, organizational skills, multitasking, personal responsibility, and character during long days bailing hay, fixing fence, and working the cattle. Early on in my career in the music industry, I attended outdoor festivals and other live events, and I would often envision, one day, hosting similar events on the same property that taught me all these life lessons. In 2005, this vision started to come to life when my dad and I converted his farm into "Brick's Off-Road Park." After four generations of farming corn to cattle, we opened the land up to dirt bikes, dune buggies, four-wheelers, and monster trucks. We've got mud holes for the rookies to play in and technical up-hill rock climbs to challenge the veterans: rolling hills, flat fields, miles of winding trails, camping facilities, and a spring-fed creek.

Turning our 450-acre farm into one of the country's best off-road park, I was able to apply my business expertise to an entirely different form of family entertainment, which attracts a completely different demographic than music. I love going there for the weekend, escaping my usual daily grind, and spending quality time with my own family, as well as our "mud family." We have experimented with live music events at the park and have plans to expand to larger events in the future, merging all my worlds.

My Hope and Goal for You

What I do in artist management is create all the spokes of the wheel between the artist and everyone connected to their career.

For years when I have been asked what a manager does, tongue-in-cheek I joke, "Managers don't do anything . . . except make sure everyone else does their jobs." But a manager is the keeper of the playbook, which makes sure everybody else understands the plan, the timing of that plan, and the execution of that plan.

I have no idea what your personal belief system may be, and I am certainly not trying to assert mine on you. But for me personally, I decided at an early age to not try and write my *own* story, but to simply get up every morning and ask God, "What am I supposed to do *today*?" Then I watch, listen, and get to work. That mindset always allowed the *best* opportunity to come my way, not the one that *I* had planned.

Over the years, I have discovered a path to teach others how to go from being a music lover with some talent to a full-fledged artist, and also help someone figure out what aspect of the music business he or she may be drawn to in the many jobs available in the industry. Countless times I have sat with a young artist, parents, investors, and in front of many university classes to help people understand what it actually takes to "do music." The average person on the outside sees the life of an artist from a one-dimensional perspective. But I'm not afraid to "pull back the curtain" and show them there is no great wizard pulling the strings. It's just hard work, determination, and passion applied to wise business principles.

I wrote this book for anyone, not just artists, who thinks they want to pursue a career in or around the music business, at any age, at any level. Even if you just want music to be a part-time passion or hobby. But hobbies don't pay the bills. There's a difference between helping out a local artist you like or being in a cover band versus finding a place in the music business that you feel lines up with your talents and then turning that into a career. You may have the ability to be an awesome booking agent,* a top label executive, or the "next big thing," but that foundation starts with understanding how the industry works together to maximize an artist's songs, brand, and career.

My hope is by the end of this book, you:

- Understand the industry, hopefully *before* you even get started,

- Learn the terminology,

- Know the goals you need to set for yourself,

- Have a clear understanding of how you can lay out a path for your future,

- Decide to get on with your own journey in the music business.

The people I know who have succeeded and sustained a career in the music business all had one major thing in common—it is also what I learned from living my own story: Don't have a Plan B. That is an absolute must in taking ownership of your career. Because if you have a Plan B, as soon as Plan A gets tough, Plan B will become your Plan A. That's just human nature. No one should want your dream to happen more than you. If I'm your coach through this book, I can't come play the game for you. You have to put in the work.

To close my story and come full circle . . . : Had I gotten

impatient and walked away from Brian that night at the camp or decided I was too good to help him out and get my hands dirty, my own music career might never have happened. No matter *what* our business may be, relationships and service are the currency through which we can best find our place in this life. I believed that truth then, and I believe it more today than ever. Keep this principle in the forefront of your mind as we walk together through the ins and outs of the music business.

I titled this chapter based on the idea that though the industry is changing dramatically in how things are done, the way that you become successful in it has not changed and will probably never change. This industry is so unique in that you get told "no" a lot and it is up to you to keep your head held high if you really want to succeed. For example, the Beatles got told "guitar groups are on the way out" and "the Beatles have no future in show business."[2] So, if arguably one of the greatest bands of all time took no for an answer, then we all would never have been able to experience the creativity that came from them. What a monumental loss that would've been. So, remember, show a strong work ethic, be a self-starter, and learn to multitask. Nothing's changed.

"Be your own artist, and always be confident in what you're doing. If you're not going to be confident, you might as well not be doing it."
—ARETHA FRANKLIN

CHAPTER TWO

THE ARTIST

If music is your dream, then no one should ever work harder than you to make it happen.

RIGHT OUT of the gate, I want to give you my definition of the word *artist**: A creative who has written or cowritten a song or songs that other people have heard and care about. An exception to this definition would be artists who are performers, like Elvis, that have never actually written a song in their career.

You may post cover* songs on YouTube. You may sing at church or weddings. You may wow your family and friends in the living room. But that's a *singer*, not an artist. So, first question based on my definition, are you a singer or an artist?

Next, I want to give you an important piece of advice. If I agreed to a meeting with you to talk about a career in music, here's the first thing I would tell you: "If you can do *anything else* other than music to make a living, do yourself a huge favor right now and go do that." If you realize you're a singer and want to just stay a singer, great. Music can be an awesome hobby, party trick, and stress reliever as you pursue other avenues of life.

I don't intend for these opening thoughts to be some kind of scare tactic, just the unbridled truth. A career in the music industry is *not* for the faint of heart. *Not* for someone who is easily offended. *Not* for someone who will give up. The music business is best pursued by a fighter. There are going to be plenty of days when you will feel like Rocky Balboa—the underdog, beat-up, cut, dizzy, and on the mat while the ref is counting.

If you do know you can walk away, be just fine, and do something else with your life, if you decide to stop reading right here, trust me, whatever you paid for this book is going to be far less money than you are likely going to burn trying to "make it." In fact, I may have just saved you thousands of dollars, a ton of time, and a lot of heartache. *You're welcome!*

I will never forget one young lady that came to an Immerse Conference several years ago. The event was a week-long crash course in Christian music that we at the Gospel Music Association once offered in the summer. During one of the Q&A sessions with industry professionals, she raised her hand. When someone on the panel called on her, she stood up, and announced, "I don't have a question, but I just want to say that I can already see what I envisioned Christian music to be, and what it actually takes to make it, are very different than I thought. I've found out what I needed to know this week, so I'm going to go back home, be grateful for this experience, and begin to pursue another path for my life." Every professional on that panel applauded and encouraged the young lady for her honesty, insight, and bravery. Remember what I said in the first chapter: Sometimes the noes can be life changing, even when they come from within our own hearts.

Alright, are you still with me? . . . Good, let's move on.

Songs: The Master Keys that Unlock Every Door

Think of five artists you regularly listen to who have had a career in his/her genre of music—pop, country, rock, alternative, hip-hop, etc.—for at least ten years. Write their names down in the spaces provided.

1.

2.

3.

4.

5.

Now that you've listed your five artists, what do you think would be the number one reason for each one's success in the music industry? Would it be: Raw talent? Producer? Record label? Manager? Booking agent? Live show? Fan base? Money invested in them? Their family? Look and style? Work ethic?

While all of these roles and factors certainly contribute to success, *none* of these are the number one reason. The answer is plain and simple. It's a song. The songs that artists are known for. S-O-N-G.

A song can become a key to unlock feelings and emotions deep inside your soul that nothing else can open. A song can cause you to travel back in time to relive a memory. A song can take you into the future to see yourself in a different place. Hear a different voice. Taste new experiences. Songs have a surreal, mystical impact on our senses, minds, hearts, and spirits like few other things in this life.

Look at your list of artists again. Chances are high that you can associate, at minimum, one massive hit for each artist. But likely several. On cue, you can sing a hit song from each artist, can't you? By heart, you know the lyrics and melody. The very reason you wrote those names down. You may have even sung a cover of one of the songs and posted it on YouTube (like hundreds, if not thousands, of other singers did too).

So, if the number one reason for success in the music business is the song, then what does it take for you to find *your* song?

First, let's cover what is not your song. You might write a great song with an amazing hook or a really clever idea, but if the words aren't believable coming from you, that's a big problem. If the message doesn't fit you, it's not your song. We see this all the time on TV vocal competitions. Some fifteen-year-old girl singing about suffering from heartache while drowning her sorrows on a bar stool. Sure, she can sing great, but the song doesn't make sense coming from her.

Not only does a song have to be great, but the person delivering the message has to be believable, relatable, and passionate about selling the lyrics. A hit has to be the perfect blend of subject matter, musical quality, a strong producer, creative style, timing in the market, the right cultural climate, relevance (musically and stylistically), and—to repeat—a good matchup with who you are.

Billboard magazine released their staff's pick of the Top 100 songs of 2020. The number one choice was "Rain on Me" by Ariana Grande and Lady Gaga, dubbing the song the year's "unofficial anthem." The staff wrote, "Its saving grace . . . [a] front-facing pop testimonial to the power of crying and persevering through your own trauma" and that it "stands apart as the song that helped millions of people cope with the uncertainty, tragedy and anxiety of an endless downpour of a year."[3] In other words, *Billboard* notes that all the components I listed above were one hundred percent on point, hitting on all cylinders, connecting with millions of people.

Because consumer awareness is enhanced by social and cultural changes, song content has to line up and speak to where people are, not where you hope they will be. Songs that break through those barriers are typically ignited by current events and social issues, just like "Rain on Me."

Over the years, I have heard young artists constantly complain, "Record labels won't talk to me because I don't have a manager" or "Booking agencies won't meet with me because I don't have a record label." Well, if you have a great song, you're believable, the subject matter is current and connectable, and you have the talent to deliver the performance on pitch with a lot of passion, everyone and everything will fall into place. Case in point, to his credit, after Jeff Moseley, founder and CEO of a Nashville-based Christian Music label, Fair Trade Services, heard "I Can Only Imagine," he took out a second mortgage on his house to make sure he had every available resource to get that song out in the strongest way possible. At the time, MercyMe had no booking agent or label, until Jeff signed them, and I had just signed on. Proof that it's all about the song.

Of course, all the "It Factor" dynamics—like personality, authenticity, and stage presence—certainly help, but the song carries the load, and everything just rides on its coattails. Legendary songwriter Harlan Howard famously described country music as "three chords and the truth."[4] He was referring to the one strength everyone knows about the genre: Great stories told through great songs can make great artists.

When the song is undeniably strong, labels jump on board, managers come to the table, and booking agents start offering shows. The song drives the momentum. Those artists you wrote down a few pages back are a success and have stayed on top because of the quality of the creative content they've consistently released. Fans will stay on the train and invite others along for the ride when they keep enjoying what the artist does. Your ability to sing their hits proves that songs connect artists with fans and fans with artists.

My experience has been that most young artists believe one of their songs is a hit when it's not, but then the reverse can also be true. They won't know, or don't know, when they *have* written a hit. Some of the most meaningful and personal songs to artists, no one else cares about. And then songs that an artist says, "Oh, I wrote that song in five minutes, and I don't really like it that much"—it's ironic how often that becomes the one he/she sings in arenas for the next twenty years. I've seen that happen time and time again.

I've also seen songs that were career-makers almost not make the record. Audio Adrenaline's lead singer's dad had to drive from Kentucky down to Nashville to tell Mark, his son, that a certain song had to make the record. The band thought it was too pop for a rock band. They were sure the song was not cool enough for their fans. But because they listened to his dad and added the song, they had a twenty-year career instead of a five-year career. Because of one song—the *right* song—"Big House."

For all these reasons, so often the first people to know a song is a hit are the fans, whether there are ten or ten thousand. On that note, let's just go ahead and get the elephant out in the middle of the room and name him: You can't play a brand-new song for your parents or significant other or grandma or BFF and expect them to say, "Wow, that is terrible. Don't let anyone else hear that." No, they all say, "That's amazing!" or "I love it!" or "You are so talented!"

In fact, be honest, that's exactly *why* you play them every single one of your songs. So you can hear them tell you those wonderful affirmations. But their opinions aren't reality at least ninety percent of the time. I once heard singer/songwriter Bob Bennett say, "People come up all the time after my shows and tell me, 'God gave me this song.' Then I hear it and know why God didn't want it anymore!" I don't care who you are, that's funny!

If you want to know how to write a great song, go back to those five artists you wrote down earlier. Look at their songs. What made you connect with them? What moves you, touches you, motivates you? Studying great songs can help you become a great songwriter.

Go Time to Go Live

So how can you get honest feedback? The answer is you need to perform your songs for people who don't know you. Total strangers. That's the only way to get an authentic response. If you can get a positive reaction from an anonymous crowd, then you are onto something. That's why a steady gig at a coffee shop, restaurant, or street corner is such a great place to hone your skills as an artist.

If you set up on the sidewalk and start singing with just an acoustic guitar, and soon a crowd gathers and forgets why they were in such a hurry, now you have a real response. And that's also how you start to build a fan base. If it's just you and a keyboard at a café, and suddenly people stop eating, stop talking, and put down their phones to listen to you, that's when you are making a genuine connection.

When you're performing your songs, don't take more time to set up the song than it takes to sing the song. In fact, don't introduce it or tell the story behind the song at all. Great songs need no setup. They speak for themselves. Let it stand on its own two feet. If one day someone hears your songs on the radio, you won't be there to set them up. Simply sing the song and let the context capture people's attention.

The next big indicator is if they come up to you afterwards to tell you they loved your set, or better yet, ask how they can find your music. When people who just heard you for the first time come up and talk to you about your songs, pay close attention to what they say. Do they bring up the same song as others or different ones? Is it the one you thought would connect with people or one that surprised you? If they talk to you about a specific song that touches them, ask why. The moments you spend listening to them share with you are incredible opportunities for market research. Companies pay big money to get that kind of feedback. If someone is offering it to you for free, get all the intel you can.

Let's say you titled a song "Growing Up," but the chorus

has the recurring word "summertime." If people keep coming up and saying, "Oh, I love that song 'Summertime,' where can I get it?" you might want to rethink the title. Fans will tell you a lot of what you need to *know*, what you need to *do*, and what you need to *not* do. Listen to them. And don't be afraid to ask questions.

You should never record and release any song until you have sung it live multiple times. You need to test, tweak, and rewrite if necessary, and then test it again. For a new artist, this rule is a must. I mentioned coffee shops, cafes, and street corners already, but here are some other potential platforms and venues:

SoundCloud* and similar platforms
You can put all the songs you want up on these platforms and then watch the streams. You'll either get them or you won't. There are plenty of stories where a song blew up and an artist was signed from one of these posts. Don't count on that. Just use this as another way to get feedback on what connects and what doesn't.

Livestream*
These events can be full productions at a studio or venue done by professionals streamed on YouTube or can be a solo performance in the living room streamed on your social media.

Writers' Round*
An event where three or four songwriters are on the stage together, taking turns performing songs they've written. (Search

"Nashville Writers Round" or "Bluebird Cafe Writers Round" on YouTube.)

Church, Civic, or City Events

Many churches, city and county governments, and other local organizations are always looking for free talent for various events. Contact your local Chamber of Commerce and let them know you're available to perform for free. Paid gigs can eventually come your way from people hearing you in these settings.

Fundraisers

Any sort of fundraising event or "telethon" where they are just trying to fill talent slots are not only great for getting an opportunity but also for giving back to your community. (And you never know who might hear you.)

Open Mic Nights*

Events where you sign up on the spot, get a number, wait your turn, and go for broke. Leave it all on the stage. You should do any and all of these that you can find as often as you can.

Open mic nights can be a great stepping stone to a writers' round. Meeting other artists and songwriters who are already involved in those circles can help you get in the door, and if you're good enough, they'll put in a good word for you.

When you go to open mic nights, don't just sing your song or do your set and go home. Your job is to hear *every* artist, pay attention to them all and their songs. Afterwards, pick out a few with whom you think you might connect, introduce yourself, and try to set up some co-writing sessions. Be brave, be confident, and put yourself out there. Don't take the noes personally. Maybe the person is too insecure or afraid to write with others? Which brings us to . . .

Songwriting 101
Make sure you don't always gravitate to the same kind of person or style of artist as yourself. If you're an introvert, write with some extroverts or vice versa. If you lean country, don't shy away from getting with a pop writer. Write with the opposite sex. Write with someone of a different race. Write with someone much younger or older. Write with two other people to check out that dynamic. (The members of country supergroup Lady A met when the three agreed to write together.) Different perspectives and diversity in creation are crucial.

So, let's say you perform a new song and don't receive a clear reaction. Possibly, you receive a negative response. That just means you should take it back home and tweak the song. Ask yourself the hard questions:

- Did it feel off somewhere in the song? Where?
- Does the chorus need a stronger hook?
- Do the lyrics need more emotional punch?
- Do the verses feel too short or too long?
- Does the melody stay in one place chordwise for too long?
- Does the chorus lift enough coming out of the verses?

Learn to take a song apart piece by piece, figure out what

works and what needs work. After several live performances and rewrites, if you aren't getting a good reaction, then it's fourth down and time to punt.

Here are two options:

Split it up into other songs. Your verse might actually be a chorus for a different song. You might have lyrics that are amazing, but the melody doesn't fit, so those become two different songs. You might end up with a first verse that fits the song, but the second verse doesn't, so you take the second and write a new song. In fact, I know of one song that was eventually split into pieces of eight new ones.

File the song away for a future cowrite. Sometimes the right writer can dig in, find some gold, and take it to a brand-new place. I've seen a great writer take two lines from an existing song and, from that, rewrite a hit. In a writing session, it's okay to say, "Hey, I have a song I want to play you that I'm not sure about. Just see if you hear a new place we could take this or if it sparks a fresh idea for you? If not, we can move on."

So, let's review: Write the song. Sing the song. Work the song. If people consistently give you a strong reaction, congratulations, you've got a winner. If not, tweak until you can't. *Got it?* Good!

The 125 Experience

One major piece of advice I have given a thousand times is that an artist needs to get a minimum of 125 shows or performances under their belt as soon as possible. These can be as simple as singing the national anthem at a civic function or sporting event. Or a house show for twelve people. Or doing a Friday night Instagram or Facebook Live. But the more you perform *live* in front of an audience, the better. Watching people's reactions in the moment is critical to honing your craft as a performer. It is also important for people to start to develop a bond with you in person. The more you can get in front of a live audience and let them get to know who you are, the more people will start to care about you, and the audience is more likely to care about your music if they first have a connection with you.

Of course, one of the biggest roadblocks to your 125 shows can be to get 125 bookings. Let's say you decide you want to sing "The Star-Spangled Banner" at a local high school football game, but what if they ask for a video of you at another high school? I suggest videoing yourself singing the anthem and then posting it on your YouTube channel. Maybe put it on your socials and tell your followers you're looking for places to perform. Having a family member, friend, or fan put in a word for you is much better than you asking for yourself. Word of mouth will always be your best friend in booking.

Your 125 shows aren't going to come together in a week or two. This is a multi step, long-term process. There will be weeks when everything falls into place and you land dates, but then weeks where it's a drought. If you know of a coffee shop or restaurant that showcases local artists, go ask how you can audition. If they never have artists perform, but you see enough room for you and your guitar in a corner, ask if they would be open to you being their first shot. No matter what, keep plugging.

During your 125 shows, you may learn and/or discover:

How to deal with all aspects of a production team. From audio, lights, video, camera to stage and road crews . . . if you do enough shows, you'll see all kinds of people:

- Easygoing vs. stressed-out

- Ducks-in-a-row vs. completely disorganized

- Consummate pros vs. well-meaning people who have no idea what they're doing

- Paid pros vs. volunteers who are just there because they want to help

- Sound engineers who are super-protective of their gear vs. a guy who just knows how to turn the power on and nothing else

- Venues that will set the stage up any way you want vs. places that are absolutely unwilling to budge on moving *anything* (This can especially be true at some churches.)

What type of audience you love to play for. Many artists have discovered that they love to perform at children's hospitals, homes for the elderly, or veterans' hospitals. A calling might come out of just looking for places to play. Musicians have started nonprofits to help them perform their own music for the audience they discovered they love to play for and people they love to serve.

You enjoy working "behind the scenes" rather than "in the spotlight." Are you like me and can't write a song to save your life? Do you enjoy crossing t's and dotting i's? Do you think more logistically and less creatively? If any of these statements resonate with you, you might be a behind-the-scenes person. But those are also the folks who make the business work.

You really aren't a very good singer. It's a tough aspect of this business, but one I want to honestly address: some people in the industry have to make the hard call that not all singers are great. A pleasant voice to sing in a choir? Yes. Draw a crowd of hundreds? No.

This is usually the hardest pill for a wannabe artist to swallow. Back in the early days of *American Idol*, Simon Cowell got a bad rap for being brutally honest. He made tough but smart decisions that benefited his business in the long run. The same applies to record executives, managers, and agents. The scene in the *I Can Only Imagine* movie where the label folks were brutally honest with Bart actually happened. That's not Hollywood fiction, that's every day in the entertainment biz.

You prefer to be in a duo or band. You may be great at harmonies and could blend well with a stronger singer, possibly someone in the circles you already know. (Duos have found amazing success in music, from Sonny & Cher to Brooks & Dunn to Dan + Shay.) Depending on the genre of music, sometimes the nature of the band's style doesn't require a great singer because it's more about the performance.

When it comes to choosing a partner for your duo/band, there are a few things to keep in mind. Once you pass the basics of their musical talent, professionalism, personal fit, etc., you just need to make sure that they are a good hang. Are they easy to be around? Do you get along with them? (Oh, have I asked if they're a good hang?)

You are better suited as a back up singer. Maybe you're not a powerhouse and aren't sure about your ability to hold your own in the spotlight. A good singer who can hear any harmony and has learned the fine art of blending his/her voice with others can make a good living as a background singer.

Here's a litmus test to check yourself on your singing ability: Choose a song that a lot of people have covered on YouTube, which fits your voice and style well. Find someone who has posted the song and gotten high ratings and positive comments. Video yourself singing the song, doing your very best. Once you've given it your best shot, watch it back, comparing your performance side by side with the other cover, analyzing your performance, pitch, range, volume, control, and power. How do you compare? Be brutally honest with yourself so someone down the line doesn't have to be a Simon Cowell to you.

Even if you find that you do, in fact, hold your own with others or are even better, this is a great way to up your game. Constantly find artists online like yourself who you think are better singers and work to match—not copy—their performance.

I can promise you that after 125 shows, you will have learned much more about the:

- Identity of who you are as an artist

- Genre or style of music you do best

- Type of audience you prefer

- Kind of songs you want to sing

- Style of songs people want to hear from you

Lastly, after you have put in your 125, you will value the roles of booking agents, managers, and labels. You'll better understand how it takes teamwork to make the dream work for a better future. You'll better understand the industry, how everything works, and the responsibilities of each party. All of this is invaluable information that you can only get one way— live performances in as many settings as possible.

If you love music, and after performing for a while, you see that being the artist is not what you thought it would be, or you realize you don't have what it takes to compete, that's okay. There are plenty of support roles in music that you might love.

Note: Interested in support roles in the industry? Explore other paths by contacting a local promoter to offer your assistance on their next show. You might be asked to:

- Be a runner*

- Help with load-in and load-out

- Sell the artist's merch

- Assist the catering/craft services* crew

- Work the box office/ticketing process day of show

You can get creative about various ways to be around music as a hobby, service, or career.

The next step after your 125 shows is to just keep going and work toward putting in your "10,000 hours," which gets you to veteran or expert level.

The Name Game

I am often asked, "We're a band. How do we decide on the right name?"

Before you announce the name of your band on social media and start designing your first album cover, the first thing you have to do is check the domain to be sure it is available. Look up any and every platform you will use, or might use, such as .com, Instagram, Twitter, Facebook, Venmo, Cash App, YouTube, and so on. Anywhere you could post, promote, and push your music.

An artist's website is crucial to gaining a fan base. If your website is "Band-A-Official.org" no professional will go to your website because they won't take you seriously. Your handles need to be as short and concise as possible, like @BandA, not @Band_A_Music_OfficialX. Before choosing a name, make sure it will be easy to find and that you can secure the name to look professional on all platforms. As far as choosing your name, think about where you're from, your given name(s) or nickname(s), catchy or meaningful phrases, types of animals/emotions/landmarks, or musical inspirations. The bottom line is a name can come from anywhere, but if you don't have the URL . . . keep looking.

An Artist's Three Key Relationships

There are at least three relationships an artist must cultivate to have a successful career.

1. The Manager

   You don't need a manager until there's so much activity in your career that you can no longer handle it all by yourself. Because most managers take a percentage of income, they aren't interested in starting with any percent of zero. They want to see an income already in place, dates on the calendar, strong social media presence, consistent and growing streams, and an artist who clearly works hard on their own without outside motivation. When all these factors are in place, a manager sees how he/she can grow what is already there. Few pros these days are interested in building someone from nothing. The pump needs to be primed and already flowing so the stream can be turned into a river.

2. The Record Label

   You don't need a record label until you have grown and maximized your music on every available platform and can't get to the next level on your own. For a label to show interest, you need a clear level of success while still having plenty of opportunity to maximize your reach. A label, along with their publishing department, can begin to pitch an artist's music for *sync** opportunities. Those can be far more lucrative than streaming revenue—dollars in sync vs. pennies in streaming. Many songwriters today are making more than some artists because they have figured out the formula for writing great songs for popular TV features and film soundtracks. There are artists/songwriters whose names you will never hear making six figures writing for sync.

3. The Booking Agent

    You don't need a booking agent until you have so many bookings coming in that you can't handle it all by yourself anymore. A full calendar you've booked yourself will get the attention of an agent. In the current climate of the music business, any good agent is going to require a track record of dates, a certain threshold of streams, and/or radio airplay to even consider you. There's no such thing anymore of getting on a major roster and the dates just start flying in. You need kindling and a spark to start a fire.

The biggest mistakes and heartaches I've seen in all my years in the music industry happen when a new artist with very little experience finds a manager who believes in him/her, gets a label deal, and lands a booking agent, all before the artist truly knows his/her identity. Once a label signs an artist, their clock is ticking. And because time is money, often both run out quickly. An artist who has been dropped by all three bases—manager, label, agent—will have a hard time getting anyone else to pay attention again.

Artist Responsibilities

I'll address the role of a manager in a later chapter, but the artist has responsibilities for their side in this relationship too. Ask questions like, "Does my manager actually have the resources and connections to do what they say?" But also, "Is my music good enough for my manager to be able to fully utilize those resources?" A manager can set you up for success, but he/she can't make you more talented or passionate.

Trust and accountability between the artist and manager are crucial. Both dynamics take time. Direct and honest conversations must take place. You have to spend time together. You have to be able to take their advice. Developing the vital relationships in your career takes time. Managers can make or break your career.

There are bad deals with good managers, and then there are bad managers where no deal is good. There are good managers with bad artists, and there are good managers and good artists in a wrong fit. You just need to make sure you are always doing all you can do for your own career, no matter what anyone else does for you. The artist who sits back and waits on a manager to bring everything to them never lasts long.

Financial Considerations for Being an Artist

Lastly, let's look at the money trail for artists, whether on your own or from these three key relationships. Before you bring anyone else into your career, exploit and maximize these (where possible) to their full potential.

Available income streams are:

- Flat guarantees* and/or percentages of live shows
- Advances and/or royalties* from a record label
- Songwriting royalties from publishing
- Sync placement payments from publishing
- Merchandise sales
- Endorsement deals
- YouTube ad money

- GoFundMe for specific projects
- Patreon (a website for artists to share their exclusive work and build connections with their fanbase) and other artist support sites

Then there are the outgoing expenses, besides what you pay yourself. As an artist, money will be paid to:

- A manager as a percentage of all or most total income
- An agent as a percentage of any booked event
- Any support personnel, from band to financial
- Cost of merchandise
- Touring expenses
- Recording expenses

Your Identity as an Artist

With streaming music, labels' finances have dwindled. Most departments at record labels are smaller than ever. All these factors mean there's less money to develop artists. If you can build a strong, loyal local or regional fan base, a label can take you to a national level. They can amplify the sound you're already making.

To do this, you need to be diligent and consistent about your overall brand*, meaning your public image as an artist. Fans must have an understanding of what they are going to get from you—from a live show to a social media post to a new line of merch. If who you are to your fans starts to be confusing or disjointed, they won't stick around to help you figure it out. They'll just replace you. Think about it—you do the same thing as a fan. Consistency is the key.

The kiss of death for any artist is to say, "I sing all kinds of music. I love it all. I can sing pop, country, rock, anything." When I hear someone say that, I assume he/she isn't an artist but the lead singer in a cover band! It's great if you are versatile enough to sing any genre, but not great if you do that all the time. Carrie Underwood can sing anything, but when she releases an album, you know it's going to be a country record. (Even her best-selling gospel hymns album is country in its style.)

As an artist, you have to be unique. You have to pick a lane and try to define yourself within that space. If you start out in Christian music and realize later you fit better in pop, or vice versa, it's okay to switch during the journey of figuring out who you are. You have time to figure this out until you have a record deal. Like it or not, agree or not, once the label puts you in a genre with a brand, you have to see that through to be successful.

That said, we have all seen veteran artists in a specific genre release an album that surprises everyone. That's because they gave the labels and their fans what they wanted for years, but got to the point in their success that won them the right to do whatever they want.

A great example is Taylor Swift. She started in country music as a teenager and wrote hits for years, became a massive success, but now what does she do? Whatever she wants to! Whatever style she wants to delve into and experiment with next, with whoever she wants to work with. Another is Rod

Stewart. Years ago, no one saw it coming when the flamboyant rock singer released *The Great American Songbook*, an album of classic standards with an orchestra. But his fan base went with him, plus he picked up a new demographic and sold millions more records.

Your job as an artist is to piece everything together so labels, booking, and management need to just come alongside you and put jet engines on the plane you've already built and have in the air.

Too many artists approach the industry with a chip on their shoulder. They come in with a love-hate thing going. That never works for long. Once you have established yourself as an artist within the industry, you can then influence the industry. But you have to earn the platform for people to actually listen. If you get off the mark, if you go too far, they stop. Like most any other industry in a capitalistic society, there is a game to be played, with rules to follow, both spoken and unspoken. So, you have to play the game, establish yourself, build your brand, learn the ropes, build a fan base, and then you can enact change and impact the culture.

Look at Bono. After establishing himself as a global rock star, he used that platform for his faith and humanitarian causes. And literally, the world listens to him *speak* the truth after he *sang* the truth for years.

To close, if you have determined that you are indeed an artist who wants to write great songs, you have to put in your 125. You can then grow to the point where you need help from the big three relationships. Then, you make sure that every day no one ever works harder than you to make your career happen.

Potential Jobs, Roles, and Positions Connected to Artists

- Songwriter
- Personal assistant to an artist (PA)
- Personal trainer for an artist
- Hair and makeup artist
- Stylist
- Personal security
- Chef/dietician/nutritionist
- Nanny
- Band member
- Session player
- Background vocalist

"The goal is to try and make the perfect song, which of course, will never happen."
—CHRIS MARTIN OF COLDPLAY[5]

CHAPTER THREE

THE SONG

A song can become a key to the doorway of the soul that nothing else will unlock.

COUNTRY ARTIST John Rich was asked to talk to his daughter's third-grade class about creative writing from a song-writer's perspective. He shared, "I held up a blank sheet of paper and a pencil and I said, 'These are two of the most powerful things in the world: a pencil and paper. The Bible started out with a pencil and a blank sheet of paper. Our Constitution was a blank sheet of paper before someone took a pencil to it. You can put anything you want on this page. It may not mean anything to anybody, or it may change the world. You have no idea, but that's the awesome power.'"[6]

As a seasoned veteran in the music business, I have witnessed that "awesome power" many times with the artists I represent—from a song impacting millions of people to changing a single life forever. And I've also seen the power of the pencil and paper change the trajectory of a songwriter's life by bringing incredible success, even with just one song.

The ultimate goal of a songwriter is to create art that transcends time and space to take listeners back to places they were a long time ago or destinations they desire to someday be. Songs are time machines that can transport us back to middle school, high school, a wedding day, the moment a child was born, or when a loved one died. For most of us, life has a soundtrack, a personal playlist that has special meaning. It's amazing when we can say, "I remember where I was and what I was doing the first time I heard that song."

A song has the power to act as a bookmark in our lives, setting an emotional, mental, and spiritual marker at a specific place in time so that a certain event is remembered forever. How many romantic comedies have we seen where the leading man looks at his lovely lady, smiles, and oozes out, "Listen . . . they're playing our song"? Yet those "our songs" would not exist without the songwriter, the creative who had to first experience the feelings and emotions in order to craft the work, hoping to impact and influence others' lives. A writer can have a singular moment of inspired creation, and then for generations, people all over the world can adopt that message as their own. Nothing creates connection between humans quite like a song.

In the Artist chapter, I drove home the power of the song and the need to develop writing as part of a successful music career. You can't talk about being an artist today without a focus on songwriting. There is an entire aspect of the industry that exists solely for the time before, during, and following the creation of a song. By the time you have a tune pop up on a playlist or hear it on the radio, most often an entire team of people have worked countless hours, and good money has been spent to get it there.

In this chapter, I want to pull back the curtain on the music publishing business, without which a songwriter's work might never see the light of day. Let's dive into the genesis of a song and the business built around the marriage of melody and lyrics.

First, some basics. Publishing involves a song's:

- Creation
- Distribution
- Placement
- Exploitation*

These are accomplished by:

- Distributing on all available streaming platforms
- Placement as a single
- Placement as a track* on an album (or released as a single, then on an album)
- Placement through sync

From these income streams, publishers then pay out a contracted portion to the songwriter.

In my experience, publishing is often an area that many artists, and sometimes even songwriters themselves, don't fully understand and value. All the more reason to dissect the methodology of this process. There are artists who have made millions from the right publishing deal, while others have lost or left millions on the table from a relationship with the wrong publisher or just a bad deal.

Signed, Sealed, Delivered

The publishing company has two responsibilities:

A publisher must curate the creation of great songs.

Publishers want to build a great collection of songs, sometimes referred to as a catalog.* Publishing companies have catalogs comprising individual songwriter/artist catalogs. Building a catalog can be done in two ways: One, they acquire existing songs. This can be one song or a writer's entire preexisting catalog with hundreds of works. Two, they work directly with songwriters in the development of their craft to build a new catalog.

A publisher must secure the talents of great writers.

Artist/writer. If a record label offers a deal to an artist who writes or cowrites his/her own songs, most often a publishing agreement comes alongside the record contract. The goal is to maximize the partnership, from the development of the artist's songs through the release of those songs, whether as their own projects or for others. This relationship can maximize an artist's talent and income.

Popular artists who have had hits recorded by others include Jessie J, who wrote "Party in the USA" released by Miley Cyrus. Ed Sheeran wrote "Love Yourself," released by Justin Bieber. Avril Lavigne wrote "Breakaway," released by Kelly Clarkson, and Ryan Tedder of OneRepublic wrote "Halo," released by Beyonce.[7] All are artists who have had massive success with their songwriting, thanks to great publishing.

Songwriter. Publishers sign exclusive agreements and then work with writers to develop their skills, build their catalogs, and place their songs. This business exists for the songwriter, whether he/she ever becomes an artist or not. I could give you ample pages of names of songwriters who have made millions in the music business that you would have never heard of unless you read deep into the credits on albums.

Historically, publishing companies have been a great connecting point for a songwriter to get a record deal. Someone who works in publishing on a regular basis with a writer might suggest to a label's A&R* rep that a songwriter has the talent to become an artist. A publishing company can strongly influence a label's decision of whether to sign someone. Whenever a label has its own publishing as an entity inside the company, then a "promote from within" scenario is beneficial for everyone because the relationship already exists.

Sometimes this is all about timing. Chris Stapleton signed his first publishing deal in 2001, shortly after moving to Nashville. When a senior VP of Universal Music Group first approached Chris about the possibility of a record contract, he said no. In an article in *Billboard* magazine, Brian Wright said, "Chris always told me he didn't want a record deal—he just wanted to be a songwriter. Every time I asked, he said, 'I don't want a record deal.'"[8] But fortunately for us all, Stapleton eventually changed his mind, and by 2015 when *Traveller* was released, in less than six months, Chris went from a relatively unknown songwriter playing clubs to a major artist singing his own hits in arenas.

Another successful songwriter who became a major artist

is Sia, who released her own album after she had penned hits for Rihanna, Celine Dion, Katy Perry, Alicia Keys, and Beyonce.[9] And then there's Julia Michaels. Before she was known as an artist, she had written hits for Nick Jonas, Keith Urban, Demi Lovato, Maroon 5, Justin Bieber, and Selena Gomez.[10]

Producer. Record producers are constantly working with artists and songwriters on new material for projects. A trend of the past several years is to literally write a record from scratch in the studio with a producer. This approach has brought the role of the producer more and more into the songwriting spotlight. Especially in the hip-hop and rap world, a producer will often be an artist's only other cowriter because they are writing the tracks in real time as they program and record the album by themselves. In fact, this makes a producer a great asset as a writer or cowriter because they can immediately produce a great demo* for the publisher.

One of the most well-known producers to come out of this growing trend has been Finneas O'Connell, Billie Eilish's brother, known professionally as just Finneas. He started his sister's meteoric rise to stardom as they worked in the bedroom of their parents' home by asking her to sing on the songs he was writing. After "Ocean Eyes" blew up on SoundCloud, they began to write together.[11] From that, she became a global artist, and he became a sought-after producer and songwriter, working with pop royalty like Justin Bieber, Demi Lovato, Selena Gomez, Halsey, and Camila Cabello, as well as releasing his own music.[12]

Studio or live musician. The amazing musicians who play in the studio and/or live for artists are sometimes signed to a publishing deal. Whether crafting incredible melodies or penning lyrical masterpieces or both, their proximity to artists often allows them the opportunity to cowrite, being at the right place at the right time. This can happen when asked to play guitar on a track in the studio and by creative osmosis being brought into the writing process, or a keys player hanging out on the tour bus being invited by the artist to help with the creation of a song.

A publishing company can bring *all* these elements together under one roof—artists, writers, producers, and musicians—to craft great songs. A reputable, connected publisher knows how to get the right people in a room to create an environment where musical magic happens.

An analogy I often use to explain the concept of a great publisher is an art gallery. A gallery seeks out existing art to bring into their displays, while also discovering artists who are creating new masterpieces to be introduced by their business. A reputable gallery always has two streams flowing: the art and the artist. That exact scenario applies to publishers with the song and the songwriters.

The Art of the Cowrite

In New York, L.A., and especially here in Nashville, there are full-time writers with publishing deals who cowrite five to ten songs every single week. A typical schedule may be a 10:00 a.m. to 2:00 p.m. cowrite and then a 2:00 p.m. to 6:00 p.m. cowrite five days a week—give or take an hour or two—if something great is in the works. Of course, a song isn't always written or finished in every session, but more often than not, a rough demo with guitar or piano and vocal is completed by the time they walk out the door.

The point person at a publishing company for a certain writer will keep his/her calendar and is constantly booking cowrites with both established pros and up-and-comers. Sought-after writers can be booked up for weeks in advance. Most publishing companies and/or labels have writer rooms* that are reserved for their people to meet and work. It's not uncommon for a writer to walk out of the room, down the hall to his rep, and say, "Hey, you got a minute to come in here and listen to this? I think we've got something for you to send to [insert artist looking for songs]."

Over the years when I have met young songwriters asking for advice, I talk about building what I call a songwriter's pyramid. The concept is to establish a firm foundation with a wide base of experiences. To write with people outside your circle who are different from you in every way in their approach, method, genre, gender, race, economic class, and so on. Be as diverse as possible. Don't say no to anyone. If it doesn't go well, you don't have to say yes twice, but you should once. To repeat a point from the Artist chapter, you need to view life and tell stories from as many unique and different perspectives as you can. I promise if you do, you'll learn a lot about music, people, *and* life!

Another huge factor in becoming a successful cowriter is to understand the importance of "being a good hang." Be kind. Be pleasant. Be positive. Be sensitive to other writers. Be on time. Work hard. Listen, listen, listen. Don't be a jerk.

Don't be a Me Monster. Don't make it all about your song and your ideas. You may be a great writer, but if someone can't wait to get out of the room after being trapped with you for four hours, they certainly won't come back for a second song. Especially here in Nashville, where a sense of "southern hospitality" is still very much alive, being a genuine, what-you-see-is-what-you-get person goes a long way. Sometimes it can even overcome a lack of talent or skill until you learn and catch up, simply because you are easy to get along with, are enjoyable as a human, and always come to the table with a few good ideas.

This principle also applies to live musicians. Some aren't amazing players, but the artist just likes having them out on the road for three months. Remember—be a good hang. Never let it be said about you, "Yeah, he/she is talented, but . . . " *No buts!*

Lastly, some writers are going to be better at melody than writing lyrics and vice versa. One of the most prolific songwriting duos of all time are Elton John and Bernie Taupin. Bernie would write the lyrics like poetry, and Elton would put his music to the words. Don Henley is known to be an amazing writer of lyrics who teamed up perfectly with Glenn Frey, Don Felder, and other Eagles' members to write their hits. Crafting great songs can literally be a 50/50 divide of joining up lyrics and melody. Regardless of how the song is written, finding the best creative partners is the key to crafting great songs.

Optimize, Maximize, and Exploit the Song

Publishing companies work hard to acquire the best songs, and then they exploit them by optimizing and maximizing their earning potential. One of the primary ways this is accomplished is by employing a person known in the industry as a song plugger,* a person who has the goal to place the song in a maximum earnings position.

Their first task is to secure a cut* of the song on a recording project. The bigger the artist, the better. Then, once it's recorded, they work to sync the song with placements across films, TV series, commercials, video games, and more.[13]

An incredible example of both these worlds colliding to create the perfect storm is Dolly Parton's song "I Will Always Love You." She originally released the song on her own record in 1974, and it went to number one on the country charts. But almost twenty years later, when Kevin Costner was producing and starring in *The Bodyguard* with Whitney Houston, and the feature song fell through at the last minute, Costner remembered Dolly's song and thought it was perfect to convey the character's feelings in the film.[14]

In 1992 when the soundtrack hit record stores at the same time the film opened in theaters, the song sold four million singles and the soundtrack sold seventeen million copies, while also winning two Grammys, all driven by that one song. No surprise that the film grossed $411 million. Dolly's estimated royalties in the '90s as the sole songwriter of "I Will Always Love You" were $10 million.[15]

The power of the song harnessed to the commercial success of the film, coupled with Whitney Houston's amazing performances of both, created an unmatched artistic synergy. This had everything to do with Dolly's songwriting and publishing, not her label or own artist career. In fact, a lot of people who were buying the song after seeing the film had no idea a country artist had penned what would become one of the biggest pop songs in history.

A publishing company tracks, collects, and pays royalties to songwriters. They send out royalty statements once a quarter or twice a year. However, it usually takes six to nine months for royalties to begin to show up from a released song. In the meantime, a writer has an account and can log in to see his/her statements of what is due them. If a songwriter has been with a publishing company for many years, with dozens or even hundreds of cuts, the statement can get fairly complicated to decipher. Typically, each line item will show the song, the source of a payment, the writer's percentage of that song, and then the royalty amount earned for that period. Because of the global reach of music, the nation where the royalty originated will also be shown. Finally, whether by a paper check or direct deposit, the writer will be paid for the designated accounting period.

Within the songwriting community, royalties have long been referred to as "mailbox money." Even if a songwriter is going through a slump or suffering from writer's block and can't seem to get the creative juices flowing, he/she could walk out to the mailbox on any given day to find a check. The crazy thing is it might be for a song written twenty years ago. *BAM! Mailbox money!*

A publishing company registers song copyrights with the U.S. Copyright Office. They also work in coordination with PROs* or Performance Rights Organizations. A PRO is a clearinghouse that acts as a middleman between the copyright holders (the publisher and songwriters) and anyone who uses those works in a "public performance." A public performance can be cover songs performed in a bar by a live band, songs played on the radio, music being streamed in a restaurant, worship music in church, or anywhere the public hears music played, whether live or through speakers, featured or in the background. PROs exist to find those avenues and collect royalties, primarily through paid licenses.

So, let's say you're sitting in your favorite restaurant and hear a classic song come on through the speakers up in the rafters. The restaurant owners are supposed to pay a fee to play that music for you. Approximately $3 billion a year is paid out for public performance. If you are a songwriter and have released music that could be played in public, you want to be sure you are getting your piece of that pie.

The "Big Three" in performance rights organizations are (in alphabetical order)

- ASCAP* (American Society of Composers, Authors, and Publishers)

- BMI* (Broadcast Music, Inc.)

- SESAC* (Society of European Stage Authors and Composers)

Each of these have the same function, but all accomplish that through slightly different methods of and approaches to licensing, collection, etc. It's similar to banking; Wells Fargo, Chase, and Bank of America all do the same thing and have the same basic function in business, yet customer service, interest rates charged, and available services can vary. In the music business, you could have three songwriters who wrote a song together, each with a different PRO. For one statement, writer #1 might get $100, writer #2 $50, and writer #3 zero. But then the next statement could be completely different due to varying factors with each PRO.

If you are a songwriter, you need to join a PRO. If you aren't sure which one to go with, ask around in your music community for referrals. Look up your favorite writers and see where they belong. The important thing is to establish a relationship and work to keep your catalog up-to-date with them. Even if you sign a publishing deal or a record contract, the PRO you belong to is up to you. Of course, a label might have some relationships in place, which may create a preference, but your relationship is most important in this particular area.

If you write Christian music, you also need to know about CCLI*—Christian Copyright Licensing International. This privately owned company started in 1988 to provide the same services as a PRO, but the public performance is the church and all ministry-related settings.[16] Like a bar that has a cover band singing popular songs for its customers to listen to, dance to, and interact with, the church offers public performances of popular Christian songs for its members almost every time it gathers.

For biblical reasons of integrity (as outlined in 1 Timothy 5) in the use of copyrights and fairness to writers and artists, CCLI collects annual fees that are paid based on the number of members of a church. A rural church with 75 members will pay significantly less than a megachurch in the city. Each participating church is required to report the songs it uses in worship services to CCLI. Then publishers are paid based on a song's activity level. At any given time on CCLI's website, you can look up the top Christian songs being sung by churches on an international scale. This provides another income stream for Christian publishers and songwriters.

I have always said that being a songwriter is one of the greatest jobs in the music industry. If I could somehow gift my children with just one talent in music, it would be to become an amazing writer. The reasons? You can:

- Be successful in the music industry but still attend every event and school function for your kids.

- Work normal hours and not be gone for months on the road.

- Set your own schedule and work with all different types of artists for decades.

- Jump on a tour bus with an artist to hammer out songs for their new record.

- Go in and out of the studio as little or as much as you want to record your demos.

- Be massively creative without paying the price of fame.

- Speak to your generation, generations from the past, and generations in the future.

- Get to retirement age and still be legitimate and relevant. If you're young and really want to be an artist, you may not understand this dynamic yet, but trust me, if you stay in this business long enough, you will one day.

At any restaurant or coffee shop in Nashville, you could be sitting next to a man or woman who has made millions in music, yet you would not know their name or recognize them. In fact, it's likely that's why, for so many years, Chris Stapleton didn't want a record deal. Many talented artists get a year or two at the top of the charts, but then for a myriad of reasons, their career starts to slide downhill and eventually out of sight. For many songwriters, as long as they keep turning out solid songs, the life expectancy of their career is far higher. Many talented men and women have written hits right up to their dying day.

So, if I were you . . . I'd be a songwriter. Like I said, it's one of the greatest jobs in the world!

The Investment and Payoff of Discipline

You could take your songs to a record label that also has in-house publishing, and say, "Hey, I'm an artist and I've got some songs for you." They might hear them and respond, "You're not really an artist yet. You're a songwriter." If they should offer you a publishing deal, that's a great way to get into the music business. That said, don't sign to a publishing company that's connected to a record label that you wouldn't want to be signed to as an artist. A label is going to be less interested in you if you've already signed your publishing to someone else. But the publisher at a label where you would want to be an artist can get you in the door.

Here's a different strategy: If you get an offer to sign to a publishing company, but you want to be on another label, take that offer over to your preferred label and say, "Hey, I've got an offer from Label X, but I'd rather be over here with you. Can we work something out?" Use the "bird in the hand" to negotiate getting where you want. As long as you haven't committed to the other company, there's no ethical or moral issue here.

Being in Nashville for so many years, I've seen a lot. I know one guy who, as he drove into town the first time and saw the Nashville city limits sign, decided right then he wasn't going to say anything until he could figure out a way to make his words rhyme. Before he called to get his cable hooked up, he sat down and wrote out how he could make everything rhyme when he talked to the cable rep. When he went to a restaurant, he looked at the menu and figured out how to make his order rhyme before he spoke to the server. *Sound crazy?* Well, fast forward twenty years to the same guy who is now a songwriter and has twelve cuts off a country music legend's double album of his top fifty songs. He's earned a good living and, from day one, made the decision to work hard to be the best writer he could be.

When another songwriter I know first came to Nashville, he decided to treat his passion and dream just like going to work every day at any business. He would get up Monday morning, get ready for work, and sit down to write by 8:00 a.m. He would work all day until he wrote a song. Whenever he finished, whether at 11:00 a.m. or 11:00 p.m., he would be done for the day. His first year here, he wrote a song every single workday, with weekends and holidays off. *That's over 250 songs in his first year!* Like any job that has a quota for the day, he got up every morning and went to work until he was done, whatever it took.

In recent years an aging group of legendary artists and songwriters have begun to accept offers to sell controlling percentages of their song catalogs, meaning their publishing rights. Investors see a growth opportunity of cashing in on the licenses of classic songs, while the artists see a massive payday now as opposed to a steady stream each month. In short, many artists in their sixties to eighties have decided they would rather have millions now than thousands each month. But, of course, you have to have a large, highly valuable catalog for that transaction to take place.[17]

In 1962, Bob Dylan signed his first songwriting deal with Leeds Publishing Company for an advance of $100. Fifty-eight years later, in December 2020, Dylan sold his entire catalog of six hundred-plus songs to Universal Music Group for an estimated $300 million.[18] What else could Bob Dylan have done to have that level of return on investment for his life's work?

Also in December 2020, Stevie Nicks sold an 80 percent share of her song catalog for an estimated $100 million to Primary Wave, an independent publisher and marketing company.[19] By the end of January 2021, Hipgnosis Songs Fund, a British company founded in 2018, had spent $1.75 billion buying stakes in 129 writers' catalogs that contained over 60,000 songs by classic pop and rock artists/writers.[20]

According to the National Music Publishers Association, in 2019 publishers collected $3.7 billion.[21] That kind of long-term return and potential has attracted capital investment from all over the world. Why? Because a tweet can crater the stock market in an hour, a "no" from one sheik can sink the oil market in a day, and when the dollar goes up, gold goes down. But no matter what happens in the world, people just keep listening to music, experiencing the power of a song, because we can always count on that emotional and spiritual connection to bring us back home.

Here's the reality when it comes to songwriting: if you can write a complete song on your own, play it for someone and see that you have touched their heart, your writing is a craft, a discipline, an art. The more you do it, the better you will become. The better writers you can write with, the better writer you will be. In short, whereas singing is a God-given talent, songwriting can be a learned discipline.

I mean this as no discouragement in being an artist, but more as an inspiration to become a great songwriter. If your songwriting pyramid can end up with a huge, wide base from interactions with hundreds of writers of all genres and styles to create a catalog of songs, you can have one of the most incredible careers on the planet that can pay you royalties for the rest of your life. Create songs that become keys to the doorways of people's souls that nothing else can unlock.

Potential Roles and Positions Connected to Music Publishing

- Songwriter
- President of the publishing company
- Director of A&R
- Assistant A&R

- Song plugger
- Copyright administrator
- Licensing department staff
- Music library organizer
- Director of foreign language translations
- Royalty and accounting department staff

"I'm learning to accept myself. I'm still in the process of learning to love who I am. And it's been really refreshing and really nice to be able to do that and be okay. I think my fans have brought that out in me."
—DUA LIPA[22]

CHAPTER FOUR

THE FANS

The bottom line is the artist's focus has to be on what the fans like, not what the artist *thinks* the fans like.

IF AN ARTIST has no one to listen to their music, come to a show, or buy their merch, are they really an artist? No. That sounds more like someone with a hobby, right? Fans are people who connect with an artist—from the casual fan who occasionally listens to the music to the superfan who listens all the time, goes to every show possible, buys every piece of merch, and tracks the artist's every move on social media, hitting "like" and commenting using "100s" with a line of fire emojis.

In 2018, the late legendary country rock superstar Charlie Daniels was interviewed by his pastor. When Charlie was asked why he never seemed to mind people coming up to him anywhere he was, the artist shared:

If someone wants an autograph, a handshake, or a hug—unless I'm running to catch a plane or something—I'm going to stop and talk to them. I've lived my dream because people enjoy what I do. That's always on my mind. If somebody says, "Hey, Charlie, I've got something I want to tell you," I'm going to stop and listen to them. I've had an incredible ride all because of people who have bought my records and my concert tickets. I am beholden to those people.[23]

While certainly culture has created a tiny minority of people who become obsessed and dangerous, most people just want to have the opportunity to connect to someone who has given them music they have lived their lives by. Bottom line—the music business does not work without fans. If the road is paved with great songs, then fans are the gas fueling the engine that drives the music industry down the road. The fans decide what moves, what stops, and what goes ninety in the fast lane.

Fans spend their hard-earned money and give time and energy to support artists by:

- Purchasing/streaming music
- Watching videos (increasing view counts)
- Buying concert tickets
- Buying upgrades for unique fan experiences such as meet and greets
- Purchasing, wearing, using, and posting official merchandise
- Buying authenticated artist memorabilia and commemorative items

- Following, sharing, and supporting on social media
- Connecting with artist endorsements and brand partnerships
- Leaving 5-star, positive reviews online
- Supporting when an artist plugs another artist or up-and-comer

The goal of anyone in the music business is to constantly offer fans the opportunity and the reason to move up from one level to the next as a fan.

Six Stages of Fandom

In order for an artist to increase their solid fanbase, he/she must recognize the casual listeners. Most of the time, someone becomes a fan of a song they hear and may not even know the artist's name. The goal for every artist, especially in the early days, is to convert casual listeners to solid fans. Let's walk through the stages:

The casual fan*

This person regularly listens to an artist's music, but the engagement stops there.

The fan*

This person knows the basic info about an artist, not just the music, and begins to connect with the brand through albums, videos, logos, and photos. Bottom line—there is engagement and brand recognition. A few bars into a song, they know who it is. A glance at a photo and they recognize the artist and/or the brand.

The true fan*

This fan includes everything above, except now they are willing to spend money to go further in the experience by buying a ticket to go see an artist live and/or purchasing a shirt or other merch item to display their connection. During 2020, many artists implored fans starting at this level to buy their merch because live shows were not possible. A lot of true fans traded what would have been ticket money for a large merch order to support artists.

The hardcore fan*

Added to everything above, this fan has some form of regular connection with the artist's music—possibly on a daily basis—goes to see the artist perform every chance they get, and will have a shirt for every tour the artist has done. Social media engagement will also take place every time an artist posts, with likes and comments from the fan, as well as communication with other fans. Online discussions can start up following a post like, "Do you think this is a hint about a new album coming?" This is usually the level at which a fan will belong to an official fan club or street team.*

The superfan*

Take all, and I mean *all*, of the above and add a deep well of knowledge about an artist's history and happenings, including his/her personal life—single or married (if single, who they date), family, where they live, all the details. This fan considers him/herself a resident expert on the artist. They know the latest and greatest, the up-to-date info—*true or not so true*. Yes, this is the level where a fan who does not understand boundaries can become a stalker.

In a *Rolling Stone* magazine article titled "Musicians Share Their Wildest Fan Stories," Ed Sheeran offered his best one:

> *A girl once chucked her iPhone at me. After the show, we wanted to give it back. When we tried to get into the phone to find a number to call, it was locked. Then we realized her screensaver was a screen grab of a text that said "ring this number." So we rang the number thinking we'd get through to someone that would know her. Instead, the phone we had started ringing. The number on the screen was for her own phone—she was hoping that I'd see it and call. Luckily, her dad ended up waiting at the back of the venue and we managed to get it back to her.*

In the same article, DJ Steve Aoki told this story, "In 2012, on . . . tour, there was a fan at one of my shows who climbed up on the roof and hung upside down just to get close enough to give me a high five in my DJ booth that was twenty feet above the ground."[24]

The moral to this story is it's okay to be a superfan, but don't get crazy!

The legacy fan*

This level is reserved for artists who have been around awhile, which means their fans have too. So all of the above, but add at least ten-plus years and a PhD in fandom. At this stage, chances are the artist may know at least the fan's first name because of years of close interaction. Typically, these fans have shown enough respect at close range over many years to make the artist feel they are safe to approach and talk. These fans also often learn details, like the artist will usually arrive at a venue at 2:00 p.m. or walk out the back door for ten minutes at about 5:00 to speak with the handful who know the schedule. These kinds of interactions help the artist feel connected to their closest fans and also give them an opportunity to feel special, which is cool for everyone.

A few years back, I had the privilege of meeting Bono. U2 has made it widely known that they have fans today that they have known well since their early days of playing small clubs back in the late '70s when no one cared who they were. Now, *that* is the true definition of legacy fans. In 2015 on U2's website, Bono wrote about their loyalty and connection to the fans:

> *U2 is a band that started out as fans. . . . We stepped out of the audience of The Clash and The Ramones. In earlier times we had fans sleeping on the floors of our hotel rooms. Later that got weird. But we've always understood who was paying our wages. U2 were the first to use new technologies like a satellite stage and billboard sized videos, to make sure the seat at the back of the house was as good as the front. But now with paparazzi and cell phone cameras it's harder to hang out except when we're on tour. The sound of a U2 audience is like the roar of a rocket launch.*[25]

A friend of mine, Marie Powers, has been a tried-and-true legacy fan of the outlaw country legend Jerry Jeff

Walker for decades. (He died in October 2020.) In 2002, Jerry Jeff put on an eBay auction for a four-day, four-person vacation in Belize, with the proceeds benefiting his music school. The event included plenty of personal time with him at his home, plus fishing and snorkeling. The last night was a private acoustic concert. Marie's boss wanted her to have the opportunity with her musical hero, so he gave her a very large budget. Bottom line—she won. Marie and three of her family members had a once-in-a-lifetime experience that they will never forget. These kinds of amazing personal encounters are what legacy fans hope for, watch out for, and will pay big money for.

An interesting and intriguing fact is that most fans, from casual to super, will never have any personal engagement, not even a few seconds for a photo opp. The only connection they have to the artist will be the music, and both the artist and the fan will be completely fine with that. Once again, that is the beauty and the power of songs.

Wisdom and Warning
Unfortunately, the majority of the stories that get shared about fans are the weird run-ins, encounters, and bizarre behavior that cause major artists to hire security. While on tour, some artists will have one or more bodyguards with them at all times, stationed outside their dressing room, bus door, and right beside them in a meet and greet. Some are even trained like Secret Service, depending on the artist and the genre, and if you make a wrong move, you'll go from standing to flat on the floor in a heartbeat.

One of the most tragic stories was Christina Grimmie. Christina had amassed a huge following on YouTube from posting covers and went on to place third in the 2014 season of *The Voice*. In June 2016, at just twenty-two years old, she was talking with fans at a meet and greet in Orlando, Florida, when a twenty-seven-year-old stalker shot her four times and then turned the gun on himself. Police later uncovered that the man had "an unrealistic infatuation" with her. One crazy fan ended a vibrant life and a wonderful talent.[26]

The moral to this story is if you are a fan, respect artists and their privacy. They are just people who we make into celebrities. So, treat them like human beings whom you respect for their art. If you are an artist or hope to become an artist, interacting with your fans is a vital part of building a career, but in the strange day in which we live, you have to be cautious. Take Jesus' advice: be as wise as serpents, and as harmless as doves.[27]

One of the unfortunate realities of the music industry for both the artist and the fan is unofficial, unauthorized, bootleg products using the artist's work, brand, or image. Those products are created by criminals, don't support the artist at all, are often of cheap quality, and hurt the brand. If someone is selling shirts out of their trunk after a show, stay away. Also today, too many online retailers are selling merchandise that has no connection to the artist at all. You also have to be very careful of third-party ticket resale sites.

Make sure everything you purchase is connected to the artist. If you are an artist who has become big enough to have people bootlegging your stuff, you can likely afford an attorney to send out cease-and-desist orders. Most of those people are scared enough by a lawyer's letter to take down anything they are selling to avoid a lawsuit, or even an arrest, depending on the circumstances. The best way to be certain you are buying legit merch from the actual artist, making sure the money will go to the artist, is to only buy from their official website or concert merch setup.

One last caution to artists or aspiring artists: Your social media is such a huge connection to your fans, likely your *only* connection to 95 percent of them. Oftentimes, once an artist signs with a label, the marketing department will want to drive the brand, and so they will ask to take over your socials and get your passwords. Sometimes they'll ask to coordinate with you to choose together what is shared. But you have to be very careful because, if you have already established a rapport with fans and they have learned your voice and style, they will be able to spot a label post a mile away.

You have likely seen posts from artists where you knew it wasn't quite right, thinking to yourself, "Ah, no, that was *not* from them." You have learned the artist well enough that you can see right through anyone posing as him/her. You should always stay in control of your own social media. Now, of course you need to listen to your label and your manager to avoid doing anything stupid or hurtful to your career. But if your posts are well received, if you're gaining more followers and engagement, then continue on. If it's not broken, don't let anyone try and fix it for you.

Building a Solid Fan Base

The bottom line is the artist's focus has to be on what the fans like, not what the artist *thinks* the fans like. When an artist is in the early stages of trying to figure out what songs to release, the fans can hold the key to the right door. As we discussed in the Artist chapter, if you sing all your songs live as many times as possible, their response and feedback will tell you everything you need to know. Your fans are going to vote, so to speak, by sharing how they feel.

Early on, the artist will have to first give the fans what they want and work to establish a solid base. Then as trust and connection grow, the artist can slowly introduce fans to the things that he/she cares about. Until then, to be blunt, the fans have no reason to care about what the artist cares about. They have to truly believe the artist cares about them as a fan first. That relationship is going to be a one-way street with very conditional love until the bridge is built. That's okay because that's how the business works.

But, once an artist has established a solid fan base and gained a sustainable platform, he/she can tell the fans about almost anything they care about, and they will reciprocate and care about those same things. The two-way street is now paved. So many artists have raised awareness and millions of dollars for good simply by telling their fans.

Two historic events in 1985 launched the connection between music and fundraising for causes with the "We Are the World" song and video released in March and the Live Aid concert event held in the UK and the U.S. in July of that year. Since then, many successful artists have made a practice of taking causes to their fans to create a synergy between great music and a valuable message.[28]

If you are going to be an artist, you have to serve the fans. The number one way to do that is to serve up great songs that move them.

One saying I have repeated over and over throughout my years in the industry is, "If they cry, they buy," meaning if you have a song that moves someone to tears, chances are great that they will buy your music, tickets to your concert, and your merchandise. And in my case with MercyMe, they might even go see a movie about that song. Or buy the book. And then the ultimate honor these days, get a tattoo of the lyrics!

If you're a fan, positions like being a street team leader or fan club president are great opportunities to learn the fan side of connection to the artist. If you're an artist with a growing fan base, watch for the right people to create those positions for your own team. Oftentimes, these people can grow with you, and a great relationship can be established.

I'm going to say this *one more time* to drive the point home—fans are the driving force behind the music business!

Potential Roles and Positions Connected to Fandom

- Music journalist
- Paid runner
- Music reviewer
- Merch vendor

Volunteer options for fans:

- Fan Club
- Street team
- Merch volunteer
- Blogger
- Podcaster
- Merch representative
- Volunteer runner

Things fans can do to support artists:

- Buy concert tickets
- Buy merch
- Wear merch
- Buy music
- Stream music
- Share music on social media

"If anyone was the Fifth Beatle, it was Brian."
—Paul McCartney on their manager, Brian Epstein[29]

CHAPTER FIVE

THE MANAGER

A manager's job is to protect and serve, helping an artist reach their goals and dreams.

OVER THE YEARS, the most frequent question I get is, "So, what does an artist manager do?" As with most titles from professional careers, especially where people may have built-in assumptions, the real answer is too long. As noted earlier, I always say with a smirk, "Well, managers don't *do* anything" . . . *pause for effect* . . . "except make sure that everyone else does *their* job." The truth is that is *exactly* what I do. And it's what any good manager should do.

But when we think of the word *manager* in any business or industry, from retail to restaurant to manufacturing, isn't that the true broad definition of the role? Making sure everyone else does their job? Management navigates the ship carrying someone else's cargo, and the better, faster, and stronger the operation, the more successful the operation can be, whether easy sailing or through rough waters.

Another analogy I use to explain a manager's job is to keep pushing the ball up the hill, making sure you don't stall out or roll backwards, all while calculating the next right step to keep moving forward.

An artist manager makes sure every entity of the music industry is doing its part to maximize the artist's career. Some days are majestic on the mountaintop, while some are messy in the mundane. Some are pure glory, while others are painfully gory.

So, how do you navigate the ship? How do you keep the ball going up the hill? Here's a comprehensive description of a manager's job:

The Four I's

The following is a helpful alliteration of four distinct roles that a manager should offer. The goal is to provide an easy-to-remember path of the key elements an artist's manager or management team provides.

Information

A manager is the keeper of the master playbook, while implementing the artist's vision. If an artist has *any* question, the manager's job is to find the answer. A good manager should be *the* source of an artist's information. The calendar is a live-and-die-by document that has to be one hundred percent accurate and solid for an artist's schedule to run smoothly and efficiently.

All incoming and outgoing info and intel flows through the manager and his/her staff. This can be everything from strategically routing* tour dates on the calendar, to reconciling a show's payout* and merch sales, to following a promoter's* instructions that an upcoming venue's stage crew is under very strict union rules.

Routing is the term for strategically mapping out tour dates as linear as possible to make sure drives are not too long between dates, while not selling markets* (cities or areas a promoter controls) too close together. For example, if you book a show two hours away the next night, the drive is easy, but you can hurt ticket sales in one of the cities. This issue is often handled by a promoter wanting a radius clause,* meaning an artist can't perform within a certain mile radius of his/her city for a set amount of time.

Show payout* is when a date is ticketed with a percentage split between the promoter and artist. At the end of the night the road manager* or tour manager* has to sit down with the promoter and reconcile expenses with income to arrive at the correct split on the profit, provided there is a profit. Often a flat guarantee is negotiated as a bottom threshold, then if a profit occurs, the split is done. Depending on the contract, this can also include merch sales for the night, if the agreement was for the venue to receive a percentage of that income. These examples prove how critical details and record keeping are to an artist's income.

Interaction

A manager is the filter through which all info and intel flows, from everyone who works with the artist on any level.

As a manager, you want your artist to be able to focus on performing and creating as much as possible, the very reason he/she is an artist. If he/she takes time off, you want them to be able to rest, refuel, and refresh to keep their creative edge. On any given day, you have to filter what communication needs to be shared with the artist and what activity in the business needs to involve them. Regardless, you become the conduit to interact with the industry *for* the artist and *to* the artist.

There are times when these dealings occur in scheduled meetings where everyone is on the same page. Other times may necessitate stepping in and speaking up, even when no one is going to like what you have to say. You have to be willing and ready to do either anytime. To be an artist manager, you have to be able to deal diplomatically with conflict, as well as choose when to compromise and when to stand your ground. But all of this interaction is done with the motive of what is best for your artist. In dealing with an industry filled with sensitive creatives, there can be days that feel like a walk on a tightrope without a net.

Intercession

A manager represents and negotiates all aspects of business for the artist.

The manager is the representative for the artist in anything that involves and impacts the artist in their career. For any meeting, such as with the record label, booking agent, etc., the manager is there to represent the artist. Most managers have some form of limited power-of-attorney to handle business and have signing privileges on behalf of the artist. This part of the job often feels like a cross between a lawyer and an ambassador, meaning you represent his/her "nation," with the job requiring a mix of being direct, discerning, and diplomatic.

Influence

A manager coaches the artist in the music business, from brand consistency to interviews to stage presence to personal crises.

In a day when celebrity and success can come quickly to an artist if he/she goes viral, or their career can suddenly take a nosedive overnight from a social media post, the manager can at times be the only voice of reason left for an artist. Everyone else is responding by either loving or hating, so you have to stay objective and protective. For that purpose, a manager can have a scary amount of influence over an artist, which must be handled with respect, wisdom, and discernment. He/she must constantly think only about what's best for their artist.

Potential relationships and aspects of the music business that an artist manager may navigate are:

- Record labels
- Music publishers
- Producers
- Engineers
- Product distribution—digital and physical
- Booking agents
- Event promoters
- Social media
- Fans—individuals, clubs, social media accounts and sites
- Artist website
- Public relations—interviews, press releases, news stories

- Touring personnel—band, tour manager, road crew
- Event venue personnel
- Merchandise—product and road team
- Literary and film agents
- Sponsors—brand, tours, one-time events
- Stylists—clothes, hair, makeup
- Video and photo shoots
- Endorsements
- Brand navigation
- All strategic partnerships

As I pointed out in the Artist chapter, management makes their living from a commission percentage of the artist's income. Most managers take a cut on anything they touch for the artist. A percentage allows the manager to make more when he/she is maximizing the artist's income, while making less if things are not going well. In business terms, this is known as a fiduciary* relationship. Merriam-Webster defines this as "a relationship in which one party places special trust, confidence, and reliance in and is influenced by another who has a fiduciary duty to act for the benefit of the party."[30]

The main place we hear of this arrangement is in financial investment. The investment firm in this setting has to make decisions based solely on what is best for the money the client has entrusted to them, not what is best for the firm. This is exactly the way the artist-manager relationship works. So, if an offer comes in for an artist that is more than he/she has ever received before, but the manager believes a new radio single going out will blow that artist up and the price will be far higher in six months, they could decide to say no. But the "no" is really "wait." Trade good money now for better money later, even if the manager's rent is due. Fiduciary. Trust. Confidence. Reliance. And often, sacrifice.

Maximizing Momentum

By now you can see being a good manager is an all-encompassing job. But being a great manager is an even tougher job. Still with all these factors in mind, there are no prerequisites for taking this role. This person could be anyone who has a relationship with the artist: a parent (often called a mom-ager or dad-ager), roommate, another family member, high school friend, etc. There are managers who started their career working in some capacity in the music industry and found an artist they really believed in. Then they developed a relationship with that artist and started working on their behalf to move their career forward. There are times, if the artist becomes successful, that manager never acquires other clients. Other times, the manager decides to start a company and sign other artists to their roster, like I did.

Young artists often think that management can guarantee a record deal and booking contract. As I stated clearly in the Artist chapter, securing a deal has more to do with the artist's talent and songs than any other factor. But if that dynamic is in place, the manager will be able to get the artist a *better* deal than the artist would alone. Relationships, track record, credibility, negotiation tactics, and experience allow most managers to get a stronger offer.

Remember this—a good manager should be able to maximize any opportunity where an artist's talent has opened a door. For example, an artist's song goes viral, and three labels quickly come calling. Alone as a starving creative, the artist might only look at the size of the advance offered and which rep he/she likes the best. For many reasons, there are limitations on how to know which label will be the best partner. But the right manager could rule out Label #1 right away because he/she knows there's a poor history of getting traction there. Label #2 has a higher advance, but the details make recoupment* almost impossible, while Label #3 has a conservative offer but a strong record of maximizing an artist's songs through multiple playlist placement and sync opportunities.

In all forms of entertainment and media, an up-front advance has to be recouped by sales before any agreed royalties begin to be paid. That includes *all* production, marketing,* and related expenses tied to the project. Anything spent toward an artist's career will be charged to the account to pay back. If a deal never recoups advance, the royalty rates are actually a moot point. The advance will be the only money received. But negotiating the best rates is crucial because, if an artist gets traction, recoupment occurs, and a strong career is established, those royalties might be paid for the next thirty years.

Once a manager has grown his/her business to a solid level of success, with a roster of established artists, then diversification and delegation can start to take place as needed. Some managers and artists get to a place where a day-to-day point person becomes necessary. This needs to happen when the artist manager can no longer keep up with the overall responsibilities of guiding the artist at thirty-thousand feet, plus handle all the details of daily tasks. Bringing in this role allows for both attention to the artist and increased opportunities for growth and expansion. The day-to-day person can become the go-to on communication and agreed-upon, specific tasks. A successful manager can also begin to hire or contract specialists in areas like social media, graphic design, accounting/bookkeeping, and legal matters.

Scooter Braun started out with only Justin Bieber when the soon-to-be pop superstar was just thirteen years old. Today, Braun's management group has upwards of thirty artists, including Ariana Grande, Kanye West, Demi Lovato, and Dan + Shay.[31] But after Colonel Tom Parker signed Elvis in 1955, "the king" was his sole client for the duration of Elvis' life, even managing the Presley estate's brand until Parker's own death in 1997.[32]

Some managers came to their clients through their primary careers that were connected to the industry, such as a music attorney, tour manager, or front-of-house engineer. For example, Chris Stapleton's current day-to-day manager started out as his road manager, as Chris was just getting started in his artist's career. Some singers or musicians meet another artist, connect, believe in them, and want to help navigate their career and put their own aside. (Remember when I said you might decide you can't compete as an artist, so you take on another role in the business? Management might be a good option if you meet the right artist.)

The obvious issue that comes into play in these cases where there is a primary career already in place is the available bandwidth of the manager. When the day job pays the bills, the manager role has to always come in second. That could potentially create a growth ceiling for the artist's career.

A key aspect of a manager's job is bringing all his/her relationships to the table for the benefit of an artist. A good manager can often bring along established, trusted connections such as:

- Reputable music attorney

- Bookkeeper (who knows the financial specifics of the music business)

- Graphic designer (for everything from logos to merch products)

- Stylist

- PR agent

- Merch company

- Production services

- Recording studios

- Video directors

- Road personnel

- Rehearsal space

Another important aspect of a manager's relationships is bringing unique opportunities to an artist. Some examples are:

- Cowrites with sought-after writers

- Tour support for established artists

- Duets/features with established artists

- TV appearances, from local morning shows to national late-night talk shows

- Auditions for film and/or TV roles

- Special features/appearances for streaming platforms— Spotify, Apple Music, Amazon

- Special appearances for online shows, such as NPR Tiny Desk, COLORS, Jam in the Van, and Mahogany Sessions

- Book publishing opportunities

- Interviews with mainstream media

Customizing a Career

An artist's needs are as diverse as music itself. Some require more attention in various areas than others, so management's job is to make sure the artist is set up for success to maximize their talents and opportunities. For example, an artist might need to be given a record budget, block off three months on their calendar, secure a studio, and then just let them hide from the world, write, and produce an incredible record. Don't mess with them, just let them do their thing while you do yours. But that same artist might need his/her hand held on a press tour because of fears and insecurities or a manager's concern of what he/she might say in the moment. For other artists, the reverse scenario could be true. Some artists are so at home on the road that when they are out, they're content and rarely need attention. That frees the manager to work on future opportunities while the tour is happening.

Some artists care a great deal about certain aspects of their career and not at all about others. Some have a lot of expertise in some areas and know nothing in others. A good manager needs to bring in help where help is needed. But where an artist wants to be involved, you let them. Where they don't, you get it covered.

The BrickHouse Brand

So far, I've given you a big picture look at the role of a manager. To close out this chapter, I want to share some of my personal philosophy of management that I have built my own career upon. These are principles that have always driven *what* I do and *how* I do it.

First, like a good police force, I believe my role is to protect and to serve. I have to protect what the artist cares about, and for my roster, the big three are:

- Faith

- Family

- Finances

When we work hard to take care of these three priorities, the rest seem to eventually fall into place. After these, the artist's goals and dreams, along with protection of their time, are very important—focusing on anything they hold near and dear to their hearts. When Jesus said in the Gospels that He did not come to be served, but to serve, that's my attitude for my artists. I have zero expectation that they should ever serve me.

That's just the nature of my job. My artists come first.

An example of protection is when the booking agent and I see that a promoter is not going to be able to sell enough tickets to cover expenses. We could hold their feet to the fire and make them pay us and lose. But while my artist might make more money that one time, we could also damage the relationship with that promoter and negatively affect that market for the next thirty years, for us and potentially other artists too, especially if the promoter goes bankrupt.

As a manager, a constant question I have to ask myself is, "Will I win the battle but lose the war?" Management is a long-term investment, so every decision needs to run through the filter of what's best in the long run for every artist.

Because of the nature of this unique relationship, coupled with the service and protection dynamic, there are times when it gets tough to separate the professional and the personal. That's why healthy boundaries are important. That said, some managers hang out with their artists and their families, while others never do, to keep the lines of separation clear. That call needs to be made by the individual on how they want to run their business. There are both pros and cons to allowing the personal to merge with the professional, and then also in keeping them separate. There's not a right or wrong, just a personal preference. I once heard one manager say, "Never hold the babies," meaning he had decided to be cautious as to how close he gets to the families. I, however, have held my fair share of babies.

To repeat and to drive home an important point—my goal is to handle all the details so the artist is free to create, record, and perform their art with as few distractions as possible.

We have each been given talents and gifts, and good managers help their artists maximize them all, even those that have not yet been discovered and need to be coached to the forefront and grown. For example, a powerhouse singer who has never written a song but has great ideas needs to be encouraged to write. Or a great writer who has a good voice might simply need vocal lessons to become as good of a vocalist as he/she is a writer.

The Two Phases of an Artist's Career

From my experience, I see my artists' careers in two phases:

- Brand Promotional Phase*
- Brand Protection Phase*

During the promotional phase, everyone involved in the artist's career promotes, promotes, promotes. The entire team pushes hard, works hard, puts in long hours, and often sacrifices their personal lives. Over the years, I have had to miss important moments with family and friends for the sake of an artist's career.

But even with all the sacrifice, time, money, and energy spent, the truth is that the majority of artists never make it out of the promotional phase. Oftentimes, when you see an artist fire everyone around them and hire a completely different team, the motive will be that the promotion phase has gone on for a long time. The idea is that the reason he/she can't break out of promotion to get traction must be because of the people around them. Granted, there are times an artist does have the wrong fit with a team, but more often than not, everyone has worked sacrificially. The artist simply can't accept that his/her level of musical talent or personal commitment might be the actual issue. That example transitions us to the next phase.

The protection phase is when traction happens in the artist's career, and everyone can start to hone in on all the elements of a balanced life, personally and professionally. The goal is for the artist to have as long of a career as possible. In this phase, we:

- Protect the brand

- Protect the reputation

- Protect the fan base

- Proactively make decisions to maintain and prolong the established career

This is why you will often hear of an artist announcing a long hiatus a few years into becoming a success. All the years of blood, sweat, and tears in the promotional phase and the first years of the protection phase have built their career to the place where a rest is not only necessary, but financially and professionally viable to keep going and growing in the years to come. This is rarely ever about an artist and their team being lazy or entitled, but more about being exhausted and their need to take a break to regroup and be able to continue on to what is next.

In both phases, figuring out how to create healthy habits in the artist is crucial, so he/she can excel in a balanced life—physically, mentally, emotionally, spiritually, financially, and professionally.

The bottom line is a manager in the music industry cannot have a bigger dream for the artist than the artist has for themselves. There's never a good reason to get an artist to a destination that is not their own vision. As a manager, when I get to sit beside an artist and watch them receive an industry award or accept a platinum record or play a packed-out iconic arena, knowing this moment seemed like an impossible dream just a few years before . . . well, it just doesn't get any better than that for me.

Potential Roles and Positions Connected to Management

- Artist manager
- Co-manager
- Day-to-day manager
- Account executive
- Management support
- Administrative assistant
- Social media director
- In-house legal team
- Accountants/bookkeepers

THE TRIFECTA

Managing Music, Movies, and Manuscripts

*After the MercyMe song "I Can Only Imagine"
became the most played and best-selling song
in the history of Christian music, it inspired
a top-grossing film and best-selling book.*

I have had the unique opportunity to manage a band with a lead singer who wrote a hit song that became a movie and a book. In this bonus section, I want to share that journey as a point of connecting the opportunities and learning experiences that can come to an artist manager.

I've always been up for a challenge, so over the years, I've had some crazy ideas thrown at me. I have learned it's smart to always "take a meeting" to hear someone out, especially when that involves one of my artists. You just never know what might happen.

Years ago, I was contacted by Cindy Bond in California, who told me she wanted to produce a movie on "the biggest song in the history of Christian music." She had two songs in consideration, and one was "I Can Only Imagine." I reached out to Bart, she flew to Nashville, and we met with her.

The producer's first question was, "Where did the song come from?" Bart told her the whole story of his childhood, his journey with his father, and his dad's salvation and death. By the end of the meeting, she said, "This is the song I want to do a movie on."

That statement launched an eight-year process, culminating in the film's release. Several times along the way, as happens with many major projects, it looked like the idea was dead. But I never totally shut it down. I would just let it marinate for a little bit, and eventually, it would come back around. Over the years, we had multiple scripts that didn't really land right for the story. I even reached a point where I quit reading them. I just let Bart tell me what he thought. He would call me and say, "Man, I couldn't even get halfway through that one."

But then the Erwin brothers were brought in, and everything changed. They got involved in the script and spent time with Bart to hear the story for themselves. One night, at around 9:00 p.m., I received an email with a script that I sent to Bart.

The next morning, I was at my office when Bart called. He had just finished reading the new script. I asked him, "Well, is it good?" He answered, "Yeah, I think it is." He drove to my office while Kim, who for years has been my "right hand" on our management team, printed off three copies. We sat down and read it out loud. By around noon, Kim had typed up our changes and sent it back to the Erwins. I remember they were blown away with our fast turnaround because they aren't used to anything involved with movies being quick. That got the ball rolling, and they began to raise money for the film, which is very common at that point in the process.

One thing I learned about movies is that the stories have to be told through the eyes of the person the film is about. The movie was through Bart's eyes, just like *The Blind Side* was told through Sandra Bullock's character's eyes. You have to choose a perspective, the one telling the story. That said, everyone involved with the film wanted anyone involved to be one hundred percent on board with the presentation. I was involved in a lot of that communication with questions like, "Do you want to be in the film or should we write you out?" and "Can we use your name?" Questions like that.

Besides permissions and raising money, casting is always a critical issue. Getting the characters accurate is so important to a film. For me, they wanted Trace Adkins from the jump, but he was hesitant, so the Erwins spent a day with him. They let him know how important he was to the film. Obviously, he eventually agreed.

Casting Bart was, of course, the toughest job, because he had to look like Bart, be a good actor, and also be able to sing great. When they landed on a Broadway actor named J. Michael Finley, Bart and his wife flew to New York to see him perform and to visit with him. The producers weren't able to land Dennis Quaid as Bart's dad until after the movie had started shooting, but that signing was vital to the film's success.

After about a week of filming, I flew to visit the set in Oklahoma. While standing at baggage claim, I saw Andy Erwin and walked over to say hi. There was a man standing next to him with his back to me. When Andy saw me, he hit the guy on the shoulder, and said, "Well, here he is. Take a look for yourself." The man turned around, looked me up and down, and then said, "I get it." It was Trace Adkins, the actor who would play me.

We spent the next day together on the set. By dinner that night, we realized we were both "cut from the same cloth," as they say. We both grew up on farms. We both played college sports. We both don't care what other people think about us.

THE TRIFECTA: MANAGING MUSIC, MOVIES, AND MANUSCRIPTS

We're both rough-around-the-edges guys. Plus he's an artist and has a manager, so that role is not foreign to him. Those factors made it easy for Trace to just jump into the role. They nailed the casting on the entire film. All told, I ended up being on the set for about twenty of the 28 shooting days.

Through the entire process, my job was to protect the MercyMe brand. I knew Bart had signed off on the script, but reading it and then seeing it come together on set, there are always going to be tweaks and changes. There were a couple of times where I had to say, "Hey, Bart wouldn't do that" or "Bart wouldn't say that." In the scene where Bart is confronted by the record labels, Trace did a take where he got bossy and yelled. I had to say, "Bro, I would protect my artist's dignity, so I wouldn't yell at them. I work for them. They're the boss. I'm just there to advise." Trace responded, "Hey, I get it." So he tweaked being aggressive and calmed down the scene. There were several times where I stepped in and offered some accuracy to how the guys were presented. I kept reminding myself that a lot of people will "meet Bart" for the first time when they see the movie, so I wanted him to be accurate on film.

Aside from calling a few people I knew who had been involved with movies, I had to navigate my way through the journey by communicating openly with everyone. One of the business partners in the production company and I had a lot of conversations, walking through the details of the deal and working through the budget for production and marketing. I also had to learn the different splits of the gross, from the theater's take to the investors to the production company. Who gets paid first and who gets paid later and how much. The movie also wanted to sponsor the band's tour that would begin around the time of the film's release. That became a separate deal as a marketing piece for the movie. I definitely had to do some research to familiarize myself with film production, but everyone involved in the film was very forthcoming with information.

As the film was starting to wrap up, and edits were being done, a discussion began for Bart to write a book to be released in tandem with the film. Bart was able to communicate many of the details that the film couldn't. A book doesn't take as long to produce as a film because there aren't a lot of moving parts. Because the book and any other ancillary pieces fell more in line with what our record label does, I handed a lot of that over to Jeff Moseley, our label president. It made sense for Jeff to get involved in those aspects that are similar to what he does every day.

As I have said and will continue to say throughout the book, the *only* reason I was involved with a film and a book was because of a great song. Isn't it amazing that a four-minute song could launch a movie that would go on to gross over $100 million and a book that would sell over two hundred thousand copies? But that is exactly why songs are so crucial to artists and the music industry.

"Just doing as well as you did last time is not good enough."
—Michael Jackson[33]

CHAPTER SIX

THE RECORD DEAL: PART I

Labels today get involved in almost every aspect of an artist's career, working hand in hand with the manager to maximize his/her brand.

WHO KNOWS if we would have ever heard of Big Machine Records had they not signed Taylor Swift. And without BMR, we may have never heard of Taylor Swift! But when they teamed up, six albums changed all their lives.[34]

The "record deal" is the phrase created many years ago to describe an artist signing a contract with a record label*. So, right out of the gate, let's define "record label" as a company that partners with artists on their music to:

- Create
- Record
- Market
- Sell

The label is the pipeline for the artist's music to be released to the public, much like the publishing company is the pipe-line for songs.

One of the biggest decisions an artist will ever make in his/her career is whether or not to sign with a record label. And, if so, with the *right* label. Most artists start with the question of "who?" *Who* will sign me? *Who* is best for me to sign with? *Who* can give me the best deal? But, first, understanding the "why" is far more important than the "who" or even the "what."

The Artist–Label Connection

Most of the time, your first impression of a label is going to be their track record, the artists who have been on their roster in the past and those currently on their roster. Initially, the most important connection between an artist and a label is going to be the A&R person who will oversee his/her recording career and will become the main contact, point person, and representative at the label. An A&R rep should be a mixture of ambassador, coach, and cheerleader all rolled into one.

A&R is constantly scouring the physical and digital world for artists, talent, fit, and potential with his/her label. For many years, artists were most often discovered while playing live in venues. Of course, the Internet has radically changed the game. Platforms like YouTube and SoundCloud are now huge magnets for A&R.

After twelve-year-old Ella Yelich-O'Connor sang lead with a group of her fellow student musicians at her school's "battle of the bands" competition, the video of the performance was posted online, and a Universal Music Group A&R rep happened onto it. He was struck by her unique vocal style and contacted her and her parents. After two years of cowriting songs under his direction, she found her musical identity and recorded her first album. At seventeen years old, she became the youngest person to ever win a Grammy for Song of the Year as the artist known as Lorde.[35] These kinds of stories are becoming more and more prevalent each year in the music business as the web makes the world both more accessible and smaller.

Regardless of how an artist is discovered, once the A&R person is convinced that all the elements and dynamics are right, he/she presents the artist to the entire team at a label for consideration. The answer could be an immediate yes, an immediate no, a not-yet-let's-wait-for-the-right-timing, or the offer of a development deal. This last option is an actual contract with a label that promises to develop the artist's career over time; hence the name.

In this arrangement, the exchange for the time and money invested by the label is that the artist is contractually obligated for the length of the agreement, and if a record is eventually recorded, royalties are usually structured in favor of the label to try and recoup their money. This can be tricky and sticky for the label and the artist. While they have the chance of ending up in a full-on deal over time, it can also become a money pit for the label and/or a career killer for the artist. But for some, like Lorde, everything comes together to create a win-win success story.

Being candid, there are some situations where a label sees some talent and just wants to make sure no one else snatches them up, but they want to wait to capitalize on them later. They offer the artist a development deal more out of defense for themselves than offense for the artist. Sometimes the artist just ends up getting put on a shelf, and his/her career is essentially paralyzed for the term of the contract. This is one of the horror stories you might hear if you hang around young artists in any of the major music cities. Of course, the right manager can know how to navigate a good deal and steer away from a bad one. But this is one of the potential pitfalls for an artist flying solo.

If an artist and a label strike a deal, most often the A&R rep stays with that artist for the remainder of the contract, being heavily involved in every aspect of the artist's recording career. That is why this relationship is critical for the artist *and* for the label. One crucial point to understand about a record label is that if you sign a contract, the clock will start ticking as soon as your signature dries on the page. Just like milk, if too much time passes, it can spoil.

To prove the adage "you just never know who might be listening," Michael Bublé was discovered when he was the singer for a prominent Canadian family's daughter's wedding reception. *Yes, he was the wedding singer.* Legendary record mogul and producer David Foster was one of the guests, and when he heard Michael sing the classic "Mack the Knife," he knew he had discovered a diamond in the rough. Following his set, the two met and Bublé's life was changed forever.[36]

Around 1990, the music industry started phasing out the 45—the small two-sided, two-song vinyl record. iTunes wasn't launched until 2003, when the digital single could be purchased. During that ten-plus years in between, the CD (compact disc) was king. If you heard a song on the radio or from a friend, you had to buy the entire CD at retail to get that one song. Imagine having to lay down ten bucks so you can listen to one song. We can't comprehend that concept anymore. Because of the monopoly of the CD, the sales volume and profit margins made labels a lot of money, so they, in turn, had huge budgets to spend to develop artists.

Through the introduction of the Internet and the digital revolution of music, artist development by labels has unfortunately become a rarity because they simply cannot afford the risk. Because of these sweeping changes, A&R have had to radically alter their tactics and look for artists who have already developed their careers to certain levels on their own—artists who have created their own fan base through social media, online presence, and live shows. The analogy I always share is that labels are looking for artists who have "gotten their own plane in the air" versus the day when the label provided the plane, crew, and runway! But to repeat my description from a previous chapter, if the A&R rep, with the label's support, can find an artist who's already in the air, then they can strap jet engines onto him/her to go farther, faster, and higher than the artist could ever go on their own.

That said, I have witnessed circumstances when a label straps those jet engines onto an artist's plane too soon, too quickly, and the entire machine disintegrates in midair. The reason can be as simple as the artist wasn't mature enough to handle the emotional stress that often comes with the demands of success. But it is certainly a beautiful sight when a label comes alongside an artist, and together, they go places that both had only dreamed they could go.

Production
The team at a record label known as the "production team" has the responsibility of gathering all the elements of a project and placing them into the right format. They upload the music, images, album

art, album credits,* and all files correctly and in a timely manner. They are to make sure any form of release happens without any issues or delays, and they track all the metadata,* meaning any and all digital information connected to the project.

Most labels have three separate creative teams inside these departments:

- Publishing: The publishing department at a label focuses on the writing process of songs from concept to completion, as we covered in the previous chapter.

- A&R: The Artists and Repertoire team puts their combined expertise into the entire recording process.

- Marketing: The marketing team directs all the aspects of the artist's branding, which typically includes all the visuals released from and about the artist. The marketing creative branding team

  » Arranges any photo shoots or video shoots

  » Assists the artist with their look, style, and fashion

  » Directs album packaging

  » Leads the artist in establishing a brand and image

  » Helps keep the artist on brand and maintain cohesiveness throughout album cycles

All of these elements take place around singles, covers,* lyric videos, performance videos, and ad campaigns. This team often has a tough job because of limited budgets and short deadlines to accomplish the label's goals.

When an artist already has a solid identity, brand, and style, the creative team can help tweak and improve everything because they have a good foundation to build on. But when an artist is new or has little direction, the team often has to create all these elements from scratch for him/her. This is why you can hear about an artist who's unhappy or disgruntled because they begin to realize that the image created for them is "not who I am." If any disconnect occurs between the artist and the label in how they are working to promote an album, there can be some real knock-down, drag-out fights. I've seen that many times throughout my years in the business, and I have worked very hard to avoid that dilemma. Proper "branding and image" is such a critical part of an artist's career and must receive the appropriate amount of attention in order for the artist and the label to be on the same page.

A talented creative team coupled with a creative artist can be a beautiful thing. As a manager, I love when that team comes to the table with great ideas. On the other side of the coin, the wrong pairing can be a total train wreck. We've all seen artists dressed in outfits or placed in photo shoots that just don't seem right for them. And then, down the road, you see a totally different look and realize, "Oh, that's who that artist is! Not those photos when they first came out. That was ridiculous. *This* looks like them and fits their music."

Their Bank and Your Brand

Here are some key elements of what a label provides an artist:

Bank

A major role that a label plays in an artist's career is to be "the bank," becoming the primary financial backer, helping the artist have the budget to get the best:

- Producer
- Engineer
- Musicians
- Look/style/image
- Video content
- Social media presence
- Publicity
- Tour support
- Brand development

Many labels today get involved in almost every aspect of an artist's career, working hand in hand with the manager to maximize his/her image.

Brand

A record label works to build the strongest brand for an artist. The brand is the overall vibe, feel, look, and style that is shown to the public. Sometimes this is exactly who the artist is. Take James Taylor; since "Fire and Rain" and "You've Got a Friend" were released in the early '70s, he's a what-you-see-is-what-you-get kind of artist. His brand has always been simply him just as he is—incredibly talented, blue-collar, guy-next-door, singer-song-writer. But sometimes an artist's brand is more like a character in a movie and not like the real person at all. Like Alice Cooper, the legendary rock star—he's actually a strong evangelical, conservative Christian who is an avid golfer. But when you look at album covers and live shows, you *never* see that image. Like most actors, you have to find interviews where they ask him about his faith and personal life to know who he actually is.

Think of one of your favorite artists. Consider how you would describe who he/she is to you and how their image makes you feel. Whatever your answer, well, that is their brand at work.

With all this information in mind, the main expenses for record labels are going to be all the elements of recording the songs and then all the aspects of marketing those projects to drive sales. Labels then make money by selling the music through singles, albums, and compilations. Of course today, the vast majority of a sale is actually digital streams; 150 streams are considered equal to the sale of a single, and 1,500 streams are equal to an album sale (150 streams x 10 songs).[37]

A Typical Record Deal

Offers from a label today are all about two components: options and songs. An option is defined as the label's legal opportunity to extend or continue the contract. The artist is not given options. For example, a label might offer an artist the option of three albums or thirty songs, whichever comes first.

Within a deal, there is the "initial period," meaning the first released recordings agreed upon. Options may follow; the label may choose to enact these potential scenarios in order to continue the contract. For a new artist with a first-time offer, that could be for just five songs with one of those released as a single promoted to radio. If the artist is successful past those five songs, the label can always pick up the option.

I touched on the term *recoupment* previously, but this is a good place to take the explanation into more detail. If an artist is given any sort of advance money, recouping or getting back that amount will be required in the contract. Recoupable means any money spent on an artist's recording career, unless you have specific percentages or limits in your contract, such as a 50/50 split on marketing expenses. So, you get really excited when your label calls your manager to say the marketing team of four people are flying in to watch you perform a sold-out show. Their airfares, hotel, rental car, and meals are all charged to your account and are recoupable on your percentage. Let me stop and say, I'm not trying to be negative or a downer, just trying to shoot you straight on how things work. Do you want the marketing team to see you live and get what you do? Of course! You want these things to happen, you just have to understand the truth about how much of this you may eventually pay.

Labels have to recoup all the costs to make your music— recording and marketing. But here's the potential good news: If the songs are great, the production is stellar, and the album is well received by the public, then the money starts to come in, and your statements eventually show all initial costs have been recouped and your royalty rate kicks in. (Remember mailbox money?) The label is now turning a profit, and you are getting your share of that take.

If your music continues to do well, and your fan base grows, after your original contract is up, your manager should be able to negotiate much higher numbers on everything. The main reason is, early on, the label took a risk on you, and they had to pad their investment the best they could. But now, you are a much safer bet and far less risk; therefore, everyone can loosen up and hopefully win a little more.

Besides the normal singles and albums that a label will

record with an artist, there are also specialty projects produced. Some examples being a Christmas album, greatest hits album, live album, or acoustic project. Other compilations may be an artist having one song on an album featuring all the artists on a label's roster. These are classified as specialty projects because they typically don't fall under the requirements for fulfilling a record contract. Timing of the release of these records or songs is usually accompanied by a specific strategy to not hinder the progress of an artist's current record release and radio singles. There are times, however, when an artist and a label are at a standoff near the end of their agreement, and a greatest hits album is released just to satisfy the contract. The artist doesn't have to produce new music for the label, but the label gets a new product to push with minimal investment.

The harsh reality today is that it's harder for a label to "break,"* or successfully launch, a new artist than at any time in the history of the music industry. There are so many artists competing on a global scale for the ears of fans. Couple that with there being less money and fewer resources for development for labels to use on artists. With the prevalence of amazing technology, along with the price of all things digital continuing to drop, artists can record incredible projects in their bedrooms. An hour after a song has been digitally mastered,* it can be uploaded to a website for twenty bucks, and fans can start listening. (Mastering will be covered in an upcoming chapter.) A savvy sense of social media presence can then produce free marketing that may hit the sweet spot for that artist's audience. All these opportunities were unfathomable just twenty years ago, proving we live in an incredible time in history for the creation and distribution of art.

(Jobs related to record labels are listed at the end of the next chapter.)

"I'm often . . . hearing about someone's new record, and I think, 'Oh boy, that's gonna be better than me.' It's a very common thing."—SIR PAUL MCCARTNEY[38]

THE RECORD DEAL: PART II

Songs can change the world. The record label can be a great partner
to help an artist create that change for the world to experience.

YEARS AGO, when the music business began to decline and
labels started to go under, everyone had to get creative about
producing as many income streams as possible. Labels began
to expand beyond just creating music. Some started to offer
management, booking, and merch to stay alive. The concept
was to become a one-stop shop under one roof for an artist.
The industry term for this kind of full-service contract is a 360
Deal,* meaning most, if not all, of an artist's career is handled
by the label. Some of these relationships produce great all-
inclusive settings, while others are subpar in some of the areas.

I've never had a problem with labels taking this approach
as long as they have actually figured out how to bring value to
the artist in any area where they are offering a service and making
money. For example, if they want to be contractually exclusive on

the merch of an artist I represent, then I want to know if they have a designer on staff so my artist no longer has to pay for design fees. They can make money on us if they are saving us money, time, and energy elsewhere. Another question would be if the label is going to have a warehouse where all the artist's merch is stored and then shipped out, as a service, for orders and tours.

Here's the one thing everyone in the music industry has to watch out for—when someone gets completely out of their lane, outside of their expertise in an area, that spells trouble. That's a roadblock on the way to success. First and foremost, a record label needs to focus on one thing—selling music. Period. If they get into other income streams and services, fine, but don't sacrifice the reason you started a record label to begin with. A merchandise company needs to focus on what? Yep, merchandise. A booking agent needs to focus on what? Yep, booking shows, having great relationships with promoters and buyers. All of the individual components of the music business have so many moving parts that very few labels can claim to do all of them effectively.

Back in the glory days, a label could spend enough marketing dollars to create an A-level artist. Now with all the noise out there, it gets harder and harder every year to get the attention of the people. The Internet has made the world smaller and smaller, so an artist in New York isn't competing for a spot on a playlist just with an artist from Kansas or California, but also with artists in Europe and Asia.

Also, genres have morphed and expanded. In country music today, there are subcategories, like traditional, country pop, bro-country, Texas, and even hick-hop. Every genre has now splintered into multiple niches. Back in the day, radio stations were the only experts telling us what country or pop or rock was. Today, while they are still in the mix, multiple avenues exist for artists to get their music out, so the paths forward are almost limitless.

Earworms and Airwaves

Record labels are made up of all the necessary departments to take an artist's project from concept to distribution. The larger the label, the more specific the roles, but all labels will have similar elements. Let's break those down.

Marketing

Marketing is simply getting the word out about the artist through as many avenues as possible. The marketing department's job is to create a strategy to implement a targeted plan around the release of an artist's music. They will utilize the artist's branding that has been developed from elements like story, image, album artwork, logo, etc., working to keep every aspect cohesive and relatable to the artist's fan base. Across-the-board consistency is critical.

Marketing includes elements such as:

- Performance videos
- Lyric videos
- Social media ad campaigns
- Contests and giveaways
- Listening events
- Points of purchase, online or retail such as Walmart and Target

- Placements and playlists on digital streaming platforms (DSPs*) such as Spotify, Apple Music, Amazon Music, Pandora, etc.
- Billboard ad campaigns
- Magazine ads, print and digital
- Radio interviews/performances (from local stations to subscriptions like Sirius XM)
- TV interviews/performances (local to national markets)
- Podcast interviews

One important note: depending on an artist's record deal, some of these expenses may be recoupable to the label.

Radio
The radio team is an extension of marketing and extremely important to the success of an artist's career.

If you had asked me several years ago if radio would still be a vital part of an artist's marketing strategy today, I would likely have said no. The reason was because everything in the music industry seemed to be moving solely toward digital platforms. With a fan or listener being able to easily curate their own personal playlist, I anticipated radio would eventually just be phased out. If someone can get in their car and plug in anything they want to listen to, why would you turn on a DJ playing whatever he or she chooses and who talks in between songs? While radio has certainly declined, it has found its own niche among all the new media and, at least for now, seems to be here to stay. The survival of radio in this new era has allowed it to continue to play an important role in directing listeners to certain music. The DSP algorithms* can introduce a listener to whatever is popular through a playlist, but the listener can also still discover artists on the radio. For most listeners, both platforms play a role in their daily lives as music consumers. Even if you personally don't listen to any form of radio, millions of people still do, which ultimately impacts the music business.

To plan the release of a song to radio, or a sequence of singles over time, the radio team will take an artist's album, listen through all the songs, and determine what they feel are the top two or three that should be pushed to radio. Once songs are narrowed down, the A&R team, particularly the artist rep, will be involved in the final selection. Some labels utilize services, which perform market testing where sampling takes place among a group of typical consumers, to see how the general public will respond to the songs; results are typically scored in a range from 1 to 5. An A&R team may have chosen Song A as the best cut for radio, but the sample group in research may have chosen Song C. This consumer data can cause a label to change their minds on the strategy.

Song testing is big in the radio world to determine what will be released to radio. If a song tests strongly in a sample group, they're going to pour more money into the machine to try to get the song up the charts. The radio department will call every week to talk to the program directors,* trying to make sure the song is gaining traction in rotation. The goal is to chart the song and help it climb as high as possible and stay there.

One of the members of my team was in a meeting where he was told that one major country artist's record label had worked with a popular DSP to identify that artist's top one percent of listeners. The label sent those subscribers three of the artist's new unreleased songs and asked them to choose the next single. Record labels are getting more scientific and specific using the digital information available today.

Obviously, a number one song is always the end goal. The label wants all the radio stations to add it around the same time. But there are early adopters, meaning some who play it early, love it, and add the song; and late adopters who finally add the song more out of peer pressure from seeing other stations move it into medium or heavy rotation. But the more in sync the song's adds* are, the better for charting the song.

You may have seen a song by an artist that has "radio edit"* beside the title. This means the label thought the song would work on radio, but they created a specific radio version that was different from the album version, and made changes like shortening the song, mixing a version with the vocal level up, or possibly using a different intro or ending, all to try and maximize it for radio.

Once the first single is chosen, the song will get uploaded to DSPs and submitted for what is known as a future "add date," meaning the date the label asks the radio stations to start playing the submitted single. Of course, the hope is that the stations will listen and decide to add the song.

Depending on the label and their marketing strategy, the radio department may schedule a radio tour where the artist and a rep from the team travel to key radio stations around the country to do in-studio, on-air interviews and performances. They usually also meet the program director and all the DJs. The goal is for an artist to get to know the folks involved in radio around the country. Those relationships are important, especially to establish a long-term career. Some artists bring a guitar or keyboard player with them for the performances. Many of the stations create video content of these performances/interviews and post them on their YouTube channel, creating new online content for marketing.

I have always advised my artists to take explicit notes anytime they visit at a radio station. Get spouses' names, kids' names, hobbies, interests, etc., and write them down. Then the next time they're at that station, use the notes as a reminder of that personal info. To establish relationships over the long haul in a career, these kinds of details matter to people. The DJ at Radio Station X is no longer just someone who interviews you once a year, but is now "Caleb who has been married for six years, has a two-year-old daughter, and is into mountain biking." In the corporate world, this is known as pre-call intelligence.

The program director* at a radio station is the gatekeeper who decides what songs will be played. Similar to the record label's testing of songs, some stations may have listener panels to test new music, normally only thirty seconds or so of each song in consideration. There are third-party testing companies that are widely used.

When a new song from an artist is added into rotation, this is called "getting an add." Each time the song plays on the radio is known as a spin.* Rotation* is the term for a radio station's current roster of played songs. There is light, medium, and heavy rotation. A song in light rotation* will only get a couple of spins per day. A few times a day is considered medium rotation.* But if you get sick of hearing a song on the radio, when it starts to

feel like a station plays a song all the time, that is heavy rotation.*
And a number one song will be in super-heavy rotation.*

All spins are reported to the weekly radio charts. The
radio department at the label will make weekly tracking calls*
to the stations, often specifically to the program director, to
inquire about activity. This tracking helps them make decisions
on whether to continue to push a single, let the single ride, or
drop the single altogether and move on to the next song. These
charts are how program directors can influence other stations
as well as the fans.

When program directors listen to new music, they are
looking for any reason to say no because there are consistently
far more songs trying to get played than there are actual spots in
their rotation. A song being deleted within the first ten seconds
is not unusual, because a good director knows what works for
their listeners—and what doesn't.

One of the easiest reasons for a director to say no is if
the artist is not signed to a label. This is why labels can act as
a first line of defense for an artist and their music. Here's the
reasoning: If the artist isn't good enough to get a label to sign
them, why should the program director take a risk on an independent artist? If a song is added, and the artist should take off,
will he/she have the resources to keep feeding the machine with
little to no help?

Also, radio programmers are in constant contact with
the teams at labels, so a program director is far more likely to
reserve rotation slots for a label he/she knows, trusts, has been
to events with, and has worked with for many years. To spell
out the rules, labels cannot pay radio to add music. They can

pay for meals for educational purposes (radio comes to town, and the label informs them of what they have going out) and giveaways to listeners. But no offers can be made of real value in exchange for favor on songs.

In contrast, as far as marketing, a massive amount of money is put behind the artists whom you start to hear in light to medium rotation on the radio. If an artist climbs the charts, then they also can get ahead of the game of selling tickets to play live. This has been true for many years and I don't know when it's ever going to change. So, remember, like I keep telling you, relationships are the key.

Today, there are many radio stations that only add one new single into rotation per month. *Yep, one per month.* Why is that? Because at the end of the day, radio stations aren't in business to break artists or keep a veteran artist in the game. They exist to make money through advertising. The larger the listening audience, the more money they can charge for ads, and the more ads they can sell. TV works the same way. (The price of Super Bowl ads is the ultimate proof.) They keep listeners by playing songs that listeners like. If they play too many new songs and lose the interest of their listeners, their market share drops, and therefore, they can't charge as much for their ads.

That said, radio stations do understand the value of helping new artists break and established artists release new singles. They also tend to like new songs to sound like the other songs that they play. There is a formula for every radio station. That's why stations have always been called "the pop station," "the rock station," or "the country station." It helps listeners to know exactly what they are going to get, with little to no surprises. For this reason, the chances of a program director taking a risk on a new artist that has a radically different sound in a certain genre is extremely slim.

If, as an artist and songwriter, you listened to a radio station for a month and then wrote a song you think would fit into the style and sound of that radio station, likely, by the time it was produced and released, the direction of that station would have changed slightly, just far enough away from your newly produced song. Again, not trying to be negative, just honest. To repeat: if you're going to be in this business, you need to understand how everything works—and doesn't.

Taking all this information into consideration, here's the game: The songwriter, artist, A&R rep, record producer, and radio department are always trying to figure out what songs the programmer might add. As you can see, program directors have a unique job as they shape the culture of music and make or break careers, not only for the artist, but also for the producer and songwriter—and ultimately, the future of record labels.

To sum up the release of a single to radio: A label devotes time, money, and energy to release a single. They record the music, test the music, set up a release schedule, send out the music, and track the song. If the song catches on and starts to climb, great. If the song doesn't work, a lot of time and money are flushed.

Pipeline to the Public

Once the record is recorded, mixed, and mastered, the production department is responsible for gathering all the elements of the release in the correct format, double- and triple-checking every detail to launch the project into the marketplace for maximum success. These elements include everything from what the consumer can access to what a platform needs to distribute the music, such as:

- Music masters
- Album packaging
- Lyrics
- Liner notes*
- Coordinated video content
- All copyright information
- All publishing information
- Barcodes

Distribution's job is to work with every potential outlet to monetize the music. In the days when physical point-of-purchase products were the norm, back when you had to go to Tower Records to get your favorite artist's new project, necessary areas of manufacturing, inventory, warehousing, and shipping were the supply chain. The goal was for all stores to have the release on the shelves when the doors opened on the drop date. For years that was on Tuesdays, until July 10, 2015, when the official release day moved to Fridays.[39]

Depending on your age, you may recall the days when artists would post a picture of themselves in a retail store buying one of their own products with a massive smile on their face and a caption like, "So excited my new CD is finally out today!" But, of course, in the digital age, while there are still a few labels offering a very small number of CDs to the handful of outlets out there that still have buyers, physical product is essentially DOA. At the same time, in the history-repeats-itself category, vinyl has seen a growing resurgence, with retail prices on new product averaging in the twenty-five-dollar range. A comeback no one in the music business saw coming was in 2020 when U.S. vinyl sales were 27.5 million units. This was up 46 percent over 2019 and thirty times over 2006, the year vinyl first reemerged. But for perspective, the 2020 number is still only three-and-a-half percent of album-equivalent music consumption per streaming.[40]

Monetizing Music

For distribution on the digital path, a label works to monetize the record through streaming via DSPs such as Spotify, Apple, Amazon, Tidal, Deezer, and YouTube Music. The distribution department of a label has to actively maintain and grow relationships with all the various outlets, large and small. Of course, placement on playlists is a huge doorway to listeners. There are so many artists today vying for those spots that connections with the gatekeepers are crucial.

Connected to a release, the placement of individual songs from a record, along with lyric videos, have become a staple product on YouTube. Many of the younger audience, especially those who cannot afford a DSP or whose parents won't spring for it, access their music solely on YouTube (a separate entity from YouTube Music, mentioned above). In the non-subscription version of YouTube, ad views come into play in this scenario, targeting the marketing of products to the demographic.

Historically and currently, the distribution department at labels operates in the background. You don't hear much about them. However, being the pipeline to the public, they are an extremely important aspect of the overall success of the music business, being the final step where fans access music. If they don't do their job, the music isn't available. They have always been one of the areas in the industry where you don't think about them until something goes wrong. If they do their jobs, you don't notice them at all.

To offer an example of how the components can be treated inside a large corporation, Sony Music, Sony Publishing, and Sony Distribution are all under the umbrella of the Sony organization, yet each entity also operates separately. With massive conglomerates like these, the right hand doesn't typically know what the left hand is doing, as they say.

Unless an artist has stipulations and exceptions spelled out in the record contract, he/she gives up all rights to sell music on their own, and distribution is exclusive to the label, including covers. If a signed artist writes a new song and records and videos an acoustic version in their living room, they can't simply post it without coordinating with their label because the label has the exclusive right to release and distribute anything the artist does.

However, those kinds of posts can create engagement with fans and marketing awareness of the artist's brand, as well as potential income through views for the artist and the label. If an artist covers and posts "Don't Stop Believing," the massively popular Journey song, someone looking for that song could discover the artist and then the artist and the music released by their label is also discovered. Basically, under a record contract, posting a video of any song falls under "distribution" and has to be coordinated with the label.

Paths of Distribution

For small labels and independent artists, third-party companies are available to handle every aspect of distributing the masters and all the production elements to the DSPs. There are services such as Distrokid, Tunecore, and CD Baby. These services work by allowing you to choose a plan (for an annual fee) based on how many artists and/or songs will be released through the account. For example, one artist or band is about twenty dollars a year, but a label with twenty bands is about $250 a year. Then you just upload the masters and all the graphic elements, including cover and lyric support. Input the drop date, and they will time the release across all time zones to hit the markets at the same time. It's easy for the label because you simply input all the percentage splits. They'll collect payments from all sources and send out the earnings.[41]

If you have a cowriter and/or producer who will get a cut of any royalty, and the person does not have an account on the service you choose, asking him/her to open one might be the best way to make sure distributions happen correctly. Also, if a PRO or other third party handles a writer's royalties, that person needs to be sure their collecting entity is made aware of the distribution and links accordingly. Because of the nature of these services being available to the general population of artists and labels, the dashboards tend to be highly user-friendly and intuitive, and help is readily available.

Digital Data

In March 1991, SoundScan began monitoring the purchase of all music. When a consumer bought a CD at Walmart, that sale was

144

logged with its specific data of price and store location. Music-related companies subscribed to the service, and every Monday, SoundScan offered the sales numbers through reports of the previous week. As an artist manager, I could look at the report and see specific information. If one of my artists sold 150 units in Minneapolis the previous week, I would see it. Tracking this kind of data allowed for synergy between radio and live shows. If you are selling incredibly well in Seattle, then guess what? You can likely sell a lot of tickets at a venue in Seattle. If sales are high in a particular market, and you also see that a station has put the new single on heavy rotation, you could connect the dots.

Today, SoundScan still exists, offering the same data monitoring in the digital world of music. Ten spins in streaming equals what used to be one sale. They adapted so we can still track how the artist is doing while using the same system of reporting.[42]

As an independent artist or a small label, all the DSPs offer this same specific data per song through the artist's or label's account. As soon as you have at least one single streaming through a service, you can see how many listeners you have per song by city and country. The analytics available directly to artists today are amazing.

The Bottom Line

Besides creating great art, the end result everyone is looking for from distribution is *selling* the art. Just for fun, as of the writing of this book, here is Soundscan's top ten albums based on unit sales since the service's launch in 1991:

1. *Metallica* by Metallica — 17,300,000
2. *Come on Over* by Shania Twain — 15,730,000

3. *Jagged Little Pill* by Alanis Morissette — 15,200,000
4. *1* by The Beatles — 13,000,000
5. *Legend* by Bob Marley — 12,300,000
6. *Millennium* by Backstreet Boys — 12,300,000
7. *The Bodyguard* (film soundtrack) by Whitney Houston — 12,140,000
8. *21* by Adele — 12,100,000
9. *Supernatural* by Santana — 11,850,000
10. *Human Clay* by Creed — 11,690,000

Celine Dion is the only artist to have two records in the top twenty, making her combined total over 20,000,000 units sold. Pop leads the field, with rock second. Country has no artist on the list unless you count Shania in her hybrid pop/country style. Eminem is the only rap/hip-hop artist in the top twenty. In more recent years, Taylor Swift and Adele have tended to dominate the year they release a project. The record for most albums sold in a single week is Adele's *25* at 3.38 million sold.[43]

Remember, distribution, whether through a record label or direct by the artist, is the single avenue through which sales/streaming numbers happen at all. If marketing is the driver, then distribution is the vehicle. But the golden road the music industry runs on is paved with what? Yep! Great songs!

Artists as Entrepreneurs
As I stated before, the amount of money that some labels invest in artists can be mind-blowing. Even in today's volatile music climate, some have millions of dollars put into their careers before the public ever hears the first song. To be clear, I believe

that an unsigned artist can release an album and spend a lot less money than a label, *but* the chances that artist is going to see the *same* level of success as someone signed to a label are not very high. I certainly wouldn't take that bet now, but who knows? I might have to soon.

One crazy exception to the rule is Lindsey Stirling, the dancing pop performance artist/violinist. With no money and every record label turning her down, she went on *America's Got Talent* in 2010, only to have Piers Morgan tell her, "The world has no place for a dancing dubstep violinist" and Sharon Osbourne to say, "I don't think what you're doing right now is enough to fill a theater in Las Vegas." But then she discovered YouTube and "Crystallize" went viral in 2012 with 140 million views, garnering her 8.5 million subscribers.[44] She told *Forbes* magazine, "I just realized I could make my career happen myself." She continued, "Then all of a sudden, all these record label people were coming out to the shows and meeting me backstage. My band thought it was really funny because they've been with multiple artists in the past and they had never seen the label trying to impress the artist so much. Usually we're the ones trying to impress them!"[45]

But after huge success in record sales and tours, just as I said in the Artist chapter, Lindsey reached the point where she outgrew what she and her team could do on their own. She signed with Lady Gaga's management and eventually agreed for her own label Lindseystomp to partner with Concord Capitol Universal.

Although it doesn't work for 99 percent of artists (in my experience), there are breakout artists like Lindsey who create successful careers without ever signing to a label. They can hire out independent contractors to do anything a label can do. But from my experience, the vast majority will spend more money, time, and energy, and the music will not get as far. And when that happens, they are less likely to make a living.

Yet if you are an artist who wants to:

- Keep total control of every aspect of your music,
- Do your own thing inside your personal calling,
- Risk that you may be limited on what you can make financially, and
- Always make sure your art is more important than money . . .

. . . then the great news is there are plenty of resources today to help you accomplish your goals as a songwriter, artist, and entrepreneur. There will be plenty of times in any artist's career where he/she has to choose art over money, and then sometimes money over art.

Once again, I want to remind you that the bottom line of any artist's success and ability to sell records—label or no label—has everything to do with what? The song! Songs can open doors. Songs can make careers. Songs can change the world. The record label can be a great partner to help an artist create art for the world to experience.

Potential Roles and Positions Connected to Record Labels

- Label president
- Director of Artist and Repertoire (A&R)
- Marketing creative branding team
  - » Marketing department manager
  - » Brand manager
  - » Content manager

- » Social media manager
- » Graphic designer
- » Stylist
- » Photographer/videographer
- Radio department
  - » Radio department manager
  - » Song Trackers
- Production team
- Operations
- Attorneys
- Accountants
- Publicist

Jobs Outside the Label
- Radio station
  - » Program director
  - » Radio on-air personality
  - » Sales team
  - » Advertisement production team

Jobs at Distribution Companies
- DSP managers
- Sales
- Marketing
- Production
- Customer service
- National account reps
- Road reps
- Phone reps

"You make your mistakes to learn how to get to the good stuff." —QUINCY JONES [46]

CHAPTER EIGHT

THE PRODUCER

*A great producer helps an artist create the most commercially
viable music that their songs will allow.*

BILL SZYMCZYK (pronounced sim-zik) produced many of
the Eagles' hit albums, including *Hotel California*, the record
that sold 32 million copies and won two Grammys. At the
2016 NAMM Show, Szymczyk talked about sitting at the
recording console between Joe Walsh and Don Felder as they
laid down the iconic guitar tracks on the title cut. He said,
"Trial and error, punch, punch, punch, 8 million times until
the end of that two days is that unbelievable guitar stuff at the
end. Actually, all the way through, but mostly at the very end
of 'Hotel California.' That's, by far, one of the highest points
of my career."[47]

By the time we hear a hit song on the radio or streaming,
one of the most important but seldom seen players in the
creation of the music is the producer.

The producer's job is to lead the artist and the A&R rep in the recording of songs, whether a single, an EP, or an entire album. For a project, the producer will help choose, write, and/or cowrite the songs and then work to make each track (recorded song) the very best it can possibly be, all while creating a cohesive and commercially viable project.

The journey to making a record usually starts with the artist's A&R rep at the label suggesting several producers who could be a good fit with the artist's style of music. The best choice is usually determined by meetings with those producers, which then can be followed up by cowriting sessions to see if they gel creatively. The producer will try to present one of his/ her best ideas, along with some production concepts that fit the artist's style. Typically, by the end of the first writing session, the producer will have created a demo of a song. Often, if the artist chooses him/her, that demo will be the beginning stage of production of the first song.

The majority of producers are independent contractors, not employees of a label or other music service. However, once a producer has success with an artist, the label will likely continue to use him/her, if a relationship wasn't previously established.

The Producer–Engineer Connection
The producer:

- Oversees the album budget (coordinated with the A&R rep)
- Chooses final songs (usually coordinated with the artist and A&R rep)
- Schedules recording dates

- Books the studio
- Hires engineers
- Hires session players
- Hires background vocalists
- Coordinates any guest artist appearances
- Records all parts of each track
- Produces overdubs*
- Mixes* the songs (or oversees the mix)
- Masters the songs (or oversees the mastering)
- Delivers the masters to the label or artist

Many producers begin their careers as an engineer or a second/assistant engineer. The job of the engineer is to:

- Set up any gear in the studio necessary to record the project the way the producer requires

- Run all the mic* cables

- Patch,* or plug in, all outboard gear the producer requires, meaning auxiliary and accessory equipment that isn't the standard hardware available in the studio but is desired for the project

- Mic drums, guitar amps, and bass amp if the bass is not patched directly into the board*

- Mic any other instruments used on the tracks (many major studios have a grand piano already mic'd up and ready)

- Set up all vocal mics for the lead singer and background vocalists; choosing a lead vocal mic can be a very specialized process according to the producer's choice and the artist's vocal style and texture

- Manage technical needs (such as label the channels on the board in the main control room specific to what will be used on the project)
- Assist the producer (keep a log of every track recorded so the project runs efficiently)
- Run interference for the producer (such as chase down and resolve issues that arise during recording)

The engineer manages all the technical aspects to help keep the producer's attention on the artist in the creative process. That said, sometimes a producer doesn't need or want an engineer. As I said earlier, he/she may have risen through the ranks as an engineer and will prefer to handle both roles. If they are working in their own studio or one used frequently, they will already know the room. Today, a lot of projects are recorded with just the producer and artist working closely together. If the project is primarily programmed,* using all digital and sampled instruments, the two may work together for months without anyone else being involved.

The Producer–Artist Connection
A producer who develops a strong relationship with an artist is an invaluable asset to his/her career. Over the years, I have heard artists refer to producers with terms of endearment, such as music gurus, father figures, therapists, marriage counselors, and even best friends. If someone has become a sought-after

full-time producer, he/she has definitely:

- Figured out how to be a good hang in the studio
- Helped artists create the most commercially viable music that their songs will allow
- Let artists feel like everything magic that happened was the artist's idea (Just kidding. *No, I'm not.)*

Many producers today have a home studio set up in a basement, bonus room, separate space above the garage, or a building behind their house. Some producers rent small studio spaces that are actually the B or C rooms in a larger studio. Regardless of where the studio is located, the artist works wherever the producer records. In the do-what-you-gotta-do-to-make-it-work category, Billie Eilish and Finneas wrote and recorded her first album in his small bedroom in their family home where she sat on the bed to cut vocals.[48] The exceptions to this "rule" are A-level artists who have their own studios. In that case, everyone involved in the record will come to the artist's location.

Building Songs from the Ground Up

The process of building all the instruments into the recorded song is called tracking.* Most often, whether programmed or live, the musical foundation of a song starts with laying down drums. Sometimes the producer will program them, and then, later in the project, those tracks will be replaced with the performance of a live drummer. Most home studios don't have enough room to set up drums or handle the noise, so at some point in the project, a larger studio will be booked for recording any large and/or loud instruments. Also, the studio can most often offer much better acoustics. Some drummers have the technology and their own space to receive the tracks from the producer, bring them up on their system, sync up with a click track,* cut live drums, and then send the cut back to the producer.

For any recording, the snare sound is always a major focal component to the sound and strength of a song. Some producers and engineers will spend literally hours working to find the right snare sound—mic'ing, tweaking, merging in a sample, and EQ-ing.* Why all this detailed work? Because so many songs are built around the drum groove. The next time a song comes on, and you immediately begin to nod your head, tap your foot, or drum your fingers on the steering wheel, it's because the drums drew you in from the very first bar of the song.

To show the importance of this aspect of the recording process and commercial success of a song, here are five iconic and globally recognized hits that begin with a drum groove. I'm betting that on one or more of these, when you simply read the title, you can "hear" the drum intro:

- Michael Jackson's "Billie Jean"
- Toto's "Rosanna"
- Stevie Wonder's "Superstition"
- Led Zeppelin's "When the Levee Breaks"
- Fleetwood Mac's "Dreams" (with the bass line)

Of course, we have to include what is probably the most infamous and iconic drum fill in music history that we all wait for and air-drum in the middle of Phil Collins' "In the Air Tonight."

Even with the prevalence and convenience of home studios, there are still plenty of projects where the producer, artist, and label will commit the money to secure a major professional studio. Live players will be brought in to cut the tracks separately or play together "as a band." Of course, if the artist *is* actually a band, especially those who tend to work more organically in their process, they will cut all their tracks this way. When someone takes that approach, you'll hear them say, "We cut our record live in the studio." That's not an oxymoron, but a method of recording. Only in rare cases are the final vocals ever recorded when the band tracks, even though the singer might sing along with them to give the players a truly live feel.

In the case where an artist is on a typical budget, and live drums are planned, the producer will book a larger studio and usually bring in a dedicated engineer. In fact, there are engineers who have a reputation for specializing in recording drums. Most major studios usually have a second engineer available who is familiar with the studio to assist in the recording.

Following the drums, typically the next instrument to be added to a track will be the bass. In the average song, you *hear* the drums but you *feel* the bass. With the massive popularity of hip-hop and rap, bass has become a much more featured component in modern music. So much so that to truly experience the work a producer and engineer put into getting super-low performances in a bass track, you have to hear the song on systems that can reproduce those frequencies.

The producer keeps building the track, now in no particular order except by preference of the producer. The producer records rhythm and lead guitars, keyboards, lead vocals, background vocals, strings, horns, percussion, and any other instruments the song may need to be completed. If live studio players are brought in to record, the approaches of how they play their parts can be different. Musicians may have been previously provided with the demos, made notes for each song, and may even come in with ideas for their parts. Or they might listen to the demos on the spot, make notes on each song, and record. Some are given chord charts such as the Nashville Number System.*[49]

Sometimes they will be given actual sheet music and will be required to play exactly what they read. Of course, this is true for string sections and orchestras, but there are also rhythm section players who are masters at sight reading* and playing on the spot.

Oftentimes, toward the end of tracking the main instruments, the producer will add overdubs, such as specific lead guitar lines, auxiliary keyboard lines, percussion, or additional vocal touches/ad libs. Overdubs is the term for recording these auxiliary parts, which are intended to add touches of color and nuance to the song. Bells and whistles, if you will. Using the building analogy, if the main rhythm tracks are the house and the vocals are the furniture, the overdubs are the decorations.

Here's an exercise for you to do: Take one of your favorite songs and, using earbuds or headphones, listen through it however many times it takes to try and pick out and write down *every* single track you can distinguish—all instruments, all vocals. Learning to actively and critically listen to train your ears to pick out *every* part of a song is a valuable learning tool for production and artistry. So often, the tasty little things a great producer mixes in are not *heard* as much as they are *felt*.

Learn to listen for the creative touches a great producer adds; the average person won't ever realize them, but they make the track very special. Besides obvious harmonies, listen for details in the vocals like doubling* or stacking,* when a lead vocal melody is sung two or more times to beef up the performance for a stronger sound. With the right producer and engineer, two to four talented singers can end up sounding like a huge choir. Case in point, the vocals at the beginning of Queen's "Bohemian Rhapsody."

Another thing producers do is add unique tracks which have been sampled and used by producers on actual tracks; a short list includes sounds from a frog, loon, woodpecker, elephant, dog, lion, a beer can opening, a soap bubble pop, and, yes, the Backstreet Boys producer even used a sampled fart that was accidently caught on a vocal mic to add to the sound of a bass line.[50]

Back in the day, as they say, once a song was tracked, trying to change the structure was almost impossible. But not anymore. Technology is a beautiful thing when songs are a group of separate files, which can be manipulated in almost any configuration. Now, that does not mean the opportunity always justifies the end result. Just because you *can* doesn't mean you *should.* That's why you'll hear stories of an artist having multiple mixes of a song. After all, it's art. But great producers know when to *start* and when to *stop* the creative process. Today's digital tools offer great flexibility and opportunity.

A Day in The Studio
When recording live instruments for a record, after getting

everything mic'd up and dialed in on the board, a producer and artist will want to track as many songs as possible. In my experience, most artists and producers will track three to five songs once they are set up and ready so they can maximize the time, money, and opportunity. Keep in mind, the label will recoup any of their expenses, so artists should think about the financial impact of their studio time as well. All this costs money, and ultimately the artist is the one paying for it, so be smart!

Once the songs have been programmed or tracked or a combination of both, the producer will start working on recording individual parts to continue building each song. For example, if a producer is a keys player, he/she might start laying down additional piano, strings, or bass tracks on their own. Sometimes these are primary tracks, and other times they are overdubs.

For vocals, most often when a producer starts to lay a rough track down, he/she will have the artist record what is known as a scratch vocal.* This will be used as a guide so the producer and players can hear the vocal line and melody as they work on the song. If all or some of the lyrics aren't finished, the artist will just sing nonsense words like "ya-ya" or "woo-woo" in the melody to show how the lead vocal will land. When you are laying down an instrument on a track you have never heard before, and there's no vocal reference, it can be easy to get lost in the song. When the track reaches a certain point in the production process, the artist will lay down the actual vocal track to replace the scratch track.

For independent artists or projects on tight budgets, someone might record several songs, from top to bottom, in a single day, especially if they have the studio reserved for eighteen to twenty-four hours. In this case, the producer has to be highly efficient and resourceful to capture what they need and keep things moving on time.

As I have stated over and over and will continue to preach, this process is still *all* about the song. While recording may have to be quick, it should never be rushed or compromised. Why spend anyone's good money on a track if you aren't going to make sure it's right? You may live with (play/perform/listen to/etc.) these songs for the rest of your career, so you don't want to regret the outcome.

When it comes to the tracks chosen for a record, most people would be amazed at the number of songs that barely make the cut on a record, but then end up becoming lightning-in-a-bottle by the time they are finished and released. There are times when, for whatever reason, the initial demo of a song just doesn't capture the team's attention. But then, at some point, a lyric gets changed, or a melody, arrangement, tempo, key, or style ends up altering the song completely. I have seen a mediocre hard-driving, upbeat song that ends up becoming an amazing ballad that blows everyone away. Again, a strong producer can hear what a song needs and what has to be done to bring out greatness.

Some songs known to have barely made the record or were a fight to get on the record are:

- Taylor Swift's "Shake It Off"
- The Rolling Stones' "I Can't Get No Satisfaction"
- Nirvana's "Smells Like Teen Spirit"
- Marvin Gaye's "What's Going On?"

- U2's "Where the Streets Have No Name"
- Bob Dylan's "Like a Rolling Stone"
- Gotye's "Somebody That I Used to Know" (his signature song that sold 8 million copies)[51]

The Psychology of Production

Great producers are worth *every* penny. After watching hundreds of these folks work over the years, the consummate pros are the ones in total control of the entire recording process. They have figured out a template to create a hit song and fashioned an environment that allows for flexibility in the song's formation, all while keeping the process moving forward and the budget intact.

A good producer is not afraid to spend a little time chasing an idea that someone comes up with, even if he/she has already tried something similar and has a good sense it won't work. But to keep everyone engaged, he/she lets the creativity ride anyway because this might be the track it finally works on. During a typical recording process, the producer has to manage a lot of moving parts, but at the end of the day, he/she knows that job one is to get everyone in the best space possible to create.

When an artist goes into the studio for the first time, they might be as giddy as a four-year-old going to Disney World. Often, the artist shows up the first day with a huge smile on his/her face, amped up, and ready to go. But by the end of the process, it may be a different story. The producer has usually pushed the artist *way* outside his/her comfort zone multiple times, creatively, lyrically, vocally, and/or emotionally.

By the producer's work ethic, the artist has:

- Been challenged like never before
- Had to change a lyric or melody they loved
- Had to change arrangements of songs
- Had to let go of what they once thought were brilliant ideas
- Possibly even had to replace one of their band members with a seasoned studio player because, for whatever reason, the artist's player just wasn't cutting it in the studio

That last scenario actually happens often, and it's always very awkward. That's why there are some producers who just say no to an artist bringing in his/her live musicians, unless it's an actual band that has been signed together. Even then, sometimes the players end up on very few of the actual tracks, or their performances get replaced later. That's why a seasoned producer has established methods to work around potentially volatile situations to keep everyone happy. Job one for the producer is to come out at the end of the recording process with music that is commercially viable, especially where a record label is involved.

Mixing the Songs

Once all the tracks have been recorded, the producer turns over all the recorded files to the mix engineer or the mixer unless, as we stated before, the producer will engineer and mix him/herself. The mixer's job is to listen to all the files and start to formulate what he/she thinks the songs should sound like, setting the individual volume levels and EQ-ing the frequencies for every track on every song. This process is usually done in a half day to a day per song, depending on the budget. The mixer has the advantage of coming into the project with "fresh ears," and the great ones have a creative gift for bringing out the very best of what the producer, artist, and musicians have captured—and what the record label wants.

A term I want to introduce here is *sonic*.* No, not the drive-in where you get sodas during happy hour. This is a musical term referring to how a song sounds. You will hear producers, artists, and labels say, "That track is the strongest, sonically, on the record." The term simply means all the right moving parts at just the right levels with the best mix possible. The opposite would be true if a song is described as being weak sonically.

Going back to our barely-made-the-album discussion—sometimes a song that is in question gets a brand-new life once the mix engineer is done with it. There is definitely an artistry to what a great mixer does.

The mix engineer will usually send out his/her first pass of a song to those in the creative loop and then let everyone chime in on how they feel about the track. The producer and artist are usually the first to give the mix engineer feedback. Other key people to hear tracks at this stage are the A&R rep, the artist's manager, the label's radio department, and anyone on the label up to and including the president.

At this stage, an artist, especially a young artist, needs to be careful who and how many people hear the song. The saying, "Too many cooks in the kitchen" is especially true in the final steps of the creative process. Plus, in the digital age, you don't want someone who is well-meaning but ignorant posting the track on social media. And no producer wants to deal with, "My mom said my vocal is too low so can we turn it up?"

Typically, there are several tweaks on any song that are suggested or requested, of which the mix engineer will actually do, but sometimes he/she won't. They need to be trusted as pros and given autonomy at this point. If anyone is going to draw hard lines with the mix engineer, it needs to be the producer. Some examples of tweaks would be a guitar line needing to increase in volume, a string section being too loud, or turns out Mama was right and the lead vocals are too soft in the chorus; ultimately that is the producer's and artist's call, not mama's.

But at the end of the day when a label is involved, they have the final say, often much to the dismay of the artist and producer. Why? Well, whoever writes the checks in any endeavor usually has the final say, right? That said, successful artists who have proven they know what works with their music and fans may get to have it their way. Usually, labels are really good about working with these artists to compromise on what the final mix should sound like without creating any lasting conflict, even though there may be stressful or tense moments during this part of the process. After all, music is art and art is subjective. But at the end of the day, the label will be marketing, releasing, and distributing the record. And you do not want them to lose excitement about the project before the release. You can't afford to win the battle and lose the war.

Sequencing the Songs
After an artist is finished with a full album, and the final mixes are complete, the next step is to sequence* the songs. This process was critical in the days of physical product, but even today with streaming, true fans will play a record through

from the first track to the last. Recently, Adele pushed for Spotify to remove the shuffle feature from album pages because she believes that song order exists to tell a story. The power of A-level artists was shown when Spotify complied with her request.[52]

By the time a project is ready to sequence, the label has probably picked out the first single that will be released to radio, which means that track will likely be placed in the top five songs on the record.

Mastering the Project

Once the sequence is established, the project is sent to be mastered. The mastering process is the final step in completing the making of an album. This is also why a final recorded song is referred to as a master.

The mastering engineer places all the songs in the sequence and then sets all the final levels. The technology he/she uses is for fine-tuning the volume and EQ of all the songs to optimize, compress, and level them out to maintain the same volume and frequency range across the same spectrum. This process is why you can listen to an entire album with your earbuds and never have to turn the volume up or down. Upbeat songs are balanced with ballads. But the opposite is true; if you listen to an album and find yourself constantly adjusting your volume, the mastering was not done well. This does not necessarily apply to older, classic albums before all the tools were developed. Back then, it was just ears and knobs, listening, tweaking, and turning. Today, you can physically see the waveforms on the computer screen and tweak accordingly.

Readying for Release

Once mastering is done, the album is "printed,"* which is the analog word for creating the final stereo version. The digital version of this process is called bouncing the tracks.* The final master is then sent to the label's production department to be married with the artwork and album packaging. The goal for the creative team, by this stage, is to have all those creative and graphic elements ready for the album's completion.

Today, in the DIY world of technology, the producer can serve as the mix engineer as well as the mastering engineer. There is incredible software available for all these end-stage processes. The bigger the label, the more likely the producer, mixer, and mastering engineer will be three different professionals, all specialists in their realm. Technology is amazing for indie artists to produce their own projects, but truly pro producers, mixers, and master-ers know how to create uniquely great art that can stand the test of time.

The Production Budget

When a label is involved, the producer is taking care of all the bills associated with the studio, musicians, background vocalists, engineers, cartage, and catering. Traditionally, mixing and mastering are the only aspects outside the framework of the album budget.

For the monetary process on an album, the producer will work with the label, artist, and manager to determine the budget. He/she will then take the total, divide it by the number of songs, come up with a per-song budget, and proceed with recording inside that framework. Different songs may have different budget amounts assigned to them in the beginning. A song may begin with the concept of a piano and vocal, so it will be slated to use far less money than a full band track. But toward the end, if everyone agrees to add real strings to the piano ballad, suddenly that song could cost more than the band track. This is why a constant accounting of the budget is critical.

The producer will, of course, have to determine his/her fee per song within that budget. Depending on the producer's track record, sometimes he/she will determine a fee but then negotiate points,* meaning a percentage of the profits the producer will receive if and when the album recoups. This can solve several issues: First, if a producer costs typically more than the label can afford, sometimes higher points can allow for less money up front but more down the road. Also, points incentivize a producer to deliver a great record for the promise of mailbox money to come. This allows for the producer to be blessed if the album is highly successful, since he/she will have had such a major hand in that occurring.

Personalized Production
A more common approach in recording today is for an artist to use multiple producers. They do this for several reasons:

- Varied styles will be represented on the record.

- A certain producer is great at ballads while another is strong with up-tempo songs.

- The preferred producer simply doesn't have the time to commit to the entire project, so the artist and label hire him/her to produce the radio singles and others to produce the remaining tracks.

- The label simply can't afford that producer for the entire project.

- If an artist and/or a label wants to experiment with a new producer, he/she can be hired for just one or two songs.

High-demand producers and engineers at the top of their game usually have to be booked far in advance. For this reason, sometimes it's better to wait for that producer to be available and push the release date of the album back. Other times, that producer isn't available for so long that you are forced to go with Plan B. And who knows? Sometimes you realize Plan B was better the whole time. For major producers who are going to get their regular fee no matter what, their interest in the artist or the songs becomes a major deciding factor. It's important that he/she gets excited about the demos or likes the artist.

Once the album is mixed, mastered, and turned in to the label, the producer's job comes to a close. It can be hard on an artist when a producer moves on to the next project. Their everyday, close relationship may not carry on outside the project. Spending literally most waking moments with the producer for months, making almost every decision about the music together, then suddenly getting radio silence can be a tough adjustment for an artist. On the other hand, once the artist gets busy promoting the album, the producer might only see the artist at a tour stop or an awards show.

Once the record is turned in, the artist has to crawl out of the dark studio, change gears, and get out there to:

- Promote the album
- Promote the single
- Tour the album
- Visit radio stations
- Do interviews
- Record liners*
- Shoot music videos
- Create content for social media and live events

Becoming a producer can be an incredibly rewarding job. A lot of producers have gotten started by finding artists or bands who wanted to make an indie record with the little money they saved up, or they may have gotten signed by a small start-up label that needed a low-cost producer. Some new indie artists or bands who have little to no cash will give up a percentage of sales on a project to a producer, like a royalty. If a young producer can afford to work for future mailbox money, that's a great option.

A lot of new artists don't really know how the recording process works, but they want a record, so that creates opportunity for a rookie producer. If the producer is also a songwriter, that's just an added bonus. If he/she's also a techie and likes to figure out different sounds and how to create them, then maybe they'll enjoy production or engineering. There are also some great technical schools that teach these skills.

Lastly, many of the sought-after producers have managers,

just like artists, overseeing their career, negotiating contracts, and creating opportunities for career growth.

As an artist manager, I love me a good producer! Over the years, I've been around some of the greats. They have a way about them that gets the very best out of both the artist and the song. And what is the music business all about, anyway? Yep! The song!

Potential Roles and Positions Connected to Production

- Music producer
- Producer's manager
- Mixing engineer
- Mastering engineer
- Studio engineer
- Second studio engineer/production assistant
- Studio manager
- Session players
- Background vocalists
- Personal assistant (to a producer)
- Album budget administrator/bookkeeper

"The true beauty of music is that it connects people. It carries a message, and we, the musicians, are the messengers."—ROY AYERS[53]

CHAPTER NINE

THE BOOKING AGENT

"A busy artist is a happy artist." — Me

ONE OF THE CLOSEST and most crucial relationships an artist should have—needs to have . . . and better have—is with his/her booking agency. Specifically with the agents who book the artist's genre of music, whether that's one person or an entire team.

Booking agents are "the face" of the artist to the live event space, meaning concert promoters, event sponsors, and talent buyers. They are also key gatekeepers to the financial health of an artist for what should be a major income stream. In the current digital world of music with with little to no physical product to sell, what was once dollars is now literally fractions of pennies. So live events have become the primary source of making money for most artists, and the more people in seats, the more money you can make, and the more merch you can sell. It all goes back to the fans, right? And fans come because of the songs!

A booking agency charges a mutually agreed upon

commission of an artist's guarantees and ticket sales. As you recall, a guarantee* is a minimum flat amount of money contracted for a performance. Ticket sales will be gross (total); those minus expenses equal net, the amount the artist actually clears financially.

A booking agency can be as small as a sole owner who handles everything. That agent, being a one person-show, has to be on the phone with promoters, do all the admin work, type up the offers,* send the offers to the manager, and issue contracts and riders.* That amount of work will limit the number of artists who can be handled without crashing the train. Bigger agencies that have multiple agents and assistants and possibly even support staff, such as a legal department or a sponsorship division, can, of course, handle large rosters.

The Buying End of Booking

It is important to understand some definitions and crucial roles in the booking process before we dive any deeper:

Promoter

These are part-time to full-time professional intermediaries in the live event world of music. There are promoters in any country where live music is played and money to be made. A promoter may work in one specific city or in a specific region of their country or, in places like Australia, an entire continent. These individuals connect an artist or a tour to a specific date at a specific venue and are responsible for the contract, marketing, promotion, ticket sales, and all the logistics necessary for the event. The promoter makes money by taking the contracted cut or percentage of what is left after all expenses incurred have been recouped and the artist's guarantee or percentage has been paid.

My general rule of thumb is that whatever the artist guarantee is, the rest of the expenses (marketing, catering, venue rent, etc.) should be double the guarantee. For a simple example, a promoter books a tour into a venue, and $100,000 is brought in through ticket sales. The artist's guarantee is $50,000, rent is $25,000, marketing is $10,000, and catering and miscellaneous expenses are $5,000. The money left goes to the promoter.

Now, I could also give you a very depressing story that happens all the time where, after paying everyone off, the promoter actually loses money. The concert promotion game is a risky business and a lucrative business all at the same time. There are plenty of promoters who have gotten rich, while many have gone bankrupt or gone under. I know promoters who have been forced to go into another line of work and spend years paying off debts. Like any industry, there are incredible people, and there are sleazeballs. If you work in the music business for very long, eventually you will encounter both.

The next time you go see a major artist, think about the promoter who's backstage, who has worked hard for months to pull off what you experienced. He/she is either really happy or very distraught, depending on whether money was made or lost.

Talent Buyer*

A talent buyer is different from a promoter in that this position typically secures artists or tours for a venue, event, or organization rather than a geographic region. They may book entertainers for a state fair or secure artists for an annual convention or conference. A talent buyer has no risk involved like the promoter. Their job is to get a specific artist for an organization or company or simply fill slots with artists on a program. Some talent buyers are out of the picture as soon as the contract is signed, while others may work closely with the actual event. Their work starts with securing artists, continues in preparing for the date, and ends after the event is played.

This position can be the point person responsible for a certain event. This could be a corporate function, annual party, benefit, or themed conference where entertainment is part of the program. Oftentimes, an event sponsor is responsible for a specific event or events as a part of their overall job, and booking artists would be one of many items on their to-do list.

Handing Over or Holding On

Okay, with those roles in mind, let's go back to the artist side. I want to do a quick review of something I told you in the Artist chapter: You don't need a booking agent until you have so many dates on the calendar and offers coming in that you can't handle the volume and the details by yourself any longer. By that point, the commission percentage you will give up to an agency can more than pay for itself by allowing you to have the time back in your life to focus on your art.

Another factor can also be that you have hit the ceiling on playing a certain-sized room, and an agency has come along that believes they can help you go to the next level in venue size. For example, within a year you moved from small coffee shops and restaurants to 1,000-cap rooms, but you've been stuck there for the past two years.

So, let's say you're ready for a booking agency, and/or one

has come after you. Here are some questions any artist needs to ask regarding this move:

- Where does the agency and/or booking agent fall in comparison to the *reputation* of other agencies in my particular genre?

- Where does the agency and/or booking agent fall in comparison to the *size* of other agencies in my particular genre?

- If the agency is not well-known or is small, are they lean, mean, and willing to hustle to fill my calendar?

- Does the agency have relationships with promoters, venues, and other connections that I don't have?

- Is there a specific agent who connects with me and "gets" my music?

I've seen artists sign with a large agency that has a popular roster and then struggle to get any dates because the lower commissions don't warrant the agents' attention. But that same agency may get them an opening slot on a tour they would have never gotten on their own.

On the other side of the coin, I've seen artists sign with a small, hungry agency that goes to work and fills up the calendar in just a few months, but they don't have connections for the big opportunities. An artist considering agencies must carefully factor in all these dynamics. One of the few reasons I would ever agree with an artist changing booking agencies is when the agreement has a key man clause,* meaning that one person is such a strategic relationship to the artist that he/she will follow that person to another agency.

Typically, starting out with the right manager who has a good relationship with several booking agencies can help an artist navigate a search for the best fit. The manager will know agencies' track records and histories to make the first choice the right choice. A large booking agency taking on an artist who doesn't have a manager is not the norm because they usually prefer that a dedicated professional is guiding the artist's career. They want someone who will work alongside the agency in strategy, planning, and negotiations. There are rare exceptions, but in most cases, a large booking agency will not take on an artist who doesn't have a manager in place. In the case where an artist signs with an agency before they sign with a manager, the agency is most likely able to help secure the manager later. The circumstances flip—agency first, then the manager.

The booking agency's primary job is to help the artist find the right venues to perform live in and, if possible, formulate a touring plan that helps him/her expand the reach and grow the brand. A new artist will typically start in small venues like coffee shops, restaurants, or clubs, with the obvious goal of moving up the food chain to increasingly larger venues.

Here's a guide to how this works in the U.S. market, using *estimated* numbers:

Small restaurants, bars, or coffee shops
Seating is typically 200 or under. Artist receives a small fee plus tips for a four-hour slot. The purchaser provides sound and house lights.

Entertainment-based bars or clubs
Seating is typically 200 to 500. Artist receives a flat guarantee, with purchaser providing sound and lights. Artist provides own transportation. A determining factor in the difference between a bar and an entertainment venue is that, at a bar, people come to drink and the music is a side activity versus a venue where people come to hear music and a bar is available. Someone booked at a bar is often paid by tips, while a venue is a flat guarantee or a cut-of-the-door charge.

Large clubs or theaters
Seating is typically 500 to 2,000. Artist receives a flat guarantee, plus a set percentage of ticket sales over a set ceiling amount. Purchaser allocates a contracted amount toward artist-provided production. Artist provides own transportation.

Arena or amphitheater (headliner on tour)
Seating is 10,000 to 25,000. Artist receives a flat guarantee versus the right to receive a set percentage of gross ticket sales after approved marketing and show expenses. Artist provides production (sound, lights, video, etc.). From early spring to late fall, outdoor amphitheaters have become popular venues for tours, with seating from 2,000 to 10,000. Many cities have strategically built amphitheaters with a capacity in between their two largest venues to offer more options. One of the most iconic outdoor concert destinations in the U.S. is Red Rocks Park and Amphitheatre in Morrison, Colorado.

Festival or Stadium
Large-scale festivals, like Coachella and Bonnaroo, have become legendary in American culture. According to Eventbrite, 32 million people attend a music festival every year. In 2015, Austin City Limits had the highest recorded attendance at 450,000, with Coachella bringing in around 200,000 people.[54] With my own artists, Creation and Lifefest are our largest events each year. With festivals, the typical offer is the artist receives a flat guarantee and festival provides production. Artist is responsible for transportation.

Stadium tours are in stadiums . . . duh. Welcome to the Big Time! You made it!

Private Event
Show me the money! These events can vary widely based on the circumstances, from corporate conventions and retreats to weddings and large family gatherings.

Church Venues
There are also the church venues of all sizes for faith-based artists. These can range anywhere from an acoustic guitar in a living room to selling out a megachurch of 10,000-plus.

There are artists who have worked hard for years and climbed the ladder all the way up from small clubs to arenas or stadiums. Interestingly, the toughest jumps to make are often the first and last levels—getting out of the small-club circuit into larger venues and then jumping from arenas to stadiums. The number of artists who can successfully sell enough tickets to make a stadium tour work financially is small.

One of the best stories is Garth Brooks, who began his career in 1985 playing bars in Tulsa, Oklahoma. On August 7, 1997, he set the record for a concert in Central Park, with 980,000 people in attendance. Today, he still sells out NFL football stadiums, and in other cities, arenas for multiple nights in a row.[55] A huge part of Garth's reputation is his energy and passion onstage. He gained that ability the hard way in his early years by working to win over bar crowds. These kinds of stories are important to share to encourage young artists to work hard and dream big.

One way for an artist to make a major jump is for a manager and/or the booking agency to secure an opening spot on a tour with a charting artist. A small-club artist might be invited to open for someone playing a tour of 1,000-seat rooms in major cities. Or an artist maxed out at the large-club level might be asked to open on an arena tour. One of the interesting aspects of this dynamic is that you can watch an artist perform a twenty-minute set as an opener in an arena, then, following the tour, pay fifteen bucks to see him/her up close in a two-hour set at a club. The arena spot can help with exposure for an artist's career, but it doesn't guarantee an immediate leap to the next level. Regardless, the artist's agency will have handled both settings and will work hard to maximize any opportunity to create new bookings.

The Role of an Agent

Agents answer the phone on incoming inquiries and offers, working to turn those calls into dates on the artist's calendar. But the majority of an agent's job is making phone calls and sending emails, scouring the landscape for opportunities for *all* of the artists on their roster. They have to constantly maintain relationships with local, regional, national, and international promoters, theaters, clubs, arenas, stadiums, festivals, fairs, and conferences.

For example, many of the state fairs around the nation bring in large crowds and have a sizable budget to book multiple stages for the season. The talent buyer for the fair might be looking to fill thirty small-stage time slots, twenty medium slots, and then a headliner for every weekend night of the fair schedule. An agent will look at his/her roster and see which artists can fill the slots the buyer is looking for. Often, an agent will make a deal for a popular headliner but work to get the buyer to agree to take on other artists for the other slots. A quantity deal is made, built around the major artist as the linchpin.

Another example, an agent knows a promoter who covers events at several venues in the Northwest, Southeast, etc. Working to route the dates on a tour, one promoter could cover four nights in four states.

Most of the medium-size to large agencies divide up the country into territories and assign agents to those. So, if there are five senior agents, they divide the fifty states up according to market size, meaning you're going to book a lot more dates in Texas than Rhode Island. The split is worked out fairly for the best connection and workload. This approach makes the agents experts on all the promoters, buyers, and venues within their territory. Occasionally, there will be a talent buyer who covers multiple states, and one agent may be assigned as a key contact so that person doesn't have to constantly deal with different agents.

Typically, agencies will also divide up their artist roster to assign what is known as a responsible agent* to each of their artists. It's like an A&R person for the booking world. This ensures that someone at the agency is committed to making sure each artist has an advocate in every conversation. The responsible agent is the main liaison to management, labels, etc. Oftentimes, an agent may have discovered a new artist and likes what they see and hear. He/she might even have gone after an artist to try and sign them for booking. Any sort of initial connection, whether through the artist or manager, can lead to that agent becoming the responsible agent. If you hear a booking agent say that he/she helped sign an artist, the majority of the time that person will be the responsible agent as well.

If a talent buyer has any sort of regular event, an agent will calendar those and reach out to say something like, "Hey, who are you thinking about having for next year? Remember, I have Artist X, Artist Y, and Artist Z. They've had an incredible year with huge hits, but we also just signed someone you have to hear."

The Anatomy of a Booking

Let's walk through a typical exchange between a promoter/buyer and a booking agent. This may begin with a call about interest in a tour or a specific artist. The agent is going to inform the promoter about the following:

Money required to secure a contract

Depending on the situation, this can be a flat guarantee, ticket split, a guaranteed minimum with a ticket split over a certain threshold of ticket sales, or a split after expenses have been covered. The minimum allows the artist or tour to know the least amount they will walk away with, but then if tickets sell well, the artist has the opportunity to profit as well as the promoter. Also depending on the situation, the agent will tell the promoter what the artist has typically been getting financially.

To move forward, the promoter makes an official offer—usually filling out an online form on the agency's website—based on all the information received from the agent. For example, the promoter may go ahead and agree to everything the agent initially asked for, or based on the promoter's specific show, he/she might not be able to meet all of the agent's initial requests. Another example, if a festival is out in the middle of nowhere and the closest hotels are an hour away, the promoter may say they will provide RVs onsite that the artist can use as a hangout/dressing room. The promoter's budget may not be able to swing the original number, so he/she might make an offer for less, hoping the artist will consider the date. If the agent feels like the offer is at least possible, he/she then sends an official offer form to the artist's manager for consideration. The agent is the first filter for any offer.

The manager then looks over the details of the offer, including all other circumstances surrounding that time frame, the money, and the logistics. If the offer seems reasonable to the manager, he/she goes over the details with the artist. A decision is made—yes, no, or a counter-offer. Countering the offer might be asking for more money, more time onstage, a better slot in the lineup, or even an entirely different date, if the agent and manager have conflicting offers on the same day.

When the numbers can't come together on an artist, a good agent will say, "Okay, we can't make this work, but I know I can get Artist A to come for that same money." They do everything they can to not lose the opportunity for the agency, even if the original artist isn't a fit.

One added detail in the contract process is that all agencies request a deposit to be paid from the promoter or buyer as a sign of good faith that the promoter is serious. Though it is not always the case, a deposit is usually common practice. They put skin in the game, so to speak. A deposit can range from 20 to 50 percent of the guarantee. The amount can depend on the details of the date. If a promoter has a solid relationship with the agency, they may require the minimum. If the date is with someone with no history, a one-off* event, or someone with a shaky past, the deposit amount goes up accordingly.

The deposit is placed into escrow, much like the money put down on a home before closing or a new car when it is ordered. The money is held in an account and used in the final disbursement of the funds. The agency will keep their cut and send the balance to the artist. The only way a deposit would come back to the promoter is if the artist cancels. The agent has to keep up with the deposit—make sure it's paid and that it's applied to the contract.

Production requirements for the artist or tour
Some artists or tours require the promoter to list all the

production on the technical rider—the addendum to the contract that states the exact sound, lights, and video the artist requires. In some situations, the artist or tour will bring a certain level of production but require the promoter to supplement with venue or rented gear. Some artists or tours travel with all their own production. When you see a major tour with five buses and fifteen semis, that's a clear sign they are traveling with every detail of their own production.

One important term you need to know is *backline*.* Backline is all the major instruments and gear of a band—drums, guitar amps, bass amps, and large keyboard rigs—that creates the "back line" of the stage in front of the curtain. The majority of the time an artist flies to perform a show, a backline list will be a part of the contract, and the promoter will rent all the necessary gear, according to the specific list the artist provides. This also connects back to the term *cartage*. In large cities, cartage companies also often provide backline for shows.

All rider requirements, such as travel, hotel,
dressing room, and meal accommodations
The rider is an addendum to the contract, which is a separate document yet a part of the whole. The contract is going to be specific to the terms that have been negotiated for the event, but the rider will be what *any* promoter will have to provide. So, event A's contract may be for $20,000 and Event B may be $30,000, but the rider will be the same and have to be provided for both dates.

The rider has become a notorious item in urban legends because of the things famous artists have asked for. And yes, some are unconditional demands as in, "If this isn't available, I don't go onstage." Rather than me throwing out a bunch of the crazy ones, just google something like "crazy things artists have asked for in their riders." You'll find plenty of light reading to entertain you for a while.

Probably the coolest and most misunderstood rider demand was on Van Halen's first major tour. The band was going to take out more production than any band had to date. Knowing many of the venues had never had that much weight on the stage, everyone's safety was a major concern. They decided to use an obscure item on the rider to test the promoter's attention to detail. On the list was a bowl of M&Ms that had to be in the dressing room among the other items, but they added one strange demand—all the brown ones had to be removed. Singer David Lee Roth explains:

> Van Halen was the first to take 850 par lamp lights—huge lights—around the country. At the time, it was the biggest production ever. If I came backstage, having been one of the architects of this lighting and staging design, and I saw brown M&Ms on the catering table, then I guarantee the promoter had not read the contract rider, and we would have to do a serious line check [of the entire stage setup].[56]

In the early stages of an artist's career, an offer might be fifty bucks to play a coffee shop ten miles from their house, and a simple "What time do you want me to start playing?" gets the ball rolling. As the artist gets bigger, and the shows become more detailed, the negotiations can become very involved. This is where a good manager and a good agent earn their keep, big-time.

Between the contract issue and the event, the agent looks for indicators that the promoter is going to have a "healthy show,"* meaning well-attended and profitable. The first indicator being that the contract and deposit were received by the deadline. Another indicator is how tickets are selling, looking for momentum to increase as the date gets closer. Most agencies do weekly ticket counts—recording the exact numbers sold versus seats remaining. Large agencies have entire departments that track ticket counts and send out weekly updates to the agent, promoter, and manager.

Whether you are an artist, agent, or promoter, there are going to be shows that make money, lose money, or break even. That's just the reality of doing business. For my artists out on a tour, we can look at presales of tickets and often see what a date is going to do. Sometimes you'll have a market that will surprise you and the walks-ups* will be strong and push you from a loss to a breakeven or from a breakeven to making money. There are going to be nights that a breakeven just keeps you rolling on to the next town. Case in point, it's better to have a break-even show in between two profitable cities than a night off traveling where everyone is just creating more expense for the tour in hotel and restaurant charges.

Some negative indicators for a contracted show are when the promoter keeps giving excuses for why the deposit hasn't been sent yet or keeps saying, "It's in the mail," yet it never arrives; also, when weekly ticket counts are not tracking well, and sales are slow. In these cases, the sooner a promoter, agent, and manager, and sometimes even the artist, can get on the same page and try to ramp up promotion, the greater the chances that the show can be saved. No one wants an artist to show up at a 1,000-seat room and play to a hundred people. That's even awkward for the people who show up!

Usually, the agent understands the markets and promoters well enough to know whether he/she should even put the artist in a situation where the promoter might not be the right person to pull off the show to begin with. That said, in all the years I've been in this business, I've never gone through an entire tour where we didn't have some kind of issue around a show that required us to get creative and do everything we could to get a decent-sized crowd there. That's why they call it work!

The Manager–Agent Connection

Managers are constantly updating agents on their artists with information such as:

- When a new record or a single is set to release
- When artists are ready to headline their own tour
- How record sales and streams are doing
- Willingness to play one-offs
- How singles are doing at radio
- Openness of playing events like festivals, fairs, conferences, or corporate or private events
- How social media is connecting with their fan base: number of followers, views, likes, replies, etc.

- The need to block time off on the calendar to write and record a new record
- The need to block time off on the calendar for rest and relaxation (or rehab)

This communication is vital for agents, so when a promoter calls for a date, he/she knows the status of that artist and what to say or not say. That said, every artist I've ever worked with has made exceptions in their schedule at one time or another when a great offer comes in, especially if it's significantly above their normal asking price. The old saying, "Everyone has their price," is certainly true. Many promoters have said to an agent, "Okay, well, how much would it take to have them leave the studio and come do my show that weekend?"

A well-connected manager with a solid reputation can get any artist signed to a booking agent at any time. But the biggest truth for the artist to understand is that having a booking agent does *not* guarantee offers are going to start pouring in right away. Why? Because the agency has to have something to create traction and demand for the artist, such as the signing of a major label deal, a single headed to radio that everyone believes will have success, or a national release date for their project. There has to be a selling point. Before that, the agent and manager might be able to book a few gigs for the artist by calling on relationships and connections. Even to get the artist on an opening act, the headliner has to have some level of belief to expose their fans to this new artist. A rough opening act is a bad look on an artist's brand and hurts everyone involved.

Finally, the sponsorship department will work to find

brand connections for artists on their roster who are a good fit for everyone involved. For example, Tractor Supply would be open to partnering with a country artist, but not a rap artist. You're more likely to sign a sneaker company up with a hip-hop artist. It's about brand and fit. A sponsor could be interested in working with an artist for just one show, such as their annual corporate conference, while someone else might be interested in a world tour that will go on for a year. Major partnerships often involve appearances at sponsor events, sponsorship of a tour, product placement in music videos, and a national TV advertising campaign. All these will be worked out in coordination with an artist's manager.

The Bullets on Booking

Let's review the duties of an agency:

- Find shows
- Route tours
- Receive and vet official offers from promoters
- Send offers to managers
- Communicate any info between the manager and the promoter
- If approved, issue the contract to the promoter with the artist rider
- Secure the signed contract and rider from the promoter and forward to the manager
- Get the deposit and place it into escrow until the date is played

- Track ticket sales
- Stay engaged with the promoter and manager as the event date gets closer, particularly if ticket sales are involved, with discussions including marketing and promotion

For everyone I have ever managed, the relationship between myself, the artist, and the record label, along with the booking agency and the responsible agent, has been absolutely critical to everyone achieving total success. When one of my artists has a single go to number one, we need a booking partner who can move strategically and quickly to maximize the momentum in the marketplace, which we've worked so hard to achieve. The timing of routing a tour many months in advance that coincides with the release of a new album is a fine art for a great agency. When an artist has garnered the number of fans to move up to the next level in the size of the venues played, I need to know the agency has the relationship and connections to make that happen. Because as I stated in the subtitle: "A busy artist is a happy artist."

Potential Roles and Positions Connected to Booking Agencies
- Agents
  - » Music
  - » Speaker
  - » TV
  - » Film
  - » Books
- Agent assistants

- Festival and fair department
- Junior agents
- Administrative staff
- Legal team
- Sponsorship team
- Social media team

"Being able to have a song on radio, but then go play a show for people that have heard the song on radio, and having it sung back to you, is—
I don't know how to describe it."
—BRETT YOUNG[57]

CHAPTER TEN

THE PROMOTER

Promoters are the financial linchpin to the overall success of touring artists.

A CLASSIC URBAN legend told by many promoters is about Alex Hodges, who managed many of the classic southern rock bands, including the legendary Allman Brothers Band. When one of their friends who had never promoted a show before wanted to book the guys, Hodges reportedly told him, "If you can take $25,000 and lay it on the driveway, pour some lighter fluid on it, light a match, watch it burn, and not succumb to the urge to stomp it out, then maybe, and only maybe, you could be a promoter." Whether or not the story is true, I can tell you from years of experience that the principle certainly is.

While we introduced the concept of a promoter in the previous chapter and covered the basics, because this role is so crucial in connecting artists to their audiences, I wanted to give the promoter its own chapter and dive deeper. Who knows? Maybe you're good with watching twenty-five grand burn, and you'll decide to become a promoter. I can tell you for sure there's no way in a manger that I could!

From my experience as a manager over the years, I think being a promoter is the one job in the music industry that comes with the *most* risks and also gets the *least* amount of accolades. If they do their job right, you never know they exist. If they slip up on a show, well, there is blood in the water, and the sharks start circling.

The basic role of the promoter is to handle all the details associated with a concert—from the first call to an agent to the cash-out at the end of the show. Once all the details are negotiated, the contract is signed, and the deposit is in escrow, that's when the real work begins for them. Here are just some of a promoter's primary responsibilities:

- Secure the venue with contract and deposit

- Line up the necessary production

- Arrange and pay for all promotion

- Line up local stagehands for day-of-show load-in and load-out of all equipment

- Book a caterer

- Work out ticket structure pricing with the venue

- Coordinate all aspects of ticketing and sales.

- Track ticket sales weekly and report those numbers to the booking agency

- Secure local runners responsible for handling errands on day of show

- Secure a licensed and bonded electrician to tie in power for all production

- Coordinate with the venue staff on details like ushers and box office

- Set load-in, sound check, meal, and load-out schedules

- Determine time that venue doors will open

- Determine number and location of ticket takers

- Secure tables, pipe and draping, etc., needed for artist's merch

- Secure and coordinate volunteers to sell merch

- Coordinate any tour sponsors and their needs

- Purchase and provide all the requirements from the artist's rider

Runners

A runner may be asked to take an artist to an afternoon movie, buy groceries, deliver the tour bus drivers to and from the hotel, get batteries for gear, make an airport pickup for a visiting A&R rep, wash clothes at a local laundromat, or find purple nail polish for the bass player's girlfriend. Think, errand-person-for-a-day and you've got it. Runners rarely ever get to see any of the show. Some are paid and some are volunteers. A crucial "must" for any runner is to be very familiar with the area. Sure, Google is great, but someone who knows where things are and how to quickly get there is critical.

The reason I am mentioning runners in detail is because

I truly believe that being a runner is the best way for people who want to be in music to accomplish several things: learn the business behind show dates, learn the amount of work it takes to be in music, and have an opportunity to network and build relationships. I always tell wanna-be artists that they need to be a runner at least once to understand the job.

My most memorable runner story happened many years ago. Out on a tour with one of my artists, I ended up with a backpack stuffed with several nights of merch cash. There was a *lot* of money inside. I knew I had to get to the bank, so I found a branch of ours in the city where we were and asked the promoter for a runner. When I walked outside, I saw a van sitting there with a guy in the driver's seat. I went over to the passenger side and jumped in. As we drove away, I realized *all* the windows were down. Then I noticed a very distinct, pungent odor. The van reeked of weed.

So, here I am, a guy with a music tour passing through town with a backpack full of cash, riding in a van that you can smell a block away. *I* would have been suspicious of me at that point!

I tried to stay cool, but inside I felt panic. Do I tell the guy to let me out on the sidewalk and figure it out from there? What should I do? I looked at him and calmly said, "Hey, please obey all traffic laws and go under the speed limit until we get to the bank, okay?" He knew I knew, and nodded as he slowed down.

Fortunately, I got to the bank, made the deposit, and made it back to the venue without incident. But that was the first and only time I thought about having to run from a runner!

Promoter Overview

The previous bullet point list is simply an overview. Specific shows will determine the advance details and day-of-show needs. Plus, the week of the show and the day of, there will be plenty of things added that were never on the to-do list. A promoter expects surprises. It's not *if* but *when*.

Because the financial margins for an artist are often notoriously thin on touring, it is important for the artist to be aligned with the right manager, booking agent, and promoter to optimize, maximize, and exploit potential net income. Agents look for the right promoters who know how to get the best deals on everything around the U.S. and also in foreign countries in the case of a world tour. The more shows a promoter does at a venue or in a specific city the better their chance of having a template for shows, such as using the same runners, caterer, printers for advertising materials, and everything else that needs to be provided at the best possible rate to help the bottom line for everyone. A promoter with solid connections will also be able to buy the best packages for promotion from radio, print, and TV. They will have also learned how to streamline social media ads for their target markets.

Most promoters start out in a specific city or region and, if they can get a few successful shows under their belt, begin to grow, getting better and more profitable the more they produce. Some are even able to become national promoters. But the majority get established in a market and become experts right where they are.

If a promoter grew up in Indianapolis, and they've been there all their life, they're going to be the best promoter, where?

In Indianapolis, right? Because they know the market. They know the days to stay away from because it might be a big local day that isn't nationwide, so they really know what's going on at the local level. For example, no one needs to book a show on a Sunday anywhere close to Green Bay when there's a home game for the Packers.

Depending on the area of the country, a promoter may have a city or region monopolized within a certain genre, having edged out all other promoters, while other areas might have solid competition. In some regions, a radio station or some other organization may be the dominant promoter. Oftentimes, established artists will work with one promoter for their tour dates. This will vary city by city and be different among artists and based on their levels.

Soft Ticket Events

There's really no stereotype for a promoter. A university student on the activities committee who has been charged with providing an artist for homecoming can learn to promote a show. A corporate employee who gets tasked to hire a major act to perform at the annual gala or in-house event can be a promoter. Someone who works at a religious organization and needs to provide talent for a camp, retreat, or conference can become a promoter. An employee of a coffee shop or restaurant could be tasked with filling the slots for their weekend acoustic shows. Often in these situations, the artist will be paid a flat guarantee, and the artist's name isn't necessarily the reason people will attend the event. Also, a ticket may not be involved, and if tickets are involved, they could be issued free just to assign seats for capacity.

These scenarios are known in the music business as soft ticket* events, meaning the artist's name normally doesn't carry the full weight of how many people attend. The event will happen regardless, but the right artist can round out a fun experience and make the event memorable. For soft tickets, there will be an overall budget, so the promoter is not working to make money from the artist or ticket sales. The artist's rider still needs to be adhered to for the event, although sometimes concessions are made during negotiations between the promoter, booking agent, and manager to achieve the overall goal of the event.

Soft ticket events are typically low stress for the artist, except when specific requests are made. If an artist is doing a corporate event for their full fee, the corporate rep promoting it might ask that at some point from stage he/she personally thank the president and his family, or make a comment about a new product that will be launching soon. Maybe even sing "Happy Birthday" to the CEO's grandmother. (Everyone's got a price.) Special requests from a soft ticket promoter need to be brought up on the front end of the offer, not ten minutes before the artist is about to go on. That's when things can get really awkward and even heated. The "ask forgiveness instead of permission" concept doesn't work well in this setting. *You want me to do what?!*

Particularly if you're a young artist, you'll work mostly on soft ticket dates, so the majority of the shows you do will be with different promoters. Being able to work with the same promoters starts to happen once you're more established and begin to do hard ticket dates.

Hard Ticket Events

It stands to reason in the music industry that if there are soft tickets, then there must be hard tickets.* Those are the typical tour dates we have already discussed at length: an artist is the draw, and tickets are sold for the performance. Why a "hard" ticket? Well, it's *harder* to get fans to part with their *hard*-earned dollars than most people think.

After a manager speaks to an artist's agency about a tour plan, then a booking agent will reach out to a promoter to say, "Hey, Artist A is going to tour in the spring of next year. What market (or markets) do you want?" They can then get specific, such as, "Check venue availability for weekends in mid-April because the tour is likely going to route through your area around that time frame." So, the promoter starts checking with building GMs (general managers) and putting available dates on hold for the weekends the booking agent suggested. Then the promoter will get back with the booking agent on the availability and capacities and work on putting offers together. Other factors are going to be how many seats are available in those venues and ticket price structures based on the popularity of the artist in those cities. These are the beginning steps of tour routing.

The entire process becomes like a long domino chain. Just one venue not being available in a single city can suddenly change the routing of the entire tour. If the artist's hometown show needs to play at the "Enormo-dome," but it's not available on the weekend they were trying to route through that area, then the manager, booking agent, and artist may decide that one show is so critical that they will reroute the entire tour to make that happen.

The optimum days of the week for tour dates are Thursday, Friday, Saturday, and Sunday. Usually, depending on the artist, tours don't do as well selling on Monday, Tuesday, or Wednesday. Booking a tour can take several weeks or even months, but once the promoter, booking agent, and manager decide on the best routing, then the dates get set, they announce the tour, and put tickets on sale.

The promoter's job is to line up all the advertising—radio spots, TV, print ads, and social media ads and posts—to have a big "on sale,"* meaning a massive first push-out to the fans. For popular major artists, you can see how critical it is to make certain the routing is set in stone because a tour can sell out in a matter of minutes. There's no room for any "uh-ohs"; there's far too much money at stake.

The promoter's ultimate goal is to line everything up to get *to* the show and then *through* the show with no hiccups. For an artist selling hard tickets, the promoter is typically paying a minimum guarantee, and then once all the expenses have been recouped, the promoter pays the artist anything due based on any agreed percentage, and then the promoter takes the profit.

The headliner split with the promoter will be an amount previously negotiated for the contract in one of these common structures: 60/40, 70/30, 80/20, or 90/10, with the artist receiving the larger percentage. The bigger the artist and the venue, the greater the artist's take, but the promoter on a 90/10 with a massive star would make more than they would on a 60/40 with a lesser artist.

There are, of course, countless ways to customize deals, by creating incentives and bonuses. A good agent and promoter will be able to get creative on the front end to arrive at the right deal for each show. Bottom line: there is no standard deal—just whatever you negotiate in the contract.

As a manager, my goal for each of my artists is to get to the point where they are doing hard ticket dates. That's how you can sustain a long-term career. This also gives artists the most flexibility to tour:

- When they want
- Where they want
- How they want
- With whom they want (openers, co-headline)

A headliner can take input from the booking agent, manager, label, accountant, and even promoters on who they suggest to take out as an opening act, but it's ultimately up to the artist. As I've stated in other parts of the book, an opening act who is a good hang and easygoing on the road is more important than any other factor. An opening act that has more streams, more views, and more radio play to help get people into seats might appear smart, but when they are trouble in the first two weeks of a three-month tour, no one cares about the stats anymore. So, if you're an aspiring artist, once again I say be kind, be flexible, be grateful, and you'll do well.

A master at the hard ticket is the band U2. They tour arenas and stadiums around the world every few years. If you want to see them, you have to buy a ticket to one of those shows. They might play Nashville on one tour and then three years later play Atlanta. But they sell out both places because people will drive for hours and even fly to their shows. They have strategically created the perfect supply and demand scenario. Another example is when the band played the Bonnaroo Music Festival in 2017, prior to the winter release of their new record; it was their first U.S. festival performance since 1983. Why? Because a festival is a soft ticket event. Did people come to Bonnaroo that year just because of U2? Well, of course. Not only was this a smart call by the festival but also of U2's management as it created a buzz around the anticipated album. But the band taking those dates will be few and far between and will depend on a huge check. Well managed; well played.

Promoter Connections

Promoters are constantly working to connect with young, up-and-coming acts. As those artists start their career and their fan base grows, the promoter hopes he/she can be the go-to for shows. If a promoter brought a brand-new act into Topeka, Kansas, and put on a small but successful show, then he/she becomes the promoter of record* in that market. Being the promoter of record usually allows for the right of first refusal* the next time that artist wants to come back through that market, hopefully at a larger venue with a higher ticket price. The goal is to grow together over the course of many years as the ticket prices grow, venue sizes get bigger, and everyone does well. But unfortunately, as much as everyone wants every artist to constantly climb the ladder, that's just not reality. Artists come and go.

That's why being a promoter is so tough, because they are constantly having to put up all the front-end money for shows, often not knowing whether they are investing or wasting their hard-earned cash. And most of the time, you can't know until the show is over. But it's such a beautiful thing when a promoter locks arms with a young artist who ends up having a really long career, and he/she is able to stay involved in several markets the promoter owns* (meaning the promoter does a lot of shows there and can benefit for many years from the success of those events).

There are occasions where a promoter and artist who have worked together on a local or regional level get along and fit well, which then eventually develops into a national relationship. That promoter can take on an entire tour, and the artist and their team work solely with that promoter. Such an exclusive connection streamlines everything for the manager, artist, booking agent, road manager, and road crew, so they are not having to constantly deal with a different promoter in every city.

Even though the contracts and riders may be close to the same, there will be subtle nuances in the different ways that promoters work. With one promoter, everyone can pull up to the next venue knowing how things are going to go. That can really fine-tune all the different aspects, from ticket prices and local stagehands to catering, dressing room setup, bus parking, and so on.

A national promoter can also approach an artist to offer, "For next year, I want to pay you X amount of dollars to do X amount of dates." This type of deal may include some sort of bonus structure paid out at the end of the agreement period for ticket sales over certain quotas. This arrangement not only offers all the perks listed above but also eliminates details like a nightly settlement. Deals like this are usually exclusive and apply only to big-name acts that a promoter can know will hit the numbers needed to work. But they also allow an artist to know a minimum amount of income they will bring in the next year.

When a promoter reaches a national level, he/she will have a team who can accomplish a large number of shows in multiple cities across the country. This might include some regional promoters who have teamed up with the national promoter. There might be a couple of national promoters who decide to form a bigger company and pool all their resources to become a powerhouse in the industry. Regardless of the who or the how on the promoter end, for an artist and a manager, it's important to work with someone who understands the artist's brand, and more importantly, the artist's fans and how to reach and connect with them to create maximum ticket sales. Once again, it all comes down to the fans.

Another reason being a promoter is the hardest job is that they have to constantly deal directly with the public and experience all the headaches that brings. Especially in our current culture of entitlement and I-want-it-now, this can be a tightrope walk between pleasing the public and responsibly representing the headliner. Promoters have been screamed at because someone's plans changed, so people demand refunds or they don't like the placement of their seats or the music is too loud—or not loud enough. Over the years, I've heard it all and know enough to say that I'm just glad I'm not a promoter.

Partnering with Promoters

As a manager representing artists, I feel like part of my job is to constantly be on the lookout for new promoters, while working to help *all* promoters be successful. If we don't, we run the risk of losing the good ones.

In working with promoters, there's no such thing as a tour where nothing goes wrong. Typically, at some point, each one is going to require that we all put our heads together to get creative to solve an issue. Regardless of what was negotiated in advance, you cannot foresee every hiccup. Therefore, it is vital to be flexible with promoters so that they can live to fight another day. If you know you are going into a show where ticket sales are light, and the promoter is not going to make enough to cover the artist's full guarantee, I've always instructed tour managers to do what they can to cut costs to help alleviate some of the promoter's expenses. I ask questions like, "Can we cut back on . . .

- Any production?
- Number of stagehands?
- Catering?
- After-show food?
- Anything on the rider?"

Sometimes you can find something to take a big bite out of a budget, but more often, a little bit in a lot of different areas can add up and help even more. If these efforts still don't get the promoter to break even, there are times I have split the loss with him/her by cutting the artist guarantee. But that only happens when the artist agrees with me, and I truly believe the promoter did everything possible to sell tickets. If the promoter just has too many shows booked, is spread too thin, and didn't give my show the attention needed, I'm less likely to consider a reduction. New artists and young artists usually don't have a lot of margin to allow for any less.

I have always been up front and honest with promoters on how things are going so that I have a good feel in advance of the day of show. We may need the artist to post some extra promotion through their social media to help sell tickets. When a show has poor sales, rarely is the promoter going to have a last-minute run on tickets at the door. That never works!

Post-Show for Promoters

Depending on the terms of the contract, when the show is wrapped, the promoter will have a final meeting with the venue to go over ticket sales and expenses. Next, he/she will meet with a tour representative (usually the tour manager or tour accountant) to review ticket sales and other expenses that need to be taken out. The point is to show all the income and expenses so they can then pay the balance of the artist guarantee. If there's any money left over, the split takes place based on the contract's terms as we previously discussed.

A well-organized promoter will have all the information ready, such as a ticket manifest (income from ticket sales at each price level), receipts for all building expenses, and receipts from all promotion for the tour representative to review the necessary information. The more detailed and clear the presentation, the better, to be above reproach with no missing or hidden income or inflated expenses. As you can clearly see, there has to be a lot of trust and accountability involved in these settlements.

If you're an artist, be nice to promoters. They want to make money. They want to sell tickets to your shows. They're not out there sitting on their hands. They're doing their best. Don't show up at a show where there are only four hundred people there and yell at the promoter because you were expecting eight hundred. Go to the promoter and tactfully ask, "What went wrong? What can we do? How can we learn from this?" And maybe, be compassionate, share the loss, and give a little bit of your guarantee back. That's long-term thinking for an artist. That's someone who wants to be in the business as a career.

I'm sure you've seen in these pages why we had to dive deeper into the role of the promoter in the music business. Let me restate yet again that they are often the financial linchpin to the overall success of artists and the music business in general. I have always been an advocate for booking agents, managers, and artists to treat promoters with respect and dignity. A good, honest promoter with a positive and upbeat staff can make the tour enjoyable for everyone, allowing the fans to focus on their favorite songs performed by their favorite artists.

Potential Roles and Positions Connected to Promoters

- Promoter
- Promoter representative
- Talent buyer
- Marketing team
- Ticketing team
- Production team
- Advancing team
- Administrative team

"I always tell people, 'The music's free. I get paid to travel.'"
—Chris Stapleton[58]

CHAPTER ELEVEN

THE TOUR

Touring is a coordinated effort among the artist, management, booking, and promoters to accomplish two things: make money and get the music in front of fans.

"I MAKE MY MONEY off of touring and merchandise. And I'm lucky I have really loyal fans that understand how it works and support," said Chance the Rapper,[59] whose project *Coloring Book* became the first streaming-only album to win a Grammy.[60] Even after winning the most coveted award in music, he stated that his primary income is from playing shows, proving the need for artists to tour.

Touring is the lifeblood of any artist's career. The annual profit/loss statement of any artist today will prove that live shows are the number one income source, regardless of how many other sources of income the artist has. In past chapters, I've shown you how managers, booking agents, and promoters initiate, oversee, and implement the touring life of an artist.

But touring is important enough to dedicate an entire chapter to it.

Any marketing dollars spent by a record label, the artist, or other sources for the sole purpose of promoting shows is going to increase brand presence in touring markets. Imagine that for six weeks prior to a live show, music fans constantly see or hear on their streaming service, social media, local radio station, and/or other digital and physical media that an artist is coming to their city; every "touch" or "impression" is valuable in today's content-saturated world. Someone who might never buy a ticket to the show could become curious and stream a song to check out an artist, and—boom—they become a first-level fan. That connection, albeit indirect, was made because the artist is touring. Obviously, once he/she is in that city, if a local TV or radio station does an interview, the opportunity for exposure increases in the market. On *Shark Tank*, they call this "customer acquisition."

For young artists, their touring schedule will likely focus on providing support to other artists, like the first act of the night playing for fifteen minutes to kick off the concert. There are two types of openers: lights up* and lights down.* Lights up means the artist walks out with the house lights up, and no tour production is used during their set. Also typically, no sound check is allowed, and the audio levels will be much lower, so people can still talk in their seats and hear the ushers tell them where they are sitting.

Of course, to state the obvious, lights down is where the house lights are brought down, and tour lighting is used at some level. Volume and quality of sound is also taken up. But if an artist can go out and capture the crowd's attention with no production, that is a clear sign of real talent and presence. That experience, while often tough work, can be an incredible learning opportunity for a young artist.

As the show progresses through the artists' sets, the production for each one is slowly increased until the headliner has *everything* placed on "ten" for them. These details are often spelled out in the contracts.

Paying Your Dues

For any artist just starting out, there are multiple avenues to playing live in front of a crowd, but they will all require a high level of commitment and dedication to hard work.

Busking.

Particularly in the three major music cities of L.A., New York, and Nashville, you can hear incredible artists on the street. This is known as busking* or being a busker. Pick a busy corner, open up the guitar case as a tip jar, and sing your heart out. Some of the most famous artists started out as buskers, such as Passenger, Ed Sheeran, Janis Joplin, and even BB King.[61]

One-Offs.

After you have gotten a little bit of attention, maybe you get an offer to play a smaller show at a coffee shop, a wedding reception, a house concert, or a bar downtown. These are called one-offs, which basically means that you're paid to do the one show and nothing more.

You're a buy-on.*

This is also called "pay to play." In this scenario, the manager and new artist agree that using resources from the new artist or record label to secure a slot on a show or a tour is worth the exposure. Buy-ons can come in many different forms. The new artist may need to provide a bus and/or trailer, production, or equipment, or simply be a part of the crew to help pull the show off by helping with load-in and load-out. They could also help with sponsorship duties, such as daily setting up the sponsorship display in the lobby, or even something as simple as promoting the tour with social media posts. In some cases, the new artist might even pay a fee in order to be added on a show/tour. A buy-on may cover a couple of bus bunks for the new artist and/or a road manager (or other support) who handles most of the details for the new artist. Everyone has to see this commitment of time and resources as an investment in the future.

You're on the tour but on your own.

In this arrangement, nothing is offered or paid for by the tour. If at the end of the night, behind the venue, you see a bunch of guys loading out into a van parked next to all the tour buses and semis, that's a dead giveaway they are on their own. The tough thing about this arrangement is the other artists and crew can sleep all night on the buses while they are driven to the next show, but this artist and team have to take turns driving and sleeping to get there on time. The shows that are hundreds of miles away can be grueling drives. Whether a solo artist with a buddy, road manager, or another player, this arrangement leads to quickly being in a zombie-like state. Sometimes a small amount of space on the merch table is made available for an item or two. Catering and some minimal production might also be worked into the contract. The currency paid is exposure.

You're on a bus, but there's no money.
Sometimes the artist is offered a bunk on a crew bus and meals, but no money is paid. Like the on-your-own tour, the only potential income stream will be a small space on a merch table. Obviously, for sheer survival, this is a much better situation than being totally on your own. As stated above, the primary payment is exposure.

You're offered a paid slot on a tour.
If an artist does begin to catch traction, rises to become a C-level or B-level act, starts getting spins at radio, and people begin recognizing his/her name, an offer might come to be a paid act on a tour and be placed in the lineup after any buy-ons or "free" acts. Playing before the headliner, a slot at a festival or fair, selling a decent amount of merchandise at shows, and actually crawling out of the lowest tax bracket might also allow an artist to be able to afford a little more support staff on the road.

No Plan B
Artists who can endure all this abuse and "pay their dues" have to love what they do and have a passion for their art. There needs to be a "No Plan B" attitude and an "I can't *not* do this with my life" mindset. But this is also why most folks don't make it beyond the early stages in their career.

In past chapters, we covered the places an artist can play as they work their way up in both soft ticket and hard ticket events. During the first few years of touring, an artist has to be out there:

- Hustling
- Making little to no money
- Surviving off T-shirt sales
- Spending a lot of time at the merch table to meet people
- Standing in the lobby shaking hands and kissing babies
- Dropping by radio stations
- Meeting industry gatekeepers
- Networking in the music community
- Staying in crappy hotels or on friends' couches
- Taking cheap early-morning flights

Tour Expansion

As an artist's career progresses, additional personnel become crucial to their touring needs. That process looks and functions differently for every artist, but once regular touring begins, one of the first hires needs to be a tour manager or road manager who will take over all the road details. This person will handle advancing* shows and making sure the date happens in accordance with the artist's rider once the manager, booking agent, and promoter have executed a performance agreement. Artists who primarily do hard ticket events usually call their person a TM (tour manager), while soft ticket artists tend to refer to their person as an RM (road manager).

Advancing means lining up everything for the show prior to arrival on day of show, working to eliminate any issues or surprises, clarifying all the production and rider needs, and answering the questions that are always going to come up, while a promoter, venue manager, or production manager* tries to make sure everything on their side is right. Advancing is well named for its meaning of taking care of everything in *advance* of the show day.

A good tour or road manager must:

- Take care of daily tasks
- Be detailed
- Be a multitasker
- Be a good planner
- Be a good communicator
- Be the boss on the day of the show
- Be the liaison between the artist and crew
- Be the liaison between the promoter or venue
- Make any necessary decisions on specific show needs at different venues
- Make last-minute decisions on any show or venue adjustments
- Pivot off certain events, such as weather, local issues, etc.
- Always keep the artist's well-being in mind
- Protect the artist while out on the road

Many of the following terms can be found in the Glossary, but they are also covered further in chapter fifteen. Here are some areas an artist could decide to grow and increase the touring budget:

- Tour support personnel such as
  » Tour/road manager
  » Front-of-house engineer*
  » Monitor engineer* or mixer (in-ears)
  » Lighting director*
  » Instrument tech (if the artist is a guitar player)
  » Full-time merch manager*
- Onstage Performers such as:
  » Band members
  » Background vocalists
  » Horn players
  » Dancers
- Production

A next-level dream for an artist might be production with video screens displaying matching graphic content for songs. Artists who want their music to be accompanied by visual enhancement may want to grow this aspect of the show more than anything else. Of course, setting up a large production, even in a club, is going to require extra help and technical savvy. One of the known principles on the road is, "If it can go wrong, it will." That's not negativity, it's reality.

The bigger an artist gets, the less the team has to wear multiple hats. For major artists, each position is hired for their expertise and concentrates solely on what the person is great at doing. But in the mid-level stages, the front-of-house engineer might also be the road manager. A guitar player might also be the merch person. The monitor mixer might be the stage manager and backline tech. Finding the balance of growing what's onstage or what's behind the scenes is a subject the right manager can also help navigate.

One additional detail is that an artist's manager and/or booking agent will typically handle any contractual issues or disagreements with the promoter prior to the show day. But on the day of the show, the road or tour manager will handle any issues that arise directly with the promoter. Only in an extreme case would the agent be contacted.

The Self-Made Tour

If an artist is a C-level or B-level act doing mostly soft ticket dates, a serious consideration must be to put together his/her own tour, as the headliner taking out a smaller act, or to produce a co-headlining arrangement so that he/she begins to establish market value and create a hard ticket track record. A booking agent can also use this as new fuel to try to increase guarantees and offers.

After all the shows have been booked, the TM/RM works with the venues to secure sound, lights, and production, which have been pre-negotiated in the initial booking contract. Next is booking any players or necessary personnel, securing a vehicle or booking flights, and packing up or ordering merchandise for the shows.

Here are some parameters for the self-made tour:

- Keep tour short at two to four packed-in weeks.

- Book into cities and venues where confidence is high on selling well.

- Protect markets by not playing soft ticket events in that region leading up to and immediately following.

- Book smaller venues to try and ensure sellouts (create demand with supply).

- Sell tickets at a safe price to ensure sell-outs (this tour isn't a time to get greedy).

- Call in all the favors possible to ensure all of the above.

- If the room isn't going to sell out on day of show, get on social media and give away tickets to create a packed room. (Once the show starts, no one will know or care who paid and who didn't.)

The goal by the end of the tour is for the booking agent to be able to honestly say that the artist packed out, for example, sixteen shows. Hopefully, the agent will also be able to add that people were turned away at the door and merch sales were huge. This narrative can ignite the booking agency and get everyone on the artist's team excited about the future. Even if a short run like this is a break-even proposition, the real goal is to begin building hard ticket value and provide positive numbers for the booking agency. Remember, a lateral move is progress when it can create an upward trend.

Now, here's what you *don't* need to do when booking your own tour. You can't stack all the odds in your favor and only play your very best markets to make it look like you can produce that result anywhere in the U.S. If an artist plays the hometown, the college town, and only around the region where he/she has built a fan base, don't paint the picture that those numbers can translate across the country. That's a recipe for disaster. If an artist gets booked into venues under false pretenses, using skewed data, the entire plan will backfire and possibly explode.

To close, my personal recommendation is that *every* mid-level artist should do a run just as I have described in this section at least once a year. Carve out the time, plan your year around it, make that block of dates a major focus, and put a lot of energy toward its success.

Reaching A-Level Status

The next and final step of an artist's career is to get to A-level. When talking about growth in touring as an artist, Jason Isbell said, "Sleeping on people's floors when you're twenty-two is fine. But when you get your life in order and have a family you want to keep a certain level of health. Touring bigger means you can keep going for longer."[62]

Here are some characteristics of an A-level artist:

- Songs are wildly successful in being received by the general public
- Content is overwhelmingly and positively consumed by fans
- Streams on all platforms are in the millions
- Songs are regularly heard on the radio (local and subscription)

- Fan base keeps growing wider and demand for content grows deeper
- Decisions are now in the artist's full control of when, how, and where tours occur
- Dates are 99 percent hard ticket
- Decisions about the opening acts are now solely up to the artist
- Hires are only for specific tour personnel covering each aspect of a show

The roles an A-level artist will have on the road:
- Tour manager (TM)
- Production manager
- Front-of-house engineer
- Monitor engineer
- Lighting director
- Content/video manager
- Stage manager*
- Merch manager
- Backline techs
- Production assistants
- Bus and semi drivers

Other potential roles:
- Dedicated techs for each band member to help with setup, during show, and tear-down

- Wardrobe and/or stylists (most A-level artists will have these)
- Caterer/nutritionist
- Personal security
- Pilots (some A-level artists fly to all their dates while all other personnel travel on buses)

Tour assets that an A-level artist may own or lease (full time or part time):
- Sound and lights
- Jet
- Buses
- Semitrucks
- Box trucks
- Staging (usually specially designed to create a custom stage)
- LED walls
- Video screens
- Stage scrim (giant veil that covers the front of stage before the show starts)
- Stage props
- Specialty production like pyro (fire), cryo (white smoke blasts), and confetti cannons

Over eighteen months in 1976 and 1977, ZZ Top brought their Worldwide Texas Tour to arenas all over the U.S., with the largest stage production to date in rock history. Each night onstage they had live animals—a buffalo, longhorn steer, two vultures, and two large rattlesnakes—all under the care of an animal handler. The vultures were tethered to perches, and the snakes were enclosed in a plexiglass case at the front edge of the stage.

Michel Priest, the tour's assistant set designer, told this story:

> [Bill Ham, the manager] was hiring nine stretch limos for every show. He would put the boys, individually, in three of them, and then six decoys in the others, just to try to make sure the band would get safely from place to place. So they had these limos all lined up backstage at Fort Worth, and as they were leading the buffalo on to the scissor lift for rehearsal, the animal jerked his nose-ring out, so he's throwing his head around in pain, snorting and wild-eyed. He sees this tall strip of light streaming in through the doors in the distance, so he heads straight for it. Between him and the light, of course, are the limos with the drivers inside. He charges right between the first two, but then gets jammed between the next two. The driver wakes from his nap, looks over, and not five inches from his eye is the face of this insane buffalo, sneezing and blowing blood all over the window. He had the presence of mind to lock the door, so it at least couldn't get inside.[63]

Ralph Fisher, the tour animal wrangler, said:

The rattlesnakes were our most dangerous animals, so we'd always make a spectacle of putting them in and out of their cage. We'd make sure one of them would escape, then we'd make a big show of recapturing it, because it made for good publicity. The headlines next day would be: "Rattlesnake escapes at ZZ Top concert." [64]

Paula Helene, the tour's stage prop manager, explained one of her tricks she used for the onstage plants:

[After a while] some of the live cacti we used on the stage were starting to look bad. So if we were staying in a hotel that had a healthy-looking cactus, in the dead of night we'd dig it up and replace it with our ailing cactus. That's how we kept good-looking cacti on the stage. [65]

My craziest tour story happened at a venue in Tyler, Texas. The room was a huge rectangle with a high ceiling, which had massive fans with large metal blades hanging throughout. During the show, one of the ceiling fans gave way and came crashing down. It landed right in front of the audio board, crushing part of the audio console, and took out the road case that was holding the Wi-Fi router. I heard the commotion on the radios and ran to check. As soon as I saw that no one was hurt and everyone was okay, I looked up to see all the other fans spinning at full power, so I immediately called for those to be shut off to avoid any other incident.

Now here's the miraculous part: The promoter had oversold the show, so the house was packed. Of all the fans that fell, it was the one over the small section where all the band's comp (guests) seats were. But no one had arrived yet. Had any of our family and friends been sitting there, someone would have died, and for sure, many would have been badly hurt. And here's the craziest part—the only seats where the fan could have fallen and *not* killed someone were those empty comp seats. That date was the first of four shows that weekend. What a way to start a run!

Regardless of the level of the artist, the goal is to create a meaningful, entertaining show that keeps people's attention and makes them want to bring their friends and family back to see the tour the next time it comes to town. This is why a lot of A-level artists have to get more and more creative to try and top what they did on the last tour, which usually translates into more money being spent on a higher level of production. While you may hear of headlining artists getting crazy paychecks for appearing at a festival like Coachella or Lollapalooza, they are spending equally crazy amounts on the production for that one show.

Now, it's time for another round of full-disclosure honesty—it doesn't matter how much production you have, the size of your LED wall, how far up your flames shoot, how much confetti you blast over the crowd, how many semis of gear you bring, how cool your tour bus is, how expensive your wardrobe is, how amazing your band performs, how cool your merchandise display is, how well routed the tour has been, or who else your front-of-house engineer has toured with—at the end of the day if you don't have songs that people want to show up to hear, your tour will be a total failure and you will end up canceling before or right after it starts. Once again, an artist's career is about *great songs* and *awesome fans*!

Growing Pains

If you are an artist or plan on being an artist, I highly recommend you build your road machine slowly over the course of several tours with a goal of never getting in over your head. If you tour too big or too fast and end up having to cancel, that move can be financially and emotionally devastating. Your brand could be damaged beyond repair and possibly take several years to recover, if at all.

Successful and long-term touring comes down to finding a healthy rhythm for the artist. This allows for financial survival as well as maintaining a healthy lifestyle around their family. A healthy rhythm also nurtures the physical, mental, emotional, and spiritual well-being of the artist, all while providing the creative time, space, and energy to keep cranking out hit songs. This requires constant, open and honest communication between the manager and artist, as well as the booking agents and promoters.

The team needs to put a touring plan in place, implement the plan, and while in the middle of execution, make any necessary adjustments for growth. The artist needs to have the freedom to say along the way to the team, "I *like* doing things like this and I *don't* like doing things like that" and "These kinds of shows energize me, while these other shows suck the life out of me." In my experience, I have found that some artists are really good at being honest and communicating what works and what doesn't for them. But even after years of touring, others still don't, or they won't draw the lines they should. It's not about becoming a prima donna, but more about fitting the touring to the artist, not vice versa.

I think I have made it abundantly clear that the road is not easy! As a matter of fact, if you don't know what you're doing, touring can be an extremely miserable life. In an interview, country music legend George Strait—who absolutely knows what he's doing—shared, "I don't mind traveling that much when I can go somewhere and stay there for a while, but touring is different. You rarely see anything. You get there early in the morning and you're resting all day, and you go in and do a sound check, and you do the show, and then bam, you're gone."[66]

I know that to a young artist the idea of jumping on a tour bus, traveling the country, and getting onstage every night sounds exciting to those who have never done it. But after about day three, you can start to feel like Bill Murray in the movie *Groundhog Day*. You'll either become his character in the first half of the movie and burn out, or you'll figure out how to be who he became in the second half. There's no in-between. If you're going to be on the road, figure out how to live your best life out there, venture outside the venue, meet the locals, and see what the great cities of this nation have to offer.

A Day in the Life

Let me give you a visual walk-through of a typical day on tour. You wake up and realize the bus is parked at the venue. You get your bags out from underneath the bus (or the back of the van). You stagger into the venue looking for any familiar signage or arrows on the ground that, hopefully, the production assistant put down to point you in the direction of your dressing room. You drop your bags and go to the bathroom (only number one is allowed on buses). Then you stumble into catering, hoping that something there seems somewhat appetizing. You sit down with some familiar faces while wiping the sleep out of your eyes. And you spend a couple of minutes trying to figure out what day it is. What town you are in. What your day will look like. Then you listen to the crew complain about how much load-in sucks because of a ramp, or stairs, or dock, or a tough union steward, or lack of volunteers. Hopefully, you have time for some personal hygiene before you finish getting dressed for the day. Next, you deal with a barrage of communication for future dates while trying to pull off the current show, last-minute ticket comp requests (freebies), and being reminded of any interviews scheduled for the day.

At some point in the afternoon, there is a sound check where you try and navigate anyone getting yelled at or quitting the band. Hopefully you have everything ready to go before doors open and the fans are let in. Next will be meet and greet where you hope no major psycho fan totally disrupts the natural flow of being able to say hello, sign something, and take a quick picture. At some point in and around all this, you may eat dinner in catering. You'll also need to change into whatever your stage clothes will be.

Once the show starts, the opening act(s) play, the evening flies by, and the headliner's set culminates with confetti cannons at the end of the last song, a final bow, and you disappear off stage into the dressing room. Later, after you take a shower, get changed, get all your stuff packed back up and out onto the bus, you can have some cold after-show food in the front lounge with everyone else. Once all the gear and production are loaded in and the drivers have returned from their hotel, then the buses start rolling out to the next city. The next day, you'll do all that all over again! Now, doesn't that sound glamorous?!

Over the years, artists usually develop a relationship with bus, sound, and lighting companies, which will become go-to people to buy or rent. They will also probably send out the same techs who will bring their gear, which will be an extension of the core touring crew. They won't be directly on the payroll, but they will probably end up feeling like family after a couple of tours.

The touring community is small so, once again, here comes some repeat advice—it's important to be a good hang. You might be the best backline tech known to man, but if you can't get along with people on a bus, chances are you won't be on a tour for long. If you ever get a reputation for being annoying, it's hard to un-ring that bell because most tour managers know each other and freely offer a thumbs-up or thumbs-down to weed out the riff-raff.

I said life on the road is not easy, but it's also not for the faint of heart. No matter how much you enjoy it, if you have *any* underlying medical conditions or lifestyle issues, such as a specific diet, this life is probably not for you. The long hours, late nights, early mornings, constantly being on the move, sleeping on a rolling bus, and jumping on early-morning flights at the end of the weekend take their toll on every area of life. Once you are back at home, you have enough time to do your laundry, fix whatever has broken while you were gone, have a quick date night, hug your kids, and then before you know it, you are right back out for the next weekend. Sometimes, depending on where you are, you don't even come home between weekends. If you are touring internationally, you may be gone for weeks at a time.

Some of the simplest things you do at home have to be planned out while you're on the road. Like, getting your laundry done on a show day while you are out on the road may seem easy enough, but you have to think about if there's time to send it out or find a place to get it done and then get back to pick it up in time before the place closes. If you miss closing time or simply forget, you'll be in another town by the time they open back up the next morning. On any days off, the hotel laundry facility with one washer and dryer means the entire crew will be lined up and down the hall to get theirs done. (I've always found it easiest to drop my laundry at a fluff-and-fold, run an errand, and come back.)

Staying healthy and practicing self-care is absolutely crucial. Finding time throughout the day to take care of some essentials is important, like personal hygiene, staying connected with family and friends, having a little alone time for reflection, journaling, reading, exercising, and resting. If you don't figure out a way to regularly do these things, chances are at some point your body and/or your mind are going to shut down on you.

The story is told of a team of explorers who wanted to travel through a remote part of the Amazon jungle. They found a local tribe and hired them to be guides and to help to carry all the necessary gear. On the morning of the third day, all the tribesmen wouldn't move. They all just sat quietly and stared at the sky. When the lead explorer asked through an interpreter why they wouldn't get up and get moving, the only answer that came back was, "We are waiting for our souls to catch up with our bodies." That, my friend, is *exactly* what you have to do on a long tour. Schedule the time to let your soul catch up with your body.

As a young artist, you play as many shows as you can, wherever you can. But when you're touring at any scale, large or small, developing and maintaining relationships with anyone influential or who has resources, who takes an interest in your music is important—a promoter who really believes in you, a business owner who consistently stays in touch to hear your needs, or a company that feels like you fit their brand. Each, any, or all of these could one day become a financial partner in helping to further your career through monetary endorsements and strategic partnerships.

Having been-there-done-that for a long time and helping my artists navigate the touring life, I look at our routing, and I schedule some fun days off along the way. Depending on the time of year and the area of the country we're going to be in, I will plan days to go snow skiing, ride motorcycles or scooters, etc. I plan fun and adventure into the tour to make the road a little easier.

Legendary classic rocker Pat Benatar, who has been touring for forty years, once said, "The soul of touring and the heart of it is basically every day like putting up a circus tent."[67] I couldn't have said it any better. I know, because I've been helping artists roll into towns all over the world and put up the circus tent for a long time.

Potential Roles and Positions Connected to Touring

- Venue Staff
  - » General manager
  - » Box office
  - » Accountant
  - » Steward
  - » Merch director
  - » Ticket takers
  - » Ushers
  - » Local crew
  - » Catering
  - » Runners
  - » Electrician
  - » Rigger
- Fair, cruise, or festival entertainment director
- Restaurant, bar, or coffee shop owner
- Talent buyer/booker for restaurant, hotel, or casino groups
- Club manager
- Church representative
- Conference coordinator
- College student activities coordinator
- Bus driver
- Truck driver
- Tour instrumentalist

(Additional artist personnel is covered further in chapter fifteen.)

"Nowadays, with the state of the music business, for any artist, whether you're up-and-coming or you've been at it for a while, you have to explore different revenues and different ways of expressing yourself."—MARY J. BLIGE[68]

CHAPTER TWELVE

THE MERCH

Aside from touring, merchandise is the primary way for an artist
to make money and expand the brand.

AT THE PEAK of Audio Adrenaline's heyday, we were scheduled to play a massive student event called DC/LA, two tandem
events held in both cities, Washington, DC, and Los Angeles.
The plans for this event had been mapped out for a year, and
we were one of the headliners. We were scheduled to play in
DC, so the week before, we sent all our merch ahead on a semi
with dc Talk's merch.

Mark Stuart, the lead singer, was struck with a bad case
of laryngitis. We monitored him closely but could tell that he
was not going to be able to sing on the day of the event. We
called and canceled. It was a huge blow to everyone. But our
merch guy was already there and set up for the day. Prior to the
announcement that Audio Adrenaline would not be coming,
the line at our tent was a trickle at best. After they announced

that Mark was sick and the band would not be performing, the fans swamped our tent. We sold out of everything we had, and the band made $25,000 that day. Losing the honorarium for that day was a tough hit, but the merch sales certainly softened the blow. And there is nothing better than a fan who is willing to pay you money to wear your shirt with your logo and help promote your brand. *Free real estate!*

Another time, I was out with MercyMe, and one of the bands on the tour called to say their van had broken down. They had made arrangements to have their merch sent ahead, and it was already set up. They informed the promoter they weren't sure if they were going to be able to make it to the show. Throughout the evening, they announced progress reports on the band's arrival. But, at one point, someone said, "Hey, when a band has a major breakdown like these guys did today, it's a hard financial hit. Show your love and go buy some of their merch to help them out to keep going and stay on the road." The fans responded, swarmed their table, and when the band finally arrived later that evening to play a late set, they were blessed by how the community had taken good care of them. Those two stories are great examples of what the right merch with the right fans can do for an artist.

In 2017, *Forbes* magazine published an article titled, "The New Role Merchandise Plays When Creating a Musician's Brand." In the piece, Mat Vlasic, CEO of Bravado, a merch company that handles products for the Rolling Stones, Prince, Drake, and Lady Gaga, said, "It's about extending an artist's brand through a global program of different consumer products. It's important to learn from other industries where they have tapped ideas around merchandising being a prominent marketing vehicle and being able to help build your brand. It's what Ralph Lauren or another fashion icon would do!"[69]

Forbes, Drake, and Ralph Lauren—all mentioned in an article about artist merch—means we are not just talking about selling cheap T-shirts out of the back of the van anymore. The development, creativity, style, design, quality, and delivery of merchandise is critical to what has become a vital income stream for artists. As we've established in past chapters, touring will obviously create the largest income stream, but if an artist is between tours or at home during the holidays, a new line being launched or a Black Friday special announced can shoot merch up to number one on the income list to be enjoyed from the comforts of the living room.

Some examples of items artists offer today are:

- T-shirts: unisex, men, women, children
- Premium shirts: fitted, raglan jerseys, long sleeve, hoodie, polo
- Jackets: denim, baseball
- Hats: dad, ball, trucker, snapback, beanie, ski
- Posters: promo shot, tour, special event, commemorative
- Miscellaneous: sticker, necklace, bracelet, pin, keychain, tote bag, socks, boxers, drumsticks, drumhead, guitar pick, flag, magnet, patch, koozie, coffee mug, license plate/holder, face mask, blanket, Christmas ornament, puzzle, custom coffee, acoustic guitar, and pretty much anything else on which you can print a logo and buy wholesale

Some artists have the same items on the road as on their website, while others offer exclusive product on a tour or on their site. Releasing a new line of merch in coordination with a soon-to-be-released album has become the norm and a great way to create synergy around a project, while also maximizing income. Particularly for this purpose, bundles have become a huge moneymaker for artists. A bundle will typically include a digital download card, LP, or CD of the new release, a T-shirt, and an autographed poster, along with any specifically branded items that coordinate with the new album. Artists will offer a range from a basic bundle to a premium bundle, with prices starting around $30 but which can go into the hundreds of dollars. Superfan (as we described in chapter nine) will buy the highest-end bundle they can possibly afford.

An artist today needs to spend a dedicated amount of time, energy, and money to curate a line of merchandise compatible and coordinated with the brand. *All* product should be part of a big-picture strategy. Testing an item in a small quantity is always wise to see what sells well before placing large orders. Yes, a small quantity will cost more, but if something doesn't connect with an artist's fans, it's better to make less profit on a few items than to lose money on a mass quantity that won't sell. Of course, like any other product in bulk, the more that is ordered, the cheaper the cost per item.

Getting quotes on several different quantities from low to high is smart in order to look at two things: total cash outlay, and profit margin per unit at each quantity level. For quotes in total dollars per quantity, always divide out to see the per-unit cost. On most products, there will be a sweet spot where unit cost, quantity, and total cost make sense and maximize your buy. Sometimes a product drops so much in price at a certain bulk that you can't afford not to buy at that quantity to capitalize on profit in the long run.

Here's a piece of advice that I have seen played out time and time again. If an artist and I work on a shirt with a designer, and we love it, if we print it up in our sizes to proudly wear, it won't sell. But then a designer shows us something we hate, but we go with it, it will sell like crazy. Moral of the story—just because you love a merch item doesn't mean the fans will. My best advice is to test anything you want to put on your table before you commit to quantities.

Merch Tour Display

Whether in one-off soft ticket events or hard ticket tours, the merch display is often the first experience and engagement for fans of an artist at a show. Think about it: You've had tickets to see one of your favorite artists for months. You're pumped for the experience. As soon as you get through the turnstiles, there in the concourse you see a huge, brightly lit display with awesomely cool new T-shirts and tour products you've never seen before. All of a sudden, that $50 you were going to spend next week on an oil change turns into a bag full of artist merch.

Exactly for this reason, on a tour, merch items need to be displayed in the most visible and easily accessible spot possible in a venue. For fans to see the display as soon as they come in the door, two key factors are light and height.

First, lighting affixed to a display is a great way to draw attention to products. Think about walking into retail stores.

There are always some kind of directed spotlights on items where they want to draw your attention. Since most music events are at night, a well-lit merch display can literally cause an artist to sell more.

The second element is height. If everything is lying down flat on tables, the only people who can see the merch are those right up at the front of a crowd. If people cannot see what an artist has available until they get up to the table, they are more likely to give up and walk away. A high percentage of merch sales at a show are impulse buys, so if people have to wait in a long line just to even see what is available, chances for making a sale drop. If a display is well-lit, and items are hung across a tall display, visible from a good distance back, then someone can already have decided what they want by the time they get to the table. This is just human nature and typical consumer behavior applied to a crowded concourse or lobby.

There are companies that sell anything needed to build a custom, high-level display merch setup. They will often design and create the display based on the artist's desires and number of products. This often includes Ultimate Support-style stands* (portable, lightweight metal with foldable legs and support arms), backdrops, body molds, mannequins, tablecloths, banners, display cases, racks, and, of course, lighting to present all the merch items in an appealing manner.

All items and the display equipment need to be packed, stored, and protected when transported. Having a damaged display or a box of crushed hats on the third night of a tour makes for a really rough and costly start. The bigger an artist gets, and the more merch sold, the bigger this investment needs to be.

Some artists, tours, and even venues have a grid system on a wall, where shirts are displayed, rather than a large backdrop with banners and mannequins. This is usually the case for club and theater shows, as the lobbies are often very small with not enough room for a wide and/or tall display. For arena tours where multiple merch stands will be set up in different concourse sections, there are usually only grids and a few select banners due to the need for so many displays.

If you're an artist, you need to always look at the number of people at your shows and then your total amount of merch sales, then divide to get the "number per head." For example, you play a club with 500 people and make $500; that's a dollar per head. You can use those numbers from each night to start to gauge your sales, plan your inventory, and chart growth. That brings us to our next section . . .

Expanding Merch with Growth

When an artist is new and starting out, he/she will be responsible for getting the merch table set up and having someone work it throughout the show. (You never want to leave a table unattended, unless you can cover it and there are ushers or security close by who are watching to prevent theft.) Often, this detail can be covered in advance by asking for help. At this stage, an artist has to always plan on having start-up cash* (change to break larger bills).

To spell out a merch must-have, an artist needs a credit card reader connected to his/her phone or an iPad. If not, money will be left on the table. A cash app option to offer fans, even besides merch, is also important, particularly if playing for tips. Many people today carry little to no cash, and most will tend to spend more money when they use a card. You need as many current, available payment options as possible. Besides common brands, such as PayPal and Square, the artist's bank might have a great option, which could integrate directly with the account, as well as offer tech support. Be sure to compare the fees charged by anyone in consideration. At any venue, getting the dedicated and secure Wi-Fi guest password is a small but critical detail. Being put into the spin cycle several minutes at a time on each transaction can literally cost an artist in sales.

Immediately following the set, the artist should go to the merch table to talk to people, sign autographs, take pictures, while also allowing a seller to fill in any details that happened during the show, such as damaged merch, questions fans had, or what has been selling well. After the crowd is gone, the artist is then responsible for doing inventory, reconciling money with the sellers (venue or third party), and getting everything packed up and ready to go to the next show. If an artist realizes something is needed, that detail should be written down and taken care of right away. Nothing's worse than getting to the next show and remembering that mediums sold out in the most popular shirt at the last show, creating wasted time and lost income.

One important encouragement I will make, particularly for a young or new artist, is that far more merch is going to be sold when he/she is at the table. The artists who decide it's not cool to be seen offstage or can't get over having to talk to people will not sell as much as the friendly folks who hang out and visit. In fact, a mediocre artist who is awesome to fans will usually do far better than the super-talented artist who's aloof and never comes out. Today, accessibility—with boundaries, of course—is critical to being successful in the music industry.

If an artist has a road or tour manager or a merch coordinator at the table to sell and handle issues, then the artist is completely free to just talk to fans. (It's always a bit awkward when in every picture of an artist taken with fans after a show, you can see a fistful of twenties in his/her hand.)

Usually somewhere between B-Level and A-level, an artist gets big enough to hire a full-time merch manager. That person's job is to live and breathe the artist's merchandise—curate, research, brainstorm new ideas, work with designers and vendors, get samples, secure pricing, make recommendations, and constantly evolve the artist's merch that's sold on the road and online. A massive responsibility is to project sales, order, ship, and keep inventory in stock and flowing. Running out of the most popular shirt is great on the last night of tour, but not on the first weekend. Also paying rush charges to vendors and shippers can quickly kill an artist's profits.

The merch manager's big-picture financial goal is to maximize the gross sales through proper inventory and margins, while minimizing the expenses from cost of goods, warehousing, damage, and shipping, so the artist's profit or net on sales is strong and the best it can be.

Another key responsibility of the merch manager is to contact the venue where the artist is playing well in advance of the show to determine all the details necessary for a smooth and profitable merch experience on the day of the show. Some of the details that need to be addressed with the venue are:

- Any merch fee that the venue or third-party seller will charge

- If fees charged, determine the split; typically, recorded product is 90/10, with soft goods (T-shirts, etc.) being 70/30 or 80/20, with the higher percentage going to the artist

- Work on negotiating the fee, if possible

- Check on the possibility of a "Most Favored Nations"* clause in the contract, meaning the lowest negotiated rate for another artist should be provided to everyone

- Dealing with any charges for space, tables, or help

- Dealing with any local taxes that must be charged and paid

- Deciding whether to absorb any of those costs or raise the prices to sustain profit

- Find out if the venue provides sellers

- If so, determine if there are any fees

- If the venue or promoter provides sellers, then determine if you are allowed to sell the merchandise with them or only allowed to "inventory in and out"* (starting and ending numbers on all merch items) and "count in and out"* (ending dollar amount minus start-up cash amount) with them. (If the venue provides people, and you can't sell with them, that's called a hall vend* or venue sell.*)

If you are allowed to provide your own sellers or volunteers, then you will need to secure them. In this case, a local radio station associated with the show or the promoter who's putting the show on can often help get people. Of course, there's always doing a call-out on social media. (It's amazing what the promise of a free T-shirt will create!) Worst-case scenario is you run backstage into catering and yell, "I need help at the merch table!" and whatever crew, band guys, or management available will usually jump in to help where they can.

Merch sellers may also be provided, for a set fee, from the paid staff of the venue who are usually required to be on-site from mid- or late-afternoon until well after the show. They will be responsible for whatever items they are given to sell at their assigned merch table. In some circumstances, if the money versus the number of items sold at the end of the night doesn't match, that shortage will be deducted from their pay. Venues have this policy to keep employees honest.

A brand-new artist might do well to only sell a couple hundred dollars in merch a night, transporting everything in cardboard boxes in their own vehicle. As an artist's career grows, often a trailer is added, with everything protected in cases, tubs, or hampers. As an A-level artist, the tour usually has a semi devoted to merch, with multiple personnel handling product. In the world of super-A-level artists, there are several semis constantly traveling back and forth to vendors, delivering merch per show, and leaving at the end of the night completely empty.

Some artists turn all their merchandise over to a company that handles everything—design, products, logistics, hiring, and firing—and simply hand the artist a check for their contracted percentage of the take. The artist has very little to do with what is provided to fans. They may give input, tweak, and approve designs, but it's up to the merch company to use their experience and expertise to create as much success as possible for both the artist and their business.

For international soft or hard ticket dates, profitability gets tough because of shipping costs, tariffs, taxes, etc. Some artists will find a merch partner in that region of the world to work with or will rely on the promoter to help coordinate providing merch for a percentage of the profit.

Songs and Sales

In an article on Spotify's website, Ed Aten, co-founder of Merchbar, and Reid Martin of the group Low Cut Connie's management team, share their thoughts:

> *Aten says the only restrictions on varieties of merch are those imposed by the artists' imaginations. . . .*
>
> *Another benefit for artists now is they can sell merch on a more a-la-carte basis, allowing them to offer more sizes and designs of shirts and heavier/bulkier items they wouldn't necessarily want to drag out on the road. "When you're putting together a tour and figuring out what you're going to carry from town to town, you've got to be really sensitive to the total number of SKUs [UPC codes] you have, the sizes you print, because it costs time and money to move that stuff around," says Martin. "Online, there's such a massive amount of fans that have different interests, desires, and sizes, that we really see there's a huge benefit to releasing a diversity of product. You're going to move a wide variety of*

types, sizes, styles, and products for different genders." . . .

Aten says, "Artists are being more responsive and more adaptive than ever before," figuring out the ways they can help themselves and their fanbases. . . . . Ingenuity is truly the limit to making the most of the current situation—and a way for artists to think bigger about how they approach merch.[70]

To explain SKU*—for a specific shirt design, each size has its own UPC, or barcode. Each specific, individual product has a SKU. If an artist is traveling alone, it's going to be easier to keep up with twenty SKUs than fifty. An artist has to constantly balance a diversity in the merch line with overwhelming fans with options.

Artists have to and want to write, create, and produce incredible music for their fans. Development of great merchandising connected to the brand can also be a creative outlet, which ultimately becomes the difference in making a living in the music business. Don't make your merch line a have-to, but a get-to. If I were you, I'd figure out how to have fun with your brand and your fans, while bringing in some cash at the same time.

Potential Roles and Positions Connected to Merchandising
- Merch manager (most likely travels)
- Assistant merch manager
- Merchandise production team
- Graphic designer
- Rep with an artist merch company
- Inventory specialists
- Merchandise models

"For the music business, social networking is brilliant.
Just when you think it's doom and gloom and you have
to spend millions of pounds on marketing and this and that,
you have this amazing thing now called fan power.
The whole world is linked through a laptop. It's amazing.
And it's free. I love it. It's absolutely brilliant."
—SIMON COWELL[71]

CHAPTER THIRTEEN

THE POST

Social media can be a deal maker or a deal breaker for an artist today.

SOCIAL MEDIA is an unbelievable resource, which can allow an artist to accomplish completely free of charge what used to take a team of publicists and marketing folks a great deal of time, money, and energy to create and disperse. Being able to engage directly with fans in almost real time to share information on tours, releases, singles, and news, as well as having the opportunity to shape culture, is near miraculous, especially compared to when I started out in the music industry. While social media certainly has its downsides and social ills, as we see every day, this digital connection to the world can be an extremely beneficial and strategic resource for any artist.

But for a new artist, someone hoping to become an artist, or anyone working with an artist in any support capacity, here's the other side of the coin: many have been turned down, or even dropped, because of poor choices in social media content.

If an artist is going to be considered by a record label, manager, publishing company, booking agency, or any other industry-related role—*trust me*—in the course of due diligence, they *will* comb through the socials looking for both the positive and the negative, the good, the bad, and the ugly.

Social media today can be a deal maker or a deal breaker. For example, if a label finds 25,000 followers and growing, along with a consistent history of smart and strategic posts that stay on brand, they consider that a major asset. I don't have to explain the other side, because likely, you know it and you've seen it.

So, if I were you, what would I do? Well, glad you asked . . .

If there is any question at all regarding social media history, then a very wise choice is to go through and clean up *every* feed, from inception of a platform to current. This move is crucial. An artist needs to view and review *every* post through the filter of answering this question: Does this post positively represent and reflect my brand? Granted, that can sometimes feel like a tightrope walk trying to appeal to everyone, while also not alienating anyone. But without using some alternate handle, an artist can't separate the "music social media" from the "personal social media."

If an artist's social media is constant drama and negativity, anyone looking to work with him/her is going to assume that what they see and read is just the tip of the iceberg. Because it usually is. As a manager, I have unfollowed artists because of what I've seen online. I don't want my name and my own brand connected to something toxic on any level.

Also, if the vibe of an artist's social media doesn't line up with his/her genre or style of music, that disconnection will be viewed as inauthentic. The question then becomes: Does the artist really know who he/she is?

Fixing the Feed

If an artist has little to no social media history, the good news is this can be "day one" of getting serious on posting the best content for a future career as well as being strategic on follows and activity. One piece of advice would be to take a few favorite artists, study their social media, and replicate a personalized version using their templates. Take a look and consider these questions:

- What do they post?
- When do they post?
- How do the posts sound?
- How do the posts feel?
- What are their patterns?
- Do they tend to be fun or serious or a mix?
- Is there a certain style to the posts?
- Is there a style to the images or graphics used?
- How do they stay consistent with their brand?
- How does the content build more growth and connection with fans?

Once an artist has cleaned up all socials, then he/she needs to set a reasonable threshold for the number of likes and level of engagement that each post must achieve. If one doesn't hit the mark, then the call needs to be made to delete. This benchmark or standard helps an artist understand how to post solid content that people will like and engage with, while also allowing future labels, managers, agents, publishers, and fans to see a very consistent and strong social media presence. So, if an artist knows that a thousand likes is a good, reasonable showing for a post, then if within a set time frame, something hasn't connected in that range, it's taken down. Everyone's memory today is super short, if not nonexistent, in the social media world, so people will quickly forget, particularly if a great post comes on the heels of a deletion.

Like any solid strategy, the goal for social media growth needs an offense and a defense: The offense is to develop healthy habits in posts to constantly increase the fan base. The defense is to avoid any negative or controversial posts that will run people off, or worse, attract haters who start leaving comments. But remember, staying focused on your music while being kind and positive is really not that hard.

Plan for Success

The best plan for social media is to:

- Create a schedule for posting.
- Plan each post to be something well-thought-out.
- Plan what is said.
- Plan what is seen.
- Plan the timing in which the message is delivered.
- Use hashtags strategically and correctly.

Obviously, there will be important moments that arise when an artist may feel the need to share something that's not on the schedule, but those occasions should be few and far between. In light of that advice, remember these points:

- Make every word count.
- Make every picture or image count.
- Don't waste any opportunity to engage with fans.
- Never react out of emotion.
- Sleep on anything before responding.
- Waiting for clarity rarely creates regrets.
- Never, and I mean never, react out of emotion.

When someone attacks on social media, the artist should never respond. Once engagement with the negative post occurs, that can never be undone. The fight has begun. An artist who has any fan base at all can rely on those folks to come to his/her defense. The best response to any toxic comment is silence from the artist, allowing room for the fans to answer. The majority of the time, they will.

When an artist has a manager or other invested person available, asking for counsel will always be a good move. He/she has to continually keep in mind that any post should not be about a *cause in the moment*, but a *career in the making*.

As far as authorship on social media, as I have stated before, *all* posts should be driven by the artist. Yes, there are companies and individual contractors that can be hired to manage social media, but the majority of fans can see right through that facade. An artist needs to be very protective of anyone to whom the feed is given. If a label wants to manage an artist's socials, then be sure it's the right person handling the accounts (for example, not an intern). Make sure they don't constantly promote other projects as if the artist is giving a shout-out. The choices of a label have to line up with the artist's brand. Regardless of how massive an artist becomes, social media is the one outlet where his/her voice needs to exclusively connect with fans.

Working with someone who specializes in social media can be great from the standpoint of understanding analytics and engagement because that's necessary information for every artist. While a professional can be beneficial, an artist should never just turn over the log-ins and walk away. Consistent involvement is crucial so posts feel authentic to the brand and fan base.

Fueling Growth

Another important aspect of social media is learning which posts are worth spending money to boost. As an artist manager, my line in the sand is drawn on whether the post is promoting an item to sell, such as a new merch product or tickets for an upcoming show. Done right, the return on investment usually makes sense. From my experience, I wouldn't recommend paying to boost anything that doesn't have a potential financial return connected. *Invest* money; never throw it away.

To stay on top of the game, artists need to constantly pay attention to any new emerging platforms that are music friendly. TikTok is a great example of an app and platform that exploded and gained fast popularity where artists could connect with fans, allow discovery by new fans, and promote their brand. Early adoption is very important because those who are in the door in the first wave often have an easier time gaining more followers as opposed to those who arrive late to the party.

Increasingly, social media has the potential to catapult a young artist into a thriving career, such as Lewis Capaldi, whose song "Someone You Loved" racked up 10 million views on YouTube. But once the song was posted on TikTok, it hit 309 million views.[72] Bottom line: millions more of Capaldi's demographic base was on TikTok instead of YouTube. That single decision of where, what, and when to post was a game-changer in his career.

Not that long ago, about the only place where fans could engage with an artist was during the two to three minutes allowed at a meet and greet prior to a show. Today, artists are expected to connect with their fans daily on multiple social media platforms. From the late-'90s to now, with AOL Messenger to Myspace to Facebook to Twitter to Instagram to Snapchat to TikTok to whatever is next, the lineage of technology continues to innovate human communication and engagement. As such a powerful artistic medium, music will always be compatible with and welcome anywhere people gather.

As social platforms progress, the younger, newer artists will need to be on the latest platform. Established veteran artists will have to maintain the status quo, like staying on Facebook and Twitter where they began, while adopting the more recent ones like Instagram and TikTok. And *everyone* will have to jump on whatever is next to stay on top. An artist ignoring any available platform is leaving cash on the table.

Social platforms have changed the way the entire industry does business, because where artists are, the music business must be. Marketing plans have to heavily involve social media. We have been handed a medium to be able to test music, track new trends, and gain valuable intel on an artist's fan base.

Smart, strategic artists train their fans on what to expect from them. Some open up and talk about almost anything, while others are more protective and draw boundaries on what they share. But however an artist decides to engage will set a standard of what fans will expect. How something starts is how it continues. Once the genie is let out of the bottle, especially on social media, it's really tough to get it back in. Yet another reason why social media needs to be created and planned out using some sort of guidelines, or maybe guardrails, is so that one doesn't drive off a cliff in the heat of the moment.

Some artists' careers have even begun because they were discovered on social media. They obviously had the X Factor, whether it was vocal, musical, and/or songwriting talent, look, style, sense of humor, or something that captured attention. Justin Bieber, The Weeknd, Tori Kelly, Charlie Puth, Alessia Cara, and 5 Seconds of Summer were all discovered on YouTube after amassing a following.[73] Shawn Mendez was discovered on Vine and Halsey on Tumblr.[74] As I stated in an earlier chapter, an A&R rep for a label no longer has to go see a show. He/she can surf the Internet from the comforts of the office and find far more talent. Going to see a live show has become the second step in order to verify ability, skill, and interaction with fans.

For this reason, a major warning for posting on social

media is to *never* execute a performance that cannot be replicated live. If an artist manipulates anything or takes a hundred tries to finally hit a high note, and then an A&R person shows up only to see it was just smoke and mirrors, that door is slammed shut. As much as an artist needs to focus on getting content up and using social media to promote the brand, the most important goal is still performing, playing, improving, and getting established as a solid, live, in-person entertainer. Posts should always be a direct reflection of actual talent, not false advertising. (Yet another reason to do the 125 shows!)

As we wrap up this vital chapter, I want to offer some basic info on how to monetize YouTube, which is current as of the writing of this book. Monetization:

- Requires a minimum of 1,000 subscribers to a channel
- Requires a minimum of 4,000 watch time hours in the past twelve months
- Requires the setup of an AdSense account that links to the channel
- Requires passing YouTube's standard review to be certain the channel meets the policies and guidelines through their Partner Program

So, can an artist be rejected? Yes.

Will YouTube give a general idea as to why? Yes.

Will they be specific? No.

But an artist can make adjustments based on the general feedback and reapply after thirty days.[75]

Allow me to reiterate this critical info about social

259

media—the best way to launch or engage an artist's career is to start (or restart) with a clean feed, be strategic about posts, schedule content, and be smart about connecting with the brand and interacting with the fan base. Social media can literally make or break, blow up or build an artist today. So, write great songs, be awesome to fans, and post the best content!

Potential Roles and Positions Connected to Social Media
- Social media manager for an artist, label, manager, or tour
- Ad specialist
- Content manager
- SEO specialist*
- Platform-specific specialist
- Branding specialist
- Graphic designer

"The image is one thing and the human being is another. It's very hard to live up to an image."—ELVIS PRESLEY[76]

CHAPTER FOURTEEN

THE PUBLICIST

**A publicist's role is to get as much free press as possible
to help spread the word about an artist's music and shows.**

A PUBLICIST or public relations company—aka PR*—is contracted for a fee to help the artist connect with as much free promotion and exposure as possible for a release, tour, or other brand announcement.

Many major record labels have an in-house* publicist or a PR department, depending on the size of their roster. A large label will have several publicists who handle multiple artists each. Small labels often have one person, or they contract with an independent publicist to use as needed. Regardless of size, the label relies on the publicist to get the word out when an artist is releasing new music or has any promotion that will benefit the label's connection to the artist.

A seasoned publicist will have a go-to network to which he/she will automatically distribute a press release or article.

THE BUSINESS BEHIND THE SONG

Following that effort, they will begin to target any other media outlets they feel might connect with the artist's release. The publicist contacts as many people as they feel would be able to spread the word through their platforms about the new music or project. The bigger the artist, the greater the reach and opportunities, including appearances, performances, and interviews.

There are the four primary avenues for publicity:

- TV—from local affiliate stations for a live performance or interview to national talk shows that book a musical guest for every episode

- Radio—from local stations to national networks to apps to subscription-based radio like Sirius XM

- Print—physical and digital articles and interviews, from local news to international magazines that center around music, like *Billboard* and *Rolling Stone*

- Online outlets—podcasts and bloggers that focus on music

Depending on the scope of the artist and project, the publicist will work to make initial contact with these entities, gauge their interest level in the artist's music, and then line up potential interaction for any sort of interview, review, or commentary.

Even when an independent artist is making calls for themselves or a manager is trying to land any publicity, an important point to remember is that *all* these outlets exist by gathering content presented to them for broadcast. They need a *lot* of content every day, every week, every month, all year long. In this world, content is king! Of course, some people or organizations may never return a call or email and might even hang up on someone, but there will always be those who, for example, need two more pieces to fulfill their monthly quota, and they would welcome an artist filling a spot. Like the Bible says in James, "You do not have because you do not ask."[77] Sometimes, it really is that simple.

If there is any possible angle to present or a doorway to get in that could create a unique spin by targeting content, those connections need to be discovered and offered. So, if a song on a new record has gotten a strong response live and is about being on the open road riding a Harley, hit up the company or go talk to a local dealer. Look at song lyrics and brainstorm *any* connections that could be made outside the normal box. Again, the only way to know for sure is to try. All anyone can do is say no.

Roles of a Publicist

A publicist's role is usually multidimensional for artists. The publicist is continually looking for positive ways to get an artist's name out to the public and increase visibility and connection.

Record Label

A record label publicist will send out press releases to all national outlets when an artist releases an album, sends a single to radio, announces a tour, wins an award, or reaches some career milestone, such as achieving gold or platinum status. Anything newsworthy is going to be pushed out for consumption.

The press release will include the artist's bio. Typically,

a label/publicist will hire a writer to write the bio if they are not writing it themselves. This might also show up on their website, on their streaming platform pages, and even on websites like Wikipedia that have entries about the artist. Bios are usually specific to an album and will be updated as each one comes out or if the artist has some new music or career update, such as receiving awards.

Tour

Tour promoters or the headlining artist will often secure a publicist or PR firm to target individual markets (targeted segments of the country) in advance of shows to increase ticket sales. The goal is to get the word out about coming to a city or region by broadcasting the location, date, and ticket outlet for local media to provide any possible mentions. This will also include scheduling artist interviews about the tour.

Brand Management

Publicists are extremely important to the overall health and stability of the artist brand in conveying all information in a concise and uniform manner. A press release usually includes quotes and statistics so that even if a one-on-one interview is not possible, the story can be told consistently. An artist doesn't want a different message created for every outlet, but rather a constant, static story. Publicists can tweak a press release to fit a certain market, but the foundation of the article should be the same.

A publicist is a key member of an artist's team, helps keep the branding consistent, and steers all interviews in the direction of what the artist is wanting to communicate. Just as management works with booking to confirm shows, and labels strategize and implement marketing plans to promote singles and albums, a publicist is going to be the sounding board of what is current in the life of an artist.

Personal Life

A publicist is critical in times of crisis. The larger the artist, the more this is true. If a death, accident, or tragedy occurs, the last thing the artist and/or his/her family will be thinking about is the media. (We've all seen the sentence "Please respect our privacy during this difficult time" a thousand times.) Because we live in a day where some outlets will make up circumstances to create click bait, getting the right information out there as soon and as wide as possible is critical. For these reasons, a publicist becomes the singular point of contact and the primary source from whom media outlets hear official messages. It is important to get your message out and be clear and concise because any confusion could lead to the social media warriors knocking on your door and saying, "You're canceled. Boom, roasted!"

Many of the super-A-level artists have personal publicists who handle anything outside of music, such as an engagement, a wedding, the birth of a child, or any branding efforts, such as a clothing line or fragrance release.

Red Carpet Events

Publicists also work with media outlets in advance of a "red carpet event." When the artist arrives, there are pre-scheduled interviews lined up so the time and opportunities can be used efficiently and effectively to maximize the moment. The publicity for an artist can be as big or even bigger than the nature of the actual event.

Specific Projects

If an artist does something outside of music—for example, if he/she writes a book—the smartest move is to secure a short-term contract with a publicist who has knowledge in that field and can focus solely on the book release.

Media Training

For the young or new artist, media training is a crucial component of launching a successful career. This is especially true if the artist is coming off anything that has created sudden notoriety like a TV show or viral video. When the media start knocking on the door and the questions begin to fly, proper preparation can save something negative from happening and getting out. Sometimes it's also good for an established artist to do a refresher course around each record. A publicist or trainer can help an artist come up with talking points that he/she can rely on to stay focused and consistent in messaging, points he/she knows to go to, regardless of the question asked. Media training is very valuable to save the artist from being diverted and distracted to get off message from what he/she is trying to convey.

To close this chapter, the difference between marketing and PR is that marketing costs money to secure, and PR is free, outside of the publicist's fees. The relationship between the PR agent and the artist is crucial to a growing career. For getting the word out about new music and live events, public relations is essential to an artist's career.

Roles and Positions Connected to PR

- Publicist
- Administrative staff
- Music journalist/reporter for media outlets
- Music-related podcast
- Music-related vlog
- Bio writer

"The blessing of your weakness is it forces you into friendships. The things that you lack, you look for in others.

—Bono[78]

CHAPTER FIFTEEN

THE ARTIST TEAM

Through all my years of working in this business, I've found most often,
from the bus drivers to the road crew to the band, everyone becomes a family.

FOR THIS FINAL CHAPTER we'll take a look, one role
at a time, at a major artist's team, and we'll walk through the
normal responsibilities. While some information may overlap
with or repeat from past chapters, ending up with a comprehensive look at what a full team can look like is a strong way to
close out this book.

Music or Entertainment Attorney

An artist is going to need a music or entertainment attorney*
or possibly a legal team, whose job is to help the artist set up
their entities and negotiate contracts with the manager, label,
publishing company, booking agent, as well as be involved with
potential growth points, such as sponsorships or a book, TV, or
film deal, plus any unique high-profile shows and appearances.
The artist's needs might change the attorney's level of involvement

271

through different stages in the career. Depending on the genre, attorneys are also involved in varying levels of dealing with show contracts, from simply composing the original draft all the way to some who are in the loop on approving every show.

The old saying "You get what you pay for" definitely applies to attorneys. While this might cost a substantial amount of up-front money to get everything set up properly, if an artist has a long career, that money is very well spent to ensure everything is done right. How things begin is how they usually continue, so making certain the *i*'s are crossed and the *i*'s are dotted is crucial to building a solid career foundation.

While I covered this topic to a degree in the Manager chapter, it's worth repeating here that an attorney also being an artist's manager has its pros and cons. A pro could be getting some "free" legal advice for a young artist, but a major negative is that attorneys are usually risk averse by nature of the role, and sometimes as an artist, you just have to close your eyes and go for it without having a full understanding of what might happen. For the most part, I view attorneys in a very positive light because they help protect artists in ways they are usually not considering. The wrong attorney can sink an artist's career or kill a great idea before it gets a chance to take off, by over-negotiating every deal point on every contract and causing people to give up and move on. Protection and caution are important, but not to the detriment of advancing a career.

An artist needs to choose an attorney who has successfully negotiated entertainment contracts. Especially in major music hubs like L.A., New York, and Nashville, there are plenty of experienced entertainment attorneys. Finding one who has handled various types of contracts with multiple major labels, along with all the various aspects of an artist's career, can save time and, in the long run, billable hours. You don't want to pay for research while your attorney tries to figure out how to handle a certain contract. (You don't need to even consider an attorney until you have put in your 125 shows.)

Business Manager

Before I introduce this role, I want to lay out a threshold for when a business manager* may be needed. One person I know in this business tells artists that until he/she is doing 150 shows a year and making at least $7,500 per show in guarantees, there's no need for consideration. The bottom line of the math is until an artist is grossing over $1 million a year, entering into this relationship is likely not advantageous to either party.

Administrative roles like the business manager and attorney are important because there may be times when they are "the only adults in the room," so to speak, who can keep the artist on track and out of trouble. A business manager handles and oversees all the bookkeeping associated with an artist's career. To lay the foundation, this role sets up all the bank accounts required and then helps the artist and his/her team understand the procedures necessary to conduct business in an efficient, timely, and professional manner. This may include action items, like who needs a credit card, what those cards can be used for, and who has access to bank accounts.

A good business manager will be meticulously organized, so when an artist returns home from the road, he/she will want the income and expenses to balance, along with the necessary receipts. Because the business manager oversees all the money, forecasting will be provided based on the contracted shows, and then everyone will be kept up-to-date on the financial health of the business.

In a healthy financial situation, the artist will be paid last after all other bills have been taken care of. A very unhealthy habit for an artist is for a business manager to approve an expense he/she really cannot afford, simply by diverting money from accounts payable and putting people off. That's a recipe for disaster, and such decisions have ruined many talented careers. A smart artist will take the advice of the business manager and balance life to arrive at a healthy financial place.

To the other side of the coin, when an artist starts to make big money, he/she also has to be careful in whom trust is placed. News reports tell us that Sting lost almost $10 million and Elton John lost $29 million due to others' mismanagement.[79] Billy Joel sued his manager, which was also his brother-in-law, for. . . *wait for it* . . . $90 million in compensatory and punitive damages after issues like secret loans, double-billed music videos, and false financial statements were discovered.[80] The more money that is made and handled, the more trust is required, and the more accountability should be created.

It is always a good idea to require two signatures on any business checks. Sometimes this policy is only implemented when the check dollar amount exceeds a certain level. That level could be $500, $1,000, $10,000, or even $100,000. It is a great way to watch your back, Jack.

A business manager should provide any reports the artist and manager request, such as accounts payable and receivable, profit/loss statement for a tour and/or the entire year, balance sheet, and list of assets and the status of each. Information needs to be kept as current as is feasible so the artist and manager can make the best decisions about any next steps, while at the same time being financially responsible.

The roles of attorneys, business managers, accountants, and bookkeepers who work within the entertainment business need to be sought out versus being hired as "someone you know." (Remember, Billy Joel's scammer was his brother-in-law at the time.) Early on in an artist's career when a business manager might not be affordable, someone trustworthy with less skill may need to handle those basic financial responsibilities. These duties can fall on the artist, band members, or a member of the family. If this is your current situation, don't freak out; this is extremely common, and I would not rush to get out of that phase too soon. But like with an attorney, if the accounting is not handled properly, things can get ugly quickly. However, it's not rocket science. If an artist and a makeshift team will follow simple wisdom, as in don't spend more than you make and always set your tax money aside as it comes in, you should never have a problem.

Tour Manager

Typically, as an artist's career grows, the first person who should be hired is the tour or road manager (TM/RM)*. To reiterate this vital information from chapter eleven, a TM is in charge of everything regarding an artist's life on the road. Once the manager and booking agent have contracted a date with a promoter, the TM then takes that information and starts making the show happen. This also includes when the manager has confirmed an appearance or interview and the artist needs to be somewhere on the day of show.

For a show, the TM secures any personnel needed for a one-off date or tour—transportation, production, band, crew, and merch. He/she makes sure all the necessary elements are in place in order for the event to be successful from load-in to load-out. This includes details such as hotels, food, and per diem.* Depending on the size of the team, the TM may delegate some of these responsibilities to other personnel, but at the end of the day, the buck stops with him/her.

A TM has to communicate well and work closely with the artist and manager to ensure that anything the artist has been confirmed to do is accomplished and carried out in line with the brand and image. As an artist manager, I have gone so far as to relinquish full control on show days to the TM, meaning once the tour day starts, I don't utilize any authority to make any changes in what the TM has implemented. That, of course, does not happen until I implicitly trust the TM. The artist has to also be one hundred percent comfortable with such a decision. The other side of that handoff is I want the TM to know that if the show has a major issue, he/she has no one else to blame. Such a level of responsibility causes some people to rise to the occasion, while others cave under the pressure.

Years ago, at an outdoor show for Audio Adrenaline, a major thunderstorm was moving into the area. Just a few songs into their set, the rain began to fall and lightning started to flash. Our TM, Ryan, was also our front-of-house engineer. I looked at him and asked, "Okay, what do you want to do?" He said, "Tell them one more song." For Audio Adrenaline, the last song was always "Big House." By the time they played the last note, we were in a monsoon.

I got the band offstage and into the dressing room. One of the guys said, "Man, I can't believe the promoter stopped us." I responded with, "The promoter didn't stop you, Ryan did." When they heard that, they all stood to go back out. Fully trusting Ryan and having handed him the authority for the show, I stepped in front of the door and said, "No, we hired Ryan to make calls like this. You have three more shows this weekend. If lightning destroys all our gear, we're sunk. We're going to trust him."

Just as I was finishing my speech, Ryan came through the door with all the band's acoustic gear. A man-on-a-mission, he said, "Guys, follow me." He led us out to a covered area near the front of the venue. He already had guys pulling large tables together and duct-taping the legs to secure them. Ryan told the guys to climb up on the tables with their acoustic instruments and perform a set. The band played for about forty-five minutes with two thousand people huddled all around them, loving every minute of one of the most memorable performances they would ever experience. We also sold more merch than we did on any other show the rest of that tour.

With all the above in consideration, a strong tour manager needs the:

- Balance of a healthy personality
- Blend of being both boss and parent
- Stability of being a bridge between management and artist
- Ability to be a hardnose in one moment and have a soft heart the next

- Capacity to be both assertive and compassionate
- Capability of being quick on the feet
- Mentality of "the buck stops here"
- Broad shoulders to carry a lot of weight

A tour manager, sometimes with the help of a production manager, will advance the date with a promoter or promoter representative, on all the details required to put on a great show. Today, that finalized information is usually put into an app called "Master Tour," so everyone on the team has access to the same information. Other apps and methods also exist. Some examples of info will be:

- Bus call times
- Flight info
- Addresses for the venues
- Meal times and locations
- Wi-Fi passwords
- Hotel info
- Sound check times
- Show times
- Interviews

Even the best TMs who have published every detail before the tour starts will still have a million moving parts to deal with once the buses roll. He/she is usually the first person in the venue and the last one out at night. The TM also has to work directly with whoever is in charge of the money to make sure that anything owed anywhere is covered and to get the cash needed for tour float* (payments for any expenses that can't be put on a credit card). The TM is the main source of contact with the promoter on the day of the show, and at the end of the night, they will settle up per the contract. If there is a tour accountant, that person will handle all those responsibilities.

A TM may have one or more assistants who help handle daily tasks such as:

- Hanging signs on dressing rooms
- Laying down or putting up arrows to navigate directions to/from the bus and around the venue
- Setting up the production office (temporary dedicated office for day of show)
- Verifying catering for each meal
- Ordering after-show food (for venue or bus)
- Making sure the buses stay stocked with essentials
- Helping with runners
- Gathering up and washing towels
- Handling requests from tour personnel
- Helping with meet and greet
- Catch all for any and every detail

Production Manager

The production manager (PM)* is in charge of sound, lights, staging, video, LED, pyro, cryo, confetti—all production elements. The PM coordinates the integration of the tour gear with the venue. He/she resolves issues such as what can be hung from the roof or what needs to be supported by lifts from the ground. The PM oversees the load-in and load-out of production, working with the building rep and local crew to ensure that the day goes as smoothly as possible to get the stage set and ready by the first sound check time. Every day, the goal is an amazing show with no glitches.

Like the TM, the PM has to make a lot of advance phone calls to make sure the building has everything needed to make the show happen. Some examples are:

- Does the loading dock have enough bays to handle the number of semitrucks?
- If not, what's the best rotation for the semis to unload to keep a constant flow of setup?
- How much power does the building have, and how far away is the source from the stage?
- Is there enough room on the stage for the full production or just partial?
- If the stage isn't big enough, what level of production will be set up?
- Can the ceiling support the weight to fly lights, sound, and LED walls?
- As cases are unpacked, where will they go for the day yet be easily available at teardown?
- Is there room backstage for empty cases, or will they have to be loaded back onto the semis?

As you can see the life of the TM and PM is details, details, details.

Stage Manager

The PM works directly with the stage manager (SM)*. The SM's responsibility is exclusively tied to the staging—platforms, ramps, risers, extensions, escape hatches, quick-change compartments, scrim, and of course, band gear for both onstage and below stage. (Some major guitarists and keyboardists have their main racks of gear below the stage.) The stage manager is the boss of how everything goes and flows on the platform, including:

- Sound check times and lengths
- Making the official call on when the show starts or countdown begins
- Managing any preshow elements, such as a local radio DJ giving a welcome and announcements
- Directing any local crew used during the show regarding set changes between acts
- Making sure the stage is one hundred percent set and ready to go for the headliner
- Assuring every safety precaution possible for artists and crew

During the show, the stage manager stands side-stage, watching like a hawk for any issues. So, if the guitar player's pedalboard suddenly goes out, he/she usually knows something is wrong at the same moment the musician does. Everyone jumps into action to solve the problem as fast as possible. Some major artists or bands have specific techs for each instrument. In that case, the guitar tech handles any issues with the guitarist, like tuning in between songs, or the drum tech changes out a broken cymbal stand.

If a tour can only afford two of the positions of TM, PM, or SM, then the production manager may also act as the stage manager. After getting the production set and ready, and once sound checks begin, the role of PM may switch to SM to ensure the sets flow smoothly. At the end of the night, the hats change again, and he/she becomes the PM for teardown and load-out. To make a budget work, any combination or merging of these roles is possible. But for a large tour, the three positions of tour manager, production manager, and stage manager are crucial to producing a seamless concert. When an artist's team realizes one role or two roles are not able to effectively get all the work done for a show, that is a clear marker that the next role should be hired. For a major artist, a tipping point will come when he/she can't afford to *not* have all three of these roles in place.

Front-of-House Engineer

The front-of-house engineer (FOH)* is the sound engineer who stands behind the audio board. He/she rules in that small domain and controls what thousands of people hear. The position of the soundboard will always be determined by the size of the venue, but will be placed near the rear of the crowd in the center. In an arena, that is typically 100 to 150 feet from the stage. The FOH engineer mixes the live audio to create the most enjoyable experience possible for the fans. He/she knows when to bump up a guitar for a solo or bring down a hot track so that whatever the artist wants, the fans hear exactly that.

Usually, at the beginning of a tour, there are rehearsals where the FOH engineer will find the right levels for each song in each set, working to get the very best mix for the live show. In reality, once the tour begins and the rooms are filled with people, acoustics and frequencies change, so it takes the FOH engineer a couple of shows to dial in the right mix. But the average fan will never hear the difference in the sound. With constant advances in technology, many boards today are automated, so changes per channel per song can be programmed in advance. Once those settings are found and/or programmed, then he/she just needs to adjust to the specific nuances of each room for each show. (Note: rehearsals are pre-tour, and sound checks are day of show.)

Another role the FOH engineer may have is, if there are several acts on the tour, each one may have their own engineer who knows and runs their show. The FOH engineer will set parameters on levels for each act using a db (decibel) meter, parameters which are sometimes spelled out in the contracts. The FOH will then stand behind each act's engineer to be sure they abide by the standards set. There are times when the FOH engineer in charge has to get strong with an act's engineer who is trying to push the limits and say, "You do that again, and I'm shutting you down. No more warnings." No engineer wants to explain to their artist that the set was cut short because they were being a jerk. Finally, the full availability of production is usually only allowed for the headliner.

Lighting Director

At most shows, right next to the audio board and the FOH is the lighting director (LD)* and his/her board, running the lights for the show. Because of the level of technology available today, most light shows have been preprogrammed in tour rehearsals, matched up with the songs, and synced with both sound and video. Of course, the particular room doesn't change the lights the way it can the audio. The only variable is: if in a particular venue (as mentioned earlier), the production manager has decided the stage can't handle the entire production, that may change the lighting setup, and adjustments will need to be made. Otherwise, the LD pulls up the program, confirms all lights are functioning normally, and makes sure the automated show runs smoothly. If manual spotlights are being utilized, the LD may also direct the spotlight operators, who are typically local hands. This is known as calling the spots.*

Monitor Engineer

No, for some reason, this role is not designated by its letters like TM, PM, SM, and LD are. The monitor engineer* is responsible for mixing the show for each individual person's onstage needs, so each one onstage can hear exactly what is needed to play their instrument or sing their parts for the best possible performance. Most bands have a click track to keep everyone on tempo, which only the musicians hear, not the audience. The click track will also serve as the count-off to the song. Some artists have backing tracks from the album, which are perfectly synced so the singer or any live musicians just have to stay locked in with the track. Some artists have both the click track and the backing track (or only a count-off into the track). Sometimes, only the drummer has the click, and everyone works off of him/her for tempo.

The majority of artists today use "in-ears," or in-ear monitors, that are custom to each person onstage. The plastic casing
in each ear houses tiny speakers, yet also acts as barriers to keep
out external sound. High-end in-ears today may have as many
as sixteen drivers (tiny speakers) in each ear. Molds are cast
from each person's ears for left and right, so the fit is custom
and exact. Because each person then has his/her own set, the
monitor engineer can give everyone their own custom mix. The
bass player may want a lot more drums than the guitar player.
The singer may want more of the main melody instrument
than anything else to help stay on pitch. Some musicians may
cut another player completely out of their in-ear mix. This mix
can be as diverse as the musicians.

Some older artists still use actual monitor speakers
onstage. While in-ears were being developed in the mid-'80s,
they didn't begin to become affordable to the majority of artists
until the mid-2000s. There appears to be a slight trend today
among acoustic and jazz musicians, as well as some young
bands who use no click or backing tracks, to return to onstage
monitors for more of an organic, live-band feel.

The monitor engineer usually stands side-stage behind
his/her board to easily make eye contact with the artist and
band during the show for minor tweaks to their in-ear/monitor
mix. The monitor engineer and the stage manager are usually
paying very close attention to the artist's and musicians' every
movement and are quick to respond to any needs. As previously stated, for the sake of budget, sometimes the production
manager will double as the monitor engineer or the monitor
engineer as the stage manager.

Band Techs

Also mentioned earlier, major artists may have dedicated band techs* per instrument, but a tour may have a single backline tech who is in charge of helping set up the band's gear: drums, amps, guitars, keyboards, pedalboards, and whatever else the band needs for the live show. This person will then help out during the performance with guitar changes between songs, tuning, and troubleshooting anything that breaks, like an amp, a drumhead, etc.

Another possible tech position is someone from a local or touring production company who works with the sound equipment and helps set up the equipment, amps, FOH, and monitor boards, and then keeps them working throughout the day and during the show. This person provides support for any production issue that may arise.

This same role may be provided by a lighting company to help get all the lights flown* or ground-supported, focused, and up and running for the concert.

Lastly, a tech might also come with the video or LED wall to help run the content shown on the video screens and make sure everything works flawlessly.

All these crucial roles join forces to put on an amazing show. If everyone does their jobs right, and all the equipment functions properly, the audience never even knows all those folks are working hard behind the scenes. Unfortunately for them, the only time you do know they exist is if there's a problem.

Ownership

One final aspect of the music business to cover is ownership* of an act from a solo artist to a ten-piece band. Like many other topics we have covered, the ways this can play out are as diverse as music itself. An act, or what people perceive to be a group or band onstage, whom everyone assumes are equal owners, might actually be just one or two of the people you see. Often, onstage performers like dancers, background vocalists, or extra musicians, such as a horn section, are not owners. Members might be paid per date or be on a set salary. Sometimes a salary is set for a number of planned dates, and then if the quarter or year ends with more shows, a final settlement is paid.

The bottom line is the owner or owners, whoever and however many there may be, are taking all the risks but also all the profit. Most fans would be surprised to know the actual business setup for many of their favorite acts. Some members of an act or a band stay committed over years and are eventually brought in as an owner. The scenarios are endless.

Obviously, this is an aspect of the music business that is normally hidden from public knowledge because, to fans, who is an owner and who isn't has zero effect on their commitment to the music and the brand.

A Musical, Dysfunctional Family

Through all my years of working in this business, I've found most often, from the bus drivers to the road crew to the band, everyone becomes a family. There are artists who have had the same people on their payroll for decades. And like any family, there can be some dysfunction, and, shall we say, some quirky family members. But over time, they develop a bond that becomes tighter than most blood relatives.

A great story of this dynamic is U2. The band that formed

in Ireland in 1976 is still the same guys onstage today. Only longtime fans may know that they were originally a five piece, with Edge's brother being the second guitarist. Realizing the group didn't need two guitarists, the brother left in 1978.[81] Even with Bono's global success as the lead singer and outspoken leader, the band has always split all the profits equally with all four members and their manager.[82] This level of equality has obviously helped the band endure a lot of hardship as a tight musical community.

One story the band tells is that early on, a record label wanted to sign them if they would replace Larry, the drummer, to which Bono reportedly had one response to the execs: "Shove it."

Another amazing story of the unity of the band was prior to a sold-out show at Sun Devils Stadium in Arizona in 1987, a credible death threat was brought to the band by the FBI. The message was delivered that if Bono sang the third verse of their song "Pride (In the Name of Love)" about Martin Luther King, Jr., that he would be shot onstage. This was before metal detectors and substantial security was at every major venue.

With the authorities' recommendation to cancel the show, a decision had to be made. But the band chose to play. In the set when the song came to that verse, Bono just closed his eyes and sang the words, later saying, "I looked up at the end of the verse and I clearly wasn't dead. But not only that . . . Adam Clayton was standing in front of me." The bass player Clayton explains why he stepped in front of Bono and was willing to take a bullet for him: "It's weird what goes through your head. Or maybe not even through your head. Maybe it's just an instinctive thing of daring someone to carry out a threat like that." Edge added about Adam's show of brotherhood: "I just thought, 'That's a mate.'"[83]. . . And that's also a sign of a true band.

Of course, from rock to pop to country to jazz to gospel, there are artists who have been performing for half a century. Legendary singer and songwriter Neil Young once stated, "It's better to burn out than to fade away."[84] Ironically, the music community has so many artists who have done neither. They love what they do and who they do it with so much that they just keep going. Jazz legend Louis Armstrong said, "Musicians don't retire; they stop when there's no more music left in them."[85] . . . *Amen.*

In closing, if you are an aspiring artist, and the reason you are reading my book is to gain a better grasp of this crazy business, my hope is that you can take your God-given passion and turn it into a long-running, successful, and impactful career. The truth is I didn't really write this to share what I know as much as I did to encourage and inspire future artists, managers, record labels, booking agents, musicians, technical geniuses, administrative gurus, and crew members to carry on this incredible, beautiful gift we have been given—the gift of music and art.

This crazy business of music will always come down to one simple, game-changing, life-changing component that artists, writers, managers, and the entire positions list longs for, prays for, hopes for, and works for: The song. The song. *That* song. The song that makes a career and will stand the test of time and outlive us all.

Potential Roles and Positions Connected to the Artist Team

- Artist

- Onstage performers
- Attorney
- Accountant
- Business manager/bookkeeper
- Tour manager
- Production assistant for the TM
- Road manager
- Production manager
- Stage manager
- Front-of-house engineer
- Lighting director
- Monitor/in-ear engineer
- Live content creator
- Videographer
- Rigger
- Set designer
- Carpenter
- Backline techs
- Production techs
- Wardrobe
- Hair and makeup
- Caterer
- Nutritionist
- Bus Driver
- Nanny
- Personal trainer
- Life coach
- Road pastor

GLOSSARY OF TERMS

#

360 Deal: a full-service contract where most, if not all, of an artist's career is handled by a record label

A

A&R: referring to Artist and Repertoire department or representative at a record label. These are label reps who search for and sign new talent, while also maintaining relationships with signed artists

Add: when a new song from an artist is placed into rotation at a radio station

Advance (Advancing): process or procedure by which a road or tour manager or other artist rep contacts a promoter to take care of everything possible "in advance" of the show day; goal of taking care of details to prepare and plan for the best show possible; reduce issues and stress on day of show

Album Credits: acknowledgements on a recording of everyone who works on the project

Algorithms: when specific to music, formulas to match music to consumers on DSPs

Artist: a creative who has written or cowritten and/or performed a song or songs that other people have heard and care about

ASCAP: acronym for American Society of Composers, Authors, and Publishers; a PRO

Attorney (Music Attorney; Entertainment Attorney): lawyer who specializes and is specifically versed in all matters of the music and entertainment business

B

Background (or Backing) Vocalists: professional singers skilled at harmonies and blending their voices to support the artist's lead vocals in the songs

Backline: all the major instruments of a band—drums, guitar amps, bass amps, and large keyboard rigs; gear that creates the "back line" of the stage in front of the curtain

Band Tech: dedicated technicians for all tour gear or for specific instruments for setup, maintenance, and teardown; helps out during the performance; troubleshoots anything during the show

BGVs: acronym for background vocals

Blockchain: a digital record of transactions utilizing "blocks" of digital info linked together in a single list called a "chain," like a digital ledger system

BMI: acronym for Broadcast Music, Inc.; a PRO

Board: a recording or live audio console

Booking Agent: "the face" of the artist to the live event space, meaning concert promoters, event sponsors, and talent buyers; key gatekeepers to the financial health of an artist for this major income stream

Bounce (Bouncing the Tracks): digital term for the final stereo version of a song or album

Brand: overall vibe, feel, look, and style of an artist that is shown to the public

Brand Promotional Phase: the season when everyone involved in the artist's career promotes, promotes, promotes; entire team pushes hard, works hard, puts in long hours, and often sacrifices their personal lives

Brand Protection Phase: the season when traction happens in the artist's career, and everyone can start to hone in on all the elements of a balanced life, personally and professionally, with the goal of having as long of a career as possible

Break: the successful launch of an artist

Business Manager: a trained professional who handles and oversees all the bookkeeping associated with an artist's career; sets up all the bank accounts required; helps the artist and his/her team understand the procedures necessary to conduct business in an efficient, timely, and professional manner

Busking (Busker): live performance for tips in a busy public place such as a street corner or subway

Buy-on: also called "pay to play," where the record label, manager, and artist agree to use artist/label resources to secure a set on a tour

C

Calling the Spots: term for a lighting director directing spotlight operators

Cartage: when pro players or producers have specific personal or rented gear delivered to a session, for example, a vintage drum kit played on a song to get a certain sound

Casual Fan: a person who regularly listens to an artist's music, but the engagement stops there

Catalog: a songwriter's total works

Catering (Craft Services): on-site food prep and service on a tour date or one-off show

GLOSSARY OF TERMS

CCLI: acronym for Christian Copyright Licensing International, a privately owned company providing the same services as a PRO for public performances of songs in church and ministry-related settings

Click Track: use of a metronome matched to a music track

Count In and Out: ending dollar amount minus start-up cash amount

Cover: performance or recording of an artist doing another artist's previously released song

Cut: placement of a song on a recording project

D

Demo: short for "demonstration," a first version or first draft to hear a song in its entirety; rarely ever becomes the final version of a song

Doubling: adding a secondary melody vocal track over the original vocal track

DSP: digital streaming platforms (also known as "digital service provider") such as Spotify, Apple Music, Amazon Music, Pandora, etc.

E

Engineer: specialized technicians responsible for all aspects of recording and completing a project; the producer focuses on the creative aspect and the engineer on the technical

EP: extended play, an EP is longer than a single but shorter than an album; typically 4-6 songs

EQ (EQ-ing): the adjustment of specific frequencies to alter the sound

Exploitation: business term for maximizing an asset

F

Fan: listens to the music like a "casual fan," but also knows the basic info about an artist, not just the music, and begins to connect with the brand through albums, videos, logos, photos, etc.

GLOSSARY OF TERMS

Fiduciary: a relationship in which one party places special trust, confidence, and reliance in and is influenced by another who has a fiduciary duty to act for the benefit of the party

Flat Guarantee: a contracted and guaranteed set amount of money paid to an artist for a performance (associated with soft ticket events)

Flown: secured from the ceiling

Front-of-house Engineer (FOH): audio engineer for an artist or tour

G

Guarantee: a flat amount of money contracted for a performance

H

Hall Vend (Venue Sell): when a venue provides its own personnel to sell merch for an artist

Hard Ticket: typical tour dates where an artist is the draw, tickets are sold, and money can be made by all involved

Hardcore Fan: includes everything listed in the definition of "casual fan," "fan," and "true fan," but has some form of regular connection with the artist's music, goes to see the artist perform every chance they get, and will have a shirt for every tour the artist has done; also regular social media engagement and online fan forums

Healthy Show: a well-attended and profitable performance

Heavy Rotation: when a song is played in a repetitive pattern on a radio station

I

In-house: professionals on a staff who work solely for that company's clients

Inventory In and Out: starting and ending numbers on all merch items

295

K

Key Man Clause: one person is such a strategic relationship to the artist that he/she will follow that person to another agency

L

Legacy Fan: includes everything listed in the definition of "casual fan," "fan," "true fan," "hardcore fan," and "Superfan," but add at least ten-plus years and a PhD in fandom; the artist may know at least the fan's first name because of years of close interaction

Light Rotation: a couple of spins per day on a radio station

Lighting Director (LD): lighting director and/or designer for all lighting production for an artist or tour

Lights Down: artist's live performance onstage with the house lights down, and tour lighting is used at some level; volume and quality of sound is also brought up

Lights Up: artist's live performance onstage with the house lights up and no actual tour production used during the set; typically, no sound check is allowed, and audio levels will be much lower

Liners: brief recorded audio or video for media promotion

Liner Notes: credits for the record and acknowledgements from the artist on a project; connected to album credits

Livestream: events can be anything from full productions at a studio or venue done by professionals to a solo performance in a living room and streamed on YouTube, social media, or other online portal

Load-in: unloading vehicles for setup of production on a tour date or one-off show

Load-out: loading up vehicles with production after tear-down from a tour date or one-off show

M

Manager: the keeper of the playbook who makes sure everybody else understands the plan, the timing of that plan, and the execution of that plan for an artist's career

Market: city or area a promoter controls

Marketing: getting the word out about an artist through as many avenues as possible

Master (Mastered, Mastering): the final step in making music into a master or mastered album wherein a professional sets all the levels and parameters of how a song will sound

Medium Rotation: a few spins per day on a radio station

Merch: the branded products an artist sells on the road

Merch Manager: the person who curates, researches, and brainstorms new ideas, works with designers and vendors, gets samples, secures pricing, makes recommendations, and constantly evolves the artist's merch that's sold on the road and online; projects sales; orders, ships, and keeps inventory in stock and flowing

Metadata: data encoded on the song so devices will recognize the song; a type of digital barcode

Mic: Microphone

Mix (Mixer, Mixes, Mixing): following all recorded performances of a song; this step is locking in all the volume levels and EQs of each track in each song to finalize the sound prior to mastering the project

Monitor Engineer: professional responsible for mixing the show for each individual person's onstage needs via in-ears or stage monitors so each one onstage can hear exactly what is needed to play their instrument or sing their parts for the best possible performance

Most Favored Nations: refers to a clause in contracts, which allows all parties to receive the lowest negotiated rate by another artist to be provided to everyone

MP3: compressed digital files

N

Nashville Number System: a method of transcribing music by denoting the scale degree on which a chord is built using numbers. (For example: in the Key of C: C=1, Dm=2-, Em=3-, F=4, G=5, Am=6-, Bdim=7dim)

O

Offer: proposal made through the booking agency for an artist to perform

On Sale: a massive first push-out of tickets for tour dates to an artist's fans

One-off: single-day travel shows that are not routed into a tour, usually with no openers or production brought by the artist

Open Mic Nights: events where you sign up on the spot, get a number, wait your turn, and "go for broke" in a live performance

Overdubs: recording auxiliary parts of a song after the primary instruments are done, intended to add touches of color and nuance to the song through added guitar, keyboard, percussion, or vocals

Owner (Ownership): an artist, band member, or investor who has legal and financial control of the name, brand, and assets

Owns: refers to a promoter's market in a city or region where substantial shows are offered

P

Patch: the process of plugging in musical gear

Per Diem: daily allotted cash payment for meals given to traveling tour personnel (not local crew)

Points: a percentage of the profits the producer receives if/when an album recoups; this is stated in the contract

PR (Publicist, Public Relations Company): a professional contracted for a fee to help the artist connect with as much promotion and exposure as possible for a release, tour, or other brand announcement

Print (Printed): analog term for creating the final stereo version of a song or album

PRO (Performance Rights Organization): clearinghouse that acts as a middleman between the copyright holder (publishers and songwriters) and anyone who uses those works where "public performance" occurs

Producer: a creative responsible for shaping an artist's songs from rough demos to final release

Production Manager (PM): the professional in charge of sound, lights, staging, video, and LED—all production elements; coordinates the integration of the tour gear with the venue; resolves issues, such as what can be hung from the roof or what needs to be supported by genie lifts from the ground; oversees the load-in and load-out of production, working with the building rep and local crew to ensure that the day goes as smoothly as possible to get the stage set and ready by the first sound check time

Program (Programmed): a performance done solely using digital and sampled instruments

Program Director: the gatekeeper at a radio station who decides the songs to be played

Promoter: professional intermediaries in the live event world of music in any country where live music is played and money is made; they may work in one specific city, in a specific region of their country, or on an entire continent; they connect an artist or a tour to a specific date at a specific venue and are responsible for the contract, marketing, promotion, ticket sales, and all the logistics necessary for the event; they make money by taking the contracted cut or percentage of what is left after all expenses incurred have been recouped and the artist's guarantee or percentage has been paid

Promoter of Record: refers to the promoter who first brought an artist to a city or region; it allows for right of first refusal the next time the artist wants to come back through that market

R

Radio Edit: custom mix of a song different from the original project for the purpose of playing on the radio

Radius Clause: terms in an agreement stating an artist can't perform within a certain mile radius of a given city or market for a set amount of time

Record Label: a company that partners with artists on their music to create, record, market, and sell music; the pipeline for the artist's music to be released to the public

Recording Studio: specialized room(s) with the acoustic environment, recording console and technology, microphones, and gear necessary to record music and vocals

Recoupment: return of funds paid out on a project

Responsible Agent: like an A&R person for the booking world; ensures that someone at the agency is committed to making sure each artist has an advocate in every conversation; is the main liaison to management, labels, etc.; may have discovered the artist

Rider: an addendum to the contract that states any needs or desires of the artist on the day of performance, which are not included in the contract or technical rider

Right of First Refusal: the promoter's option to decide if they want to promote the next show after they have already brought an artist to a city or region

Road Manager (RM): similar to a tour manager, but this term is often used for those who work with lesser-known artists who do mostly soft ticket dates

Rotation: a radio station's current roster of played songs

Routing: strategic mapping out of tour dates as linear as possible to make sure drives are not too long between shows, while also not selling markets (cities) too close together

Royalty: an agreed percentage paid out from the income of an asset, in this case, songs

Runner: an on-site assistant for the day on a tour date or one-off show (name derived from running errands)

S

Scratch Vocal: temporary lead vocal track used only as a guide for players to hear the melody as they work on the song but will ultimately be replaced by the final vocal

SEO Specialist: a "search engine specialist" whose job is to make sure any search about an organization shows up, as high as possible, in the search results

Sequence: final placement or order of songs in the track listing

SESAC: acronym for Society of European Stage Authors and Composers; a PRO

Session Players: musicians required to play on the songs—rhythm section, strings, any instrument needed

Show Pay-out: Profit split per agreement on a ticketed date between the promoter and artist, following reconciliation of expenses with income and payment of any threshold guarantee (associated with hard ticket events)

Sight Reading: a performance played solely from sheet music never seen before

SKU: stands for stock-keeping unit; UPC (universal product code) for each individual merch item

Soft Ticket: an event where the artist's name normally doesn't carry the full weight of how many people attend; event will happen regardless, but the right artist can round out a fun experience and make the event memorable; there will be an overall budget, so the promoter is not working to make money from the artist or ticket sales; artist's rider still needs to be adhered to for the event, but sometimes concessions are made during negotiations between the promoter, booking agent, and manager to achieve the overall goal of the event

Song Plugger: a professional who works to connect a publisher's songs to recording artists for placement

Sonic (Sonically): musical term referring to how a song sounds

SoundCloud: online platform where an artist can post songs for free access

Spin: the single broadcast of a song on the radio

Stacking: adding multiple vocal tracks (or instruments) to create a stronger sound (more tracks created than with doubling)

Stage Manager (SM): a professional who works exclusively with staging—platforms, ramps, risers, extensions, escape hatches, quick-change compartments, scrim, and of course, band gear for both onstage and below stage; boss of how everything goes and flows on the platform

Start-up Cash: change to break larger bills

Street Team: group of fans who can be called upon to get the word out about a project, etc.

Superfan: includes everything listed in the definition of "casual fan," "fan," "true fan," "hardcore fan," and "Superfan," adding a deep well of knowledge about an artist's history and happenings, including his/her personal life; considers him/herself a resident expert on the artist

Super-heavy Rotation: when a song is at the top of the chart and played more than any other song on a radio station

Sync: short for synchronization, this is the marriage of a song to a visual image on TV, film, commercials, and games

T

Talent Buyer: secures artists or tours for a venue, event, or organization; may be someone on staff, such as for a state fair, or a contracted person for an annual convention or conference; has no risk involved (like a promoter does); point person responsible for a certain event, like a corporate function, annual party, benefit, or themed conference where entertainment is part of the program; responsible for a specific event or events as a part of their overall job, and booking artists would be one of many items on their to-do list

Technical Rider: an addendum to the contract stating the exact sound, lights, and video the artist requires

Tour Float: cash payments made for any tour/event expenses that can't be put on a credit card

Tour Manager (TM): a professional who takes care of all aspects of life on the road for a touring artist; associated with hard ticket event artists

Track: a recorded song

Tracking: the process of building all the instruments into the recorded song

Tracking Calls: communication made between the radio department at a label and radio stations to inquire about the activity of a song

True Fan: includes everything from the "casual fan" and "fan" descriptions, except now they are willing to spend money to go further into the experience by buying a ticket to go see an artist live and/or purchasing a shirt or other merch item to display their connection

U

Ultimate Support-style Stands: portable, lightweight metal equipment with foldable legs and support arms

W

Walk-ups: people who show up at the actual event and buy a face-value ticket at the box office of the venue

WAV: uncompressed digital files

Writer Room: a space provided at a record label or publisher reserved for songwriters to meet and work

Writers' Round: events where three or four songwriters are on the stage together, taking turns performing songs they've written (search "Nashville Writers Round" or "Bluebird Café Writers Round" on YouTube)

BONUS SECTION: INDUSTRY INTERVIEWS

Conversation — Mark Nicholas
Head of Publishing at Integrity Music

"The song is king. It's about telling a great story."

The following is an interview with Mark Nicholas, a friend and respected veteran who has survived and thrived for many years in the music business.

Brickell: Mark, tell us in your own words what a publisher does and your process with a song.

Mark: Publishers are in the business of intellectual property. From a broad stroke, what a publisher often does is help develop a song, see a song come to be created. While this did not used to be the case, today, the vast majority of artists are also songwriters, so we use all our resources to help them create great songs.

A lot of our work is coming alongside an artist, a songwriter, and helping them collaborate with other people, to find the right creative pairings to craft great songs. We have to understand what the artist needs and wants to say, and surround them with the right people to help those songs be born into wonderful art. And especially in Nashville, the song is king. It's about telling a great story.

With intellectual property, which is what songs are, when it comes to a master recording, an analogy would be that you would prefer to hold a broad stock portfolio versus a single share of a stock, right? You want a great song to be monetized in as many ways as possible versus landing in one fixed property. Think of it also like one store versus a franchise. We want to get as much momentum and mileage as we can from every song in our catalog.

But as a publisher, once a song is ready, we have to move from the creative into the administrative. The first thing is to register that song with the Performing Rights Organizations. Second, we send it to our sub-publisher network around the world. The song gets registered in all those other territories. Someone then has the opportunity to submit any kind of public performance of that song, theoretically, anywhere on the planet and be monetized. Those organizations hold blanket licenses with radio, TV, and streaming services with the performances being tracked, again theoretically, which assigns part of the licensing income to that song. That then flows to the publisher, and then the publisher pays out the writer's share. An interesting side fact is that when an artist performs live, the venue pays performance rights through a PRO, creating another income stream for the artist.

That's stage one—positioning the song on a global level to receive income. Next comes the opportunity for other artists to hear the song and record their own version. If so, they have to come to the publisher and request a license. We then charge applicable fees. This licensing and collection of money is also in the administrative, the stewardship aspect.

A publisher's goal is to exploit or maximize a song and find new ways for it to make money. For example, if I have a Christmas song like "Little Drummer Boy," to maximize its earnings I would send it to all the print companies for opportunities, like school bands, etc. My goal is for that song to be in every Christmas program through the purchase of PDFs of the sheet music for their bands to play.

You could also send the song to TV supervisors to hopefully get "Little Drummer Boy" placed in the field on something like a good Hallmark or Netflix Christmas movie. You could send it to advertising agencies to try and land a seasonal Target commercial. Of course, you have to have a master of that song to be able to pitch, to have a corresponding recording of it. To promote a song, you need an actual produced master. A voice memo demo from a phone is not going to work. With that, you might be able to find other people to record the song, but you can't really do anything to promote it until you actually have a master.

Brickell: Talk about an artist who records someone else's song and that process with you as a publisher.

Mark: To be clear, you can record any song that has been previously recorded without technically asking for permission. However, to do so without asking first, you're agreeing to what is called compulsory licensing. This is basically governmentally set rules, whereby you have to account to me. Let's say Joe Schmo records one of my writer's songs but doesn't come to me for a license. You then have to account for the statutory mechanical rate to me every month, or your compulsory licenses become null and void. So, it's always better if you just ask permission of the publisher, because we can't technically say no. Then you pay quarterly without accounting, for example, the number of plays on Spotify. There's no crazy math involved unless you enact the compulsory licensing.

Brickell: We've heard a lot the past few years about the MLC Act or the Mechanical Licensing Collective that's responsible for administering the new blanket compulsory license for the use of musical works by digital music services. I had the privilege of being in Washington when the bill was signed into law. Explain it from your viewpoint.

Mark: In regards to the MLC Act, it's about people not being able to even know where to go to get the license, right? Even if they wanted to. They searched and searched and searched but couldn't find it, so they just record the song anyway. So the songwriter doesn't get paid. But now there's a central location everybody can work through.

Brickell: Take us through the organizational or personnel aspect of publishing.

Mark: In a publishing company, especially a larger organization, there will be a creative director in publishing who is like the A&R person for a record label—the talent acquisition rep and also the developer. So your creative director is usually the one responsible for signing the songwriters and also for getting them into the creative ecosystem, into relationships or a group. We have one creative director in our company. Other larger companies may have two or three people in that position.

I've seen creative directors that are basically salesmen, more money oriented, but are really good. They're just out hustling. And some are like me, a glorified music fan that just wanted to be involved in the music business.

So you have a creative team and an administrative team. Depending on the size of your company, you could have somebody who might be a one-stop shop—they register the songs, send them to sub-publishers, license songs, collect royalties, process royalties, literally do everything.

Brickell: In the Christian music space where you work, how do the PROs connect to radio?

Mark: Within Christian music in the U.S., there's approximately a thousand radio stations. Of those, less than two hundred or so are actually reporting stations, the major-market stations. So that means the PROs are only tracking twenty percent of the stations on their payouts. You still have another eight hundred stations across the country who are just paying an annual license fee that goes into the general fund, but the PROs are only paying based on the reports from the top two hundred stations.

Brickell: To close, what's your advice to any hopeful songwriter?

Mark: My advice to songwriters is wherever you are and however old you are, write as much as you can on your own before you work with other people. You need to learn and know your own skill set and your own voice before you start jumping into cowrites. You'll be glad you honed your craft outside of a writer's room, especially if you move to Nashville and start cowriting. Then when that happens wherever you are, you need to find your own community, one that fits you and your primary style.

To sum up Mark's talking points, publishers:
- Are in the business of intellectual property
- Help to develop a song from creation to release
- Help find creative partnerships for songwriters
- Work the creative and administrative sides of the song
- Register songs with PROs
- Send a song to sub-publishers all over the world
- Deal with public performance licenses
- Deal with requests to record songs
- Collect money from all income streams
- Exploit songs to make maximum money
- Work with songs in all forms of print
- Work with songs in sync—film, TV, and digital platforms

Conversation — Jeff Moseley
Founder and CEO of Fair Trade Services

*"Today, a record company is not about starting a locomotive
from a standstill, but about recognizing the machines
that are already moving, where people are already saying yes,
and then adding fuel to that fire."*

Jeff Moseley is a forty-plus-year veteran in Christian music.
For twenty years and counting, I have worked closely with
Jeff. He founded INO Records in 1999 and in 2011 established Fair Trade Services, the label he owns and operates today.
They maintain a strong roster of recording artists from diverse
musical styles who are "committed to spiritual significance,
cultural relevance, and artistic excellence." I sat down with Jeff
to get his take on record labels. Here's our conversation.

Brickell: What are the right questions for an artist to ask about
a label?

Jeff: Here are the first questions an artist needs to ask themselves about a potential label:

- Does this label have expertise in my particular genre?
- Is there room for me on their roster, or has someone
  already filled the spot I offer?
- Do they have the capacity, the bandwidth, to give me
  plenty of time and attention?
- Am I just in it for the biggest check, or am I okay being
  the biggest fish in a small pond?

- Are they passionate about me and my music?
- Do they bring a specific expertise to my career?
- Do they have the finances to give my project the best shot?
- Am I okay if they have less passion, but better connections, therefore, possibly a better fit for me?

One thing I'd like to address for new artists is that they're going to look at a certain label and see the other artists on that roster and decide that label may not be the right place for them, or they'll say, "I want to be like Artist X, so I want to be at that label." When you're choosing a label, you have to look at their capabilities. You have to look at factors, such as how many artists they are capable of handling and their expertise in terms of genres. Do you want to be one of four of the same type of artist or be the only one like you for them to focus on? And going where they can write the biggest check is sometimes the absolute wrong thing to do.

Artists may find a label that has the passion for who they are, but maybe not the expertise for the artist's genre or the finances needed to break them. Or maybe someone has the expertise and the finances, but no passion for who you are and your music. Politics can be involved, but you're trying to find a place that has a passion for you.

Brickell: What do you think are the biggest differences between twenty years ago versus today in trying to break an artist?

Jeff: Well, years ago, when you tried to break an artist, a label could shoot at the target and hit the paper on the first try, and then shoot again for the rings, and eventually work your way into the bull's-eye. Today, you have to nail it the first time and be right on the money. It's super competitive. You have one try to get it right. For that reason, it's best if artist development happens off the grid, outside the label, with management first, and then we can come alongside to take it to the next level.

Brickell: I use the bank analogy a lot when I talk about the financial aspect of labels. How do you see that?

Jeff: The big difference in that analogy with a record label is if you borrow money from a bank, one way or another, you will have to pay it back. With most record labels, if they can't recoup and lose money on you, you don't have to pay them back, even if they drop you. They just cut their losses and move on.

Brickell: Talk to me about publishing inside a label.

Jeff: A publishing department could have one or two people or up to twenty, depending on the label's size. The creative director in a publishing department typically works with a songwriter to help them develop cowrites and pitch songs to other artists. Some departments are specialized to the point that there are people that do nothing but work to fit songs to potential artists looking to record.

Then there's also music administration, which secures the copyrights, makes sure the copyrights are registered with the appropriate people, and then also manages the money to be sure it flows correctly. So you've got people that help create songs, the ones that pitch the songs, and then those who administer the flow of income from songs. They typically issue mechanical licenses so that other artists can record their songs, and then make sure they collect the revenue.

As far as signing publishing with the record label, today, they may or may not require the artist to sign over all or a portion of their publishing. But placing publishing with the label is just a reality. But obviously, the more established an artist and the bigger the sales, the more weight they have to get a bigger royalty rate. They have a chance to dictate the terms, rather than the terms being dictated to them.

Brickell: What's your take on radio today?

Jeff: Radio's goal is to attract the largest amount of listeners. That's why it is still relevant and one of the most important factors for artists. With radio you are either "broadcasting" or "narrowcasting." You want the maximum amount of people gathered around a central theme or idea in a readily accessible way. Top 20 is only going to have twenty songs, not thirty. There are a limited number of opportunities to go to radio with a single for an artist on a roster.

Brickell: Talk about the primary areas of a label.

Jeff: There are four main departments: A&R, creative services, brand management, and commerce. A&R helps the artist create the record and have responsibilities they have to get right, like:

- Help the artist discover what kind of record they want to make
- Try to make a record for the artist's target audience
- Hire the right producer to best articulate the record
- Work with the artist and producer to come up with the best songs to articulate the philosophy of the record
- Oversee the project financially to stay on budget
- Oversee the project creatively to stay on brand
- Work to keep the project on the agreed timeline to hit the targeted release date

Creative services typically works with the other departments to help with anything to do with an artist's image, such as facilitating a photo shoot, video shoot, wardrobe, etc. Then we have marketing and typically what we call brand management. And then also radio and video. Marketing needs to understand the personal brand and essence of the artist, the core of who the artist is. Personal brand must filter through everything in the marketing umbrella.

In brand management, there's the marketing director or manager who works to ensure the artist's brand is best articulated through all elements of the marketing. He or she also makes sure a coherent story is being presented for people to understand and then how to tell that story correctly, to create a line behind the brand. Sometimes that is organic if you've worked with someone a lot, while other times, with a new artist, you have to figure it out. The brand manager also works with artists on buying advertising, anything to promote a record, being responsible for overall promotion.

For radio, that team will also typically:

- Make sure to choose the right radio signals for maximum airplay
- Call the stations that get maximum airplay
- Work with those stations, whether terrestrial or satellite, toward positioning on websites and promotions
- Make phone calls and personal visits to radio stations with or without the artist, depending on circumstances
- Develop and maintain a relationship with stations to understand and intersect with their needs

Brand management also works with an artist's video content, which today is a strong marketing tool as well as a monetized income stream. Someone will oversee the creation of video, help make sure they are placed in the appropriate and optimized places, and then be certain they are monetized correctly.

Another category is what I call commerce. They are the people typically involved with the DSPs, anywhere music can be monetized from the master. So there's the four areas under marketing. Some have brand managers with a team, while in some companies a department may be just one person.

In creative services, all these people will have roles that overlap, but the creative director is going to make sure that photo shoots, videos, and covers are done correctly. Then the production department is going to make sure that data is correct, that it's ingested properly at all the commerce sites, the DSPs, YouTube, etc., because we live in a world of metadata, and if the metadata is incorrect, you don't get paid.

Brickell: Define metadata for us.

Jeff: Sure, that's data that's encoded on the song so that machines will recognize the song. Like a barcode, so to speak. We also use blockchain* technology, which is a digital record of transactions. Individual records called blocks are linked together in a single list called a chain. Each transaction added to a blockchain is validated by multiple computers on the Internet. It's like a digital ledger system. While blockchain is not fully maximized yet, we can put in all the songwriters, all the splits on songs, all the percentages, who it goes to and when, and when it gets to us. So, for example, it is possible when Sirius XM plays a song one time, immediately fifty bank accounts show up with .001 cent or whatever the monetary amount might be. With this technology, you don't need accountants for the royalty departments, although you will need someone eventually to verify the distribution.

Brickell: How do you decide when to offer an artist a contract?

Jeff: So our job is to find out where there's movement, where there's excitement, where there's something local that can become regional, or regional artists that can become national. If people are voting yes already, we think we can take them to the next level. Shovel more coal into a train that's moving in the right direction. A record company has to put out a lot of energy and time on their artists.

Once an artist is signed and the journey begins, artistry doesn't typically go step-by-step. It stays on the same plane, and then jumps four or five steps, and then plateaus, and then five or six steps. You have to invest, invest, invest. And then one day, wow, we move forward incredibly. It's very different.

When all that I just described is happening, we'll sign that artist's record contract. Typically today, a record company will commit to one record with the option, or right of first refusal, for more. Meaning that if things go well on that first record, we have the option to do another record. But if the record doesn't do well, we don't have any obligation. So, a typical deal is going to be one record, plus some number of options, typically not over four.

The hardest part for any label is trying to break a new artist, the initial launch of an artist. It's the beginning of getting them going. But when it comes to an ending, typically the market tells us that it's over before we even recognize it.

Brickell: How do you decide what direction to take an artist once he or she is signed?

Jeff: A really good record company has to spend time with an artist to understand their psyche, where they are coming from, where they want to go, and what they want to do with their music. Who they feel they're called to be. You have to ask probing questions, work with them, help them arrive at that point so they can figure it all out. Rarely does an artist walk in the door fully formed and fully fashioned right. So it requires wisdom and discernment and a lot of conversation. Also, as an artist changes through the years, the person that first walked in the door will change and not stay the same. Life happens, real life changes us.

One of the biggest mistakes a record company can make is their ongoing perception of an artist. If they come in the label at twenty-three years old, they're treated as if they're twenty-three. But if they stay for years and now are a forty-five-year-old with four kids, you can't keep treating and branding that artist like they are twenty-three. Wow, that's a major mistake. There's twenty-two more years of experience you can't ignore. I've seen that happen a lot.

One thing I have said over the years—while a record company's job is to help an artist figure out who they're going to be, if at the end of the project, you see our fingerprints on a record, that means we held it too tightly. Because at our best we're editors, not creators. It's not about us, it's about the artists. And so you really shouldn't see us. We should be invisible behind them, behind the curtain. Our job is just to help guide that process, to get them where they need to go, to develop a path to success as straight and as quickly as possible. And then our job is to walk alongside, just to remind the artist where their path is. If they're veering off intentionally, okay, that's fine. But if they just veered off and didn't realize it, we need to help get them back.

In the old days, we lived in a broadcast society. Then we moved into a narrowcast society, but now we're going to a micro-cast society. An artist can no longer say, "My audience is everybody," because you ain't for everybody. If you try, you will have nobody to listen. And so you've got to narrowcast or micro-cast. And there are some norms you can't ignore. There needs to be a cohesive and coherent story throughout what you say you're going to do. If you're a middle-of-the-road artist, it would be a branding challenge to show up with tattoos and earrings in a leather jacket. That would be tough to sell. Just like if you're a rock act, you can't show up in a polyester suit.

Most artists walk in the door with dreams of a gold record with every album and single, but the number one goal of a label should be to make enough money to do their next project.

Brickell: What are the income streams for a label?

Jeff: Currently, from the sale of physical products, digital downloads, and streaming, with the latter being by far the biggest. With a traditional record deal, the label is going to fund the record, pay for making the record, for the artwork, marketing, and production. In exchange, the artist receives a royalty rate, a percentage of the sales. You have to recoup all that money, typically the entire production budget, and probably 30 or 40 percent of the marketing budget. You have to recoup at your artist's royalty rate. So, for a simple example, if $100 comes in, with your royalty rate being 15 percent, you get $15. But if the record label has spent $30 on the record, you don't get it. Because your $15 goes to repay their $30. So you still "owe" the record label $15. But if the record doesn't work, you don't have to pay the record company back the remaining $15.

So, when money comes in through, primarily streaming, we pay the artists, typically quarterly. We say, "Here's the expenses. Here's the income. Here's your percentage of the income. Let's apply your percentage of the income to your expenses. We'll write you a check, if the income is greater than expenses. We don't write you a check if it's not." In streaming, of course, we aren't paying for manufacturing of a physical product, so there's not as many deductions. So we define an album as ten to twelve masters (complete recorded songs) and an EP* as three to six songs. Because there is so little physical product, the distribution aspect today in partnering with larger companies, like a Sony, ends up being more about connecting for radio, TV, and film syncs. Today, you typically lose money on the first record and can break even on the second one, like a learning curve. But the marketplace is so crowded and so hypercompetitive that if you aren't sighted in on the target correctly on the first outing, you probably won't make it.

Brickell: So with all you just shared in mind, to you, what is a record label's *primary* role?

Jeff: In my opinion, a record company's job is to recognize talent that is being voted on out there by the public. Again, it's like a locomotive. Once a 100-ton locomotive is already going down the track, it's easier to just shovel coal in to increase speed. Today, a record company is not about starting a locomotive from a standstill, but about recognizing the machines that are already moving. Where people are already saying yes and then adding fuel to that fire. A label has to have the vision to look at a machine and foresee if and when it can get financially sustainable and, ultimately, profitable.

Scan this QR code to connect to an informative article about Jeff and me.

Conversation — Brown Bannister
Fourteen-Time Grammy-Winning Producer

"As a producer, I am a friend, counselor, therapist, and advocate."

Brown is a legend in the production world. He has won fourteen Grammy Awards and twenty-five Dove Awards and has been inducted into the Gospel Music Hall of Fame. The following are some nuggets of wisdom from a conversation we had about the world of recording.

Brickell: How do you approach producing?

Brown: Well, there's different types of producers, just like there's different types of managers and different types of artists. You know when you hear the Secretary of the Treasury or the Secretary of Defense or Secretary of State being asked policy questions, and they answer with, "I serve at the pleasure of the president." Well, as a producer, I have creative and fiduciary responsibilities to multiple parties, but at the end of the day, I serve at the pleasure of the artist I am working with at the time. For me, since day one, I have just really tried to serve the artist.

Brickell: What about the record label?

Brown: Of course, to a degree, I have to also serve the record label because they're paying for the record. At times, a producer's role is, in a sense, dealing with a sort of divided interest between the artist and the label. But, if you're trying to listen to everybody, hopefully you're going to do the right thing for all parties—manager, label, artist.

Brickell: How do you explain what a producer does?

Brown: The best analogy I have come up with over the years for what a producer does is like being a combination of the architect and general contractor of a construction project. You're working in tandem with the artist and other creatives to come up with a design for the project. You have to lay out what you envision for the artist and the project. But then you're also the general contractor, hiring all the subs, the musicians . . . you're hiring an arranger, the studio, an engineer, all the necessary creatives for the project. There's so many moving pieces to making records. Recording is a lot like building a house. Over the years, I have all these relationships with skilled craftsmen, decades of vetting people, finding the best people for a specific task. Every project is different, so you choose what people are best for the job you are doing.

Brickell: Over the years, as you have produced so many records, what has changed the most?

Brown: Obviously, technology has changed, and keeps changing, the way records are made. That's one of the major realities for producers, especially young producers. They're putting the drums together, then playing guitar, but then fixing it because they're not really a guitar player, yet they can do it and make it work through editing. Particularly young producers today are recording everything with the artists, mixing the record, doing everything. They're amazing.

But what you don't get in that situation is all the other creative minds in the room that are all working together. All agreeing: "Let's make this thing as good as we can. I've got this idea." Someone else says, "Oh wow! I never thought of that. That's a great idea. Yeah, let's go that direction." With the new approach, you don't get that community of ideas. For years, we depended on that dynamic and thought we couldn't make a record any other way. If those people didn't show up, there was no record. So I feel like that's one of the downsides of technology. Don't get me wrong—I mean there's so many upsides, it's so much more accessible for people to put out content and be producers and artists. But we just have to realize there are always going to be trade-offs either way.

Brickell: How do you approach an artist in their craft?

Brown: The other important aspect of production is deciding what the content is going to be. A lot of times, the artist is involved in the writing. But man, that is such a tricky thing to tell them that their songs are good or that they need to just keep working on their songs. That's a huge part of the process when you work with artists, publishers, and the A&R person. To sum up, the producer's job is to empower new artists, but the artist's job is to take ownership and be the CEO of his or her mission and brand. Sometimes today, an artist's voice can just become a vehicle for the producer, and the producer sees themselves as the celebrity. But again, I come back to the idea that a producer's job is to serve at the pleasure of the artist. Yes, the label matters a great deal, but because you are in the creative process, oftentimes for months, it's about the artist and the songs. As a producer, especially as a veteran in the music business, I am a friend, counselor, therapist, and advocate.

Conversation — Mike Snider
Partner with William Morris Endeavor
and Head of the Christian Division

"A good agent is part of the strategy
in an artist's career, in the mix on everything."

Mike and I have worked closely together for twenty years and counting. He is head of the Christian Music Division at William Morris Endeavor (WME). His career in the music industry spans two decades-plus, from road manager to label executive, manager, and agent. Mike and his then wife, Lisa Jones Snider, ran Third Coast Artists Agency from 1999 to 2012. TCAA was purchased by Paradigm Agency in 2012, and in 2014, he brought his team to WME. Here's my conversation with Mike.

Brickell: Let's talk about signing artists today.

Mike: The majority of the artists we work with today have a manager, but many of them also have a publisher because songwriting has become such a huge focus. WME is signing acts with publishing deals that don't have record deals. It's gotten so competitive on the agency side that we're sometimes even the first ones in on an artist before they get a record label or a manager because, if something has given an artist traction, we have to move quickly to not lose the opportunity.

Brickell: How do you see the role of agent fit with an artist's team?

Mike: I work closely with all the managers on offers and answer all the questions before they take it to the artist. I really believe that the artist, manager, and agent relationship is the most important, even though we end up spending a lot of time with an artist's record label. But the plan when a new record is released is usually straightforward—a new record, new promotion, new tour. We're constantly working as a team in a 365-day relationship.

Brickell: How do you see your relationship with the artists you represent?

Mike: Booking today is the artist's lifeblood. As an agency, we're a major part of an artist raising their family because, today, booking shows is where the most money comes from. That's changed a lot over the years. Our role for an artist is protecting their markets, working with ticket prices, ticket increases, guarantee increases, all that goes along with managing and growing that income stream.

We're also traditionally the first voice out into the world for an artist, sometimes even before the record comes out. We're the first contact, from promoters, radio stations, and incoming calls from people who hear about an artist. Before a manager or a label ever talks to anyone, we're an artist's first connection with the outside world in booking shows. Like you said, the "face" of the artist.

Brickell: How is the role of an agent different today than in years past?

Mike: A good agent is part of the strategy in an artist's career, in the mix on everything—all aspects of what the artist is doing—album releases, tours, singles, who you open for, who opens for you, who to tour with, specialty projects, marketing meetings, even the best time in the year or career to take time off. We're usually in the loop or asked to speak into these things. We've literally become an extension of the management team for many artists.

As a full-service agency, we're now often involved in talent, literary, digital, sponsorships, book deals, podcasts, and TV and film opportunities. Here in Nashville, in L.A. and New York, agents are handling things like that, even though, especially here in Nashville, managers are still heavily involved. We've moved from just booking dates to being leaned on to deliver these kinds of deals.

Conversation — Jacob Reiser
Owner of Rush Concerts

The big question I want answered when the show is over:
"Did the fans walk out happy?" That's the endgame.

I have worked with Jacob and/or his father, Cliff, through their promotions company, Rush Concerts, for my entire career. They are Ohio-based promoters who have expanded their reach nationwide and have promoted shows in every state in the United States. They have always been willing to be creative in working with artists, managers, and booking agents to help get artists on the road and doing shows to try and help launch their career as well as sustain a twenty-plus-year career.

Brickell: Tell us how you got started.

Jacob: I have been around live music and entertainment my entire life. My dad was doing concerts and promoting boxing when I was a little boy. I was always right by his side. That continued after he took a job running the only arena at the time in Columbus, Ohio. I started working alongside my dad officially in 1999, right after graduating from college. My first and only job I've had. I couldn't imagine doing anything else.

Brickell: Talk about your role and what's required of you.

Jacob: To me, the first and most important role as a promoter is talent buying. My goal is to work with the best talent and team (managers and agents). Surround myself with the best. I have learned that as a promoter you really have to sell yourself. As in any business, the music industry is about relationships, which are built over the long haul, by showing that you're honest and willing to do everything it takes to make an event successful, which is no small task.

There are so many details that make an event successful, starting with the right talent, booking them into the right room in the right city at the right time. Making sure that we have covered all the bases on advertising, pricing tickets correctly, and then making sure the day of the show is as smooth as possible. When the artist and support staff are on the road, our goal is to make them feel as at home as possible. I tell my staff that on show day no job is more important than any other job. Everything must be done to the best of our ability to make an event successful.

Brickell: What's your strategy as a promoter?

Jacob: As a promoter, I rely on managers to find talent. I don't know how to do that. I don't know what sounds good and what doesn't. I think *all* music sounds good. I can't bring in artists that I like, but rather what the public will buy tickets to see. As with managers, promoters are always trying to figure out who's going to be the "next big thing." If I'm working with a manager's number one talent, I'm going to work with their number five talent as well. I trust the managers I work with and want to help them build up their next artist to be a headlining talent.

Brickell: How do you approach working with artist managers?

Jacob: I want to hear from the manager and from the booking agent. But the first time I hear about an artist, I know I'm going to be asked to do what I do, to take a shot. And promoters are always trying to figure out who's going to be the "next big thing." When trying to book an artist, especially for the first time, you have to look at the artist's history in your region. And on a brand-new artist, a promoter can typically pay the artist a little less and make a bigger percentage to better cover the risk.

Brickell: How do you approach working with artists for the long run?

Jacob: A promoter ultimately works for the artist. To be able to work with artists for an extended period of time, you need to have their trust. You do that by maximizing ticket sales, which then maximizes what an artist can make. You have to have success.

Brickell: Talk about your process in booking artists.

Jacob: Ideally, you want to have a great reputation in the business so that agents are calling you and telling you what tours they have going out. After you have decided that you want to go after a tour, or even just a few dates on a tour, the first thing you do is find out if the venue you are wanting to go to is available. We get that on hold and then work on a deal with the venue. After we have our expenses, we are ready to make an offer to the band. It's a good idea to really pay attention to gross versus expenses. Can both the artist and promoter make money? For that, ticket prices are key. What do we think people are willing to pay? We don't want to underprice, and we certainly don't want to overprice. We try to find the sweet spot.

After we have all of our expenses and have inserted pricing into the offer, we submit the offer. Once an offer is accepted, we start working on the date. We send the artist rider to the venue and begin working on ticketing. We need to make sure that the stage is properly placed so the seating and scaling of ticket prices is spot on.

After ticketing is set, we decide on an on-sale date. When we know the on-sale date, we begin working on the budget for advertising the show. How are we going to let people know that the artist we are working with is coming to their town? Our belief at Rush Concerts is that we spend a big chunk of our advertising budget during the on-sale push. We believe that if you a sell a lot of tickets right away, you've got more people advertising by word of mouth on your behalf.

Once we are on sale, hopefully tickets are flying out the door. Next, we begin working on the advance of the show. As the promoter, we are the liaison between the building and the tour. All communication flows through us, and we want to make sure both the venue and artist are well represented.

Brickell: What about growth and gauging your success as a promoter?

Jacob: If tickets go on sale and sell out, the public's opinion is, "Oh my gosh, this artist is huge!" There's more talk, there's more people saying they couldn't get tickets than are going. So then you see the effect the next time the artist comes through. You move from a small venue to a theater. Then the theater sells out. Our next move is arenas or larger theaters. For us, the ideal time between an artist playing in a city is every eighteen months, with two years being the optimum span.

There's no template for every show. Each show is different. So you start with your marketing plan to see what worked last time and what didn't. You need to make different decisions for each city. But the big question for me as a promoter that I want answered when the show is over: "Did the fans walk out happy?" *That's* the endgame.

Conversation — Velvet Kelm
President of The Media Collective

(Key components for the media plan, biographies, and publicist role sections were created with the help of Velvet's fellow PR colleagues Jules Wortman and Sarita M. Stewart.)

"When it comes to media, it's all about the story."

The Media Collective was born in May 2002, when Velvet Kelm purchased The Resource Agency's music-based public relations division, a firm she has successfully headed since its inception in 2000. Velvet's vast experience in PR and artist management and development has made her the first stop for many big names in Nashville and beyond, by offering full- service public relations services to their clients both inside and outside the music industry. As her resume proves, she has been personally involved in the development of some of the music industry's top talent, while also branching out to offer authors and organizations the benefit of her years of expertise.

Brickell: Let's start by talking about being a publicist at a label versus independent.

Velvet: The role of public relations can be a little bit different, depending on whether you're at a label or not. I can speak to both because I was at a label for almost seven years, where I got my start. Many of the bigger artists have diversified careers—recording artist, author, endorsements, etc. An independent publicist oversees the various press pieces involved and usually has a direct, hands-on relationship with the client. They may be hired for a specific specialty, such as TV booking, or strong connections within a certain music genre, and generally can work for a myriad of clients, whether the music artist has a recording deal or is an independent artist.

A label publicist helps to secure overall publicity for artists on a label, and they drive publicity for the label as well. Labels generally hire independent publicists to generate publicity for individual artist campaigns, and the label publicist works in conjunction with the independent publicist on the artist's record-related issues.

Brickell: Talk about your role from your unique perspective.

Velvet: The music publicist is in the business of helping his or her client build their image and works to communicate the client's information and imagery to the media as well as the larger public. The value of publicity is priceless. It can be challenging for an artist to garner attention for new music due to the plethora of music being released and, as such, difficult for an artist to cut through the fragmented music marketplace without the services of a music publicist. PR is one of the most important components around an artist's music release.

A great publicist wears many hats. Here's a short list of traits that most successful publicists have:

- Excellent written and verbal communication skills
- Organized with an eye for detail
- The ability to mesh with all types of people/personalities and be a team player
- Aggressive and unafraid of being told no
- The ability to think past obstacles and apply out-of-the-box creative planning
- A mind trained to remember names and faces
- Deep media relationships formed over many years of trust-building through various projects and clients
- Well respected for their honesty and fairness to both clients and journalists
- Well-read and up-to-date on current events (both pop culture and world news)
- Competitive by nature
- Big-Picture Thinking with the ability to think through

a situation strategically, especially challenging ones; to visualize the stated media goals, no matter the stage of the campaign; and to be flexible to change the pitch angle as needed

Brickell: There are so many outlets today for you to pitch to. How do you manage that? How does that play into a new media campaign for an artist? Walk us through that process.

Velvet: Media outlets today are hit from every direction, daily, by thousands of things, and you're competing with everything else out there for their attention. One of the most annoying things for the media is when you pitch them something that just doesn't fit their outlet. It's really important to know your client and their story, but it's just as important to know the media to whom you're pitching and whether or not it's a fit. The more you can be informed about who it is you're pitching, the better. This is where crafting a media plan and blueprint comes into play, such as:

Media Plan—Once the publicist signs a client, a targeted media plan should be created. If possible, the publicist should sit down with the artist and his or her team prior to constructing the media plan. This can be helpful in gaining a better understanding of the artist and/or project. This process allows the publicist to help shape the story direction and pitch angles around the project.

A publicist develops a customized media plan based on the artist's unique strengths. The goal is to reach the widest demographic of the public possible via as many communication channels as possible. The plan should include customized pitches to journalists or media outlets most likely to publish the story.

Media Plan Blueprint—The media plan serves as a blueprint to help ensure that all team members have a shared focus on the project's rollout. The plan should look different for each project, taking into consideration various factors, such as music genre, how much recorded material has been released previously, etc. The publicist spearheads the process of preparing a tailored campaign to fit the goals and needs around the music release, tour, or event.

Brickell: Of course, there are also so many ways to communicate to the people in your outlets. How do you know who to pitch, and as long as you've been doing this, I'm sure you've had to navigate how this has changed?

Velvet: With all the different forms of communication that exist today, I have to communicate based on whom I'm reaching out to, like whether they have a preference of phone, email, text, social media, etc. Clearly when I started in the early 2000s we weren't using all these methods, so there are, of course, so many more ways to communicate today.

In terms of publicity, media is a collective term used to describe agencies of mass communication that reach an audience. This includes:

- Books

- Magazines
- Newspapers
- Podcasts
- Radio
- Television
- Internet
- Streaming platforms
- Social media

In a traditional path, the publicist serves as a buffer between the client and the media as highlighted below. They communicate the desired client message into a media pitch.

ARTIST > PUBLICIST > MEDIA > AUDIENCE

As far as knowing who to pitch, when creating the campaign/plan, media angles should include a general discussion of the press strategy as well as the story angles for focus on the media campaign. Once you know that, you can create your media targets, which is who the publicist plans to strategically approach. You generally have two groups:

Level One Media Targets: these focus on potential placements around the artist's music-release activities

Level Two Media Targets: if the artist plans to tour (whether in person or via livestreams) make sure to include a second round of media targets

Brickell: Explain why an artist needs an updated bio for every project.

Velvet: The artist's biography serves as one of the cornerstones of a publicity campaign and tells the artist's story. This entices the reader to learn more about the artist and his or her music and should convey the substance of what the artist is all about. The bio also often serves as a starting point for a journalist to obtain background content or to help generate questions for interview purposes. It's also a publicity tool, which helps the publicist (and usually others on the artist's team) to control the artist's narrative to the outside world.

Publicists are responsible for coordinating and overseeing the editorial coverage for their artists and need to ensure that all necessary materials needed to service the media are gathered *prior* to beginning the media campaign. Most common campaign assets today include:

- Artist biography
- MP3* of recorded music (album) or WAV* of recorded music (album)
- High-resolution album artwork
- High-resolution folder of publicity photos (with cited photographer credit)
- Liner notes
- Lyrics
- Streaming link to the album (SoundCloud, etc.)
- Links to videos used for premiere (unlisted YouTube links are best, as they are easy to share with media members and can be kept private)

338

Brickell: Let's talk about tour press.

Velvet: Tour press is actually one of the most cut-and-dry types of PR you can do. Because you have something very specific happening within a market, and the press in that market generally tends to respond well. For the most part, local press are going to be happy to cover an event. As with all pitches, it's important to be prepared and have core angles that fit with the local event/area, bio and photos of the talent, all details for the event (time, date, ticket info, etc.) when you are pitching.

Brickell: Tell us your thoughts about media training for an artist.

Velvet: Most people are not born knowing how to talk to the press. Sure, some are better than others, but it's always important to learn how. Even a few of the artists who are consummate pros will do media training before a press campaign begins, just to refresh. It's so important because, especially for newer artists, it really helps you to hone in on what it is you want to say. I will tell an artist, "You need to know why you're here, why you're doing this, why you've created this project, what inspired you, and what it is you want to get across. Then say it in a concise way." Media training helps an artist keep it together, know where he or she is going with their message, and stay away from any tangents.

Some media outlets can ask a crazy question, looking for a controversial answer on a topic that has nothing to do with the project. If an artist is confident on their talking points and what they need to say, then staying on track is easier. No matter what somebody asks, an artist needs to be honest, but can learn how to answer how he or she wants to answer. The key is taking the time to know what the answer is. I know the phrase "talking points" can sound programmed, but it's really just about having easy-to-remember go-to thoughts for what he or she actually wants to say that is authentic to who they are.

In general today, there are just so many controversial topics, it can be so easy to get backed into a corner. An artist needs to learn how to respond with, "I don't want to answer that" in a gracious way. If I have an artist with an interview request, where I feel like the outlet has a controversial or divisive agenda that will not be beneficial, we just say no.

Brickell: What seems to be the one thing most artists want you to land for them?

Velvet: One of the questions a lot of artists ask me is how do they get on late-night TV. Everyone always thinks it's the cool thing to get on a TV talk show. But my experience is there's no guarantee getting on one of those shows will move the needle for the artist. While it usually won't necessarily sell records or gain streams, late-night TV can give an artist credibility and potentially bring other opportunities. Note here, however, like all media, late-night TV will expect you to pitch them someone that fits their show/audience as well, so make sure you have the stats, the style, and the story to fit before you pitch.

Brickell: To wrap up, you got your degree here in Nashville, but how did you actually launch into your career at a label?

Velvet: An internship! As is so often the case with higher learning, I got more in my first year of an internship at a record label than I did in four years at a university. Even though I was at a great school, you just learn more when you're on the case. It was on-the-job training, and it just grew from there. If you show you're willing to work hard, learn, do what is asked—which in my case, early on, was a lot of mailings, errands, and faxing—you will gain respect.

NOTES

CHAPTER ONE

1. "I Can Only Imagine (2018)," The Numbers, https://www.the-numbers.com/movie/I-Can-Only-Imagine-(2018).
2. The Beatles, *The Beatles Anthology* (San Francisco: Chronicle Books, 2000).

CHAPTER TWO

3. S. D., Billboard Staff, "The 100 Best Songs of 2020," Billboard Charts, December 8, 2020, https://www.billboard.com/articles/news/list/9494940/best-songs-2020-top-100/.
4. Darby Sparkman, "Harlan Howard: The Legendary Songwriter Who Coined 'Three Chords and the Truth'" *Wide Open Country*, April 7, 2021, https://www.wideopencountry.com/harlan-howard/.

CHAPTER THREE

5. John Hamlin, "A Look at the 'Mystery' of Coldplay," *CBS News*, August 13, 2009, https://www.cbsnews.com/news/a-look-at-the-mystery-of-coldplay/.
6. Jim Beviglia, "Songwriter U: John Rich Shares His Process of Writing Hit Songs," *American Songwriter*, February 2021, https://americansongwriter.com/songwriter-u-john-rich-shares-his-process-of-writing-hit-songs/.

7. "23 Songs that Were Secretly Written by Huge Stars," *Yahoo! Best Life*, May 14, 2019, https://www.yahoo.com/now/23-songs-were-secretly-written-230028895.html.

8. Rob Tannenbaum, "Chris Stapleton on Being the Accidental Country Star: 'The Lesson Is, Make Music That You Love,'" *Billboard*, February 4, 2016, https://www.billboard.com/articles/news/magazine-feature/6866048/chris-stapleton-grammys-on-traveller-success.

9. James Pagatpatan, "The Best 15 Songs Sia Furler Wrote for Other Artists," *Spinditty*, November 20, 2021, https://spinditty.com/artists-bands/The-Best-Songs-Sia-Wrote-for-Other-Artists.

10. Jana Fisher, "16 Songs You Didn't Know Were Written by Julia Michels," *Soundigest*, February 7, 2019, https://soundigest.com/2019/02/07/songs-written-by-julia-michels/.

11. Jem Aswad, "Billie Eilish and Her Brother and Co-Writer, Finneas, Get Deep About Their Music and What's Next," *Variety*, December 4, 2019, https://variety.com/2019/music/news/billie-eilish-finneas-oconnell-songwriting-1203421768/.

12. Callie Ahlgrim, "25 songs you probably didn't know were written and produced by Billie Eillish's brother," *Insider*, October 15, 2021, https://www.insider.com/finneas-oconnell-songs-wrote-produced-billie-eilish-brother.

13. We introduced the term *cut* [or *sync*] in the in the Artist chapter as well as earlier because it's so important to understand.

14. "Whitney Houston: How Dolly Parton Song Landed on *The Bodyguard* Soundtrack," CMT, February 12, 2012, http://www.cmt.com/news/1679096/whitney-houston-how-dolly-parton-song-landed-on-the-bodyguard-soundtrack/.

15. Hope Ngo, "This Is How Much Money Dolly Parton Is Actually Worth," The List, August 11, 2020, https://www.thelist.com/177398/this-is-how-much-money-dolly-parton-is-actually-worth/.

16. "About Christian Copyright Licensing International'," CCLI, https://us.ccli.com/about-ccli/

17. "What's Behind the Boom in Song Catalog Sales? (And Should I Sell Mine?) Billboard Insights, https://static.billboard.com/files/2020/02/insights_billboard-1582901163.pdf.

18. Ben Sisario, "Bob Dylan Sells His Songwriting Catalog in Blockbuster Deal," *The New York Times*, December 7, 2020, https://www.nytimes.com/2020/12/07/arts/music/bob-dylan-universal-music.html.

19. Cathy Applefeld Olson, "Stevie Nicks Sells Majority Stake in Songwriting Catalog," *Forbes*, December 4, 2020, https://www.forbes.com/

sites/cathyolson/2020/12/04/stevie-nicks-sells-
majority-stake-in-songwriting-catalog/?sh=5373b143239a.

20. Georg Szalai, "Hipgnosis Is Buying Music Libraries—and Plans
to Spend $1 Billion More," *The Hollywood Reporter*, February 18,
2021, https://www.hollywoodreporter.com/business/business-news/
hipgnosis-songs-fund-buying-music-catalogs-plans-to-spend-
more-4133850/.

21. Ben Sisario, "Bob Dylan Sells His Songwriting Catalog in Blockbuster
Deal."

CHAPTER FOUR

22. "Dua Lipa Quotes," BrainyQuote, https://www.brainyquote.com/
quotes/dua_lipa_908961.

23. "A Legend and His Pastor—An Interview with Charlie Daniels and
Pastor Allen Jackson," Allen Jackson Ministries, January 5, 2018,
https://www.youtube.com/watch?v=oDdLs-ZOnxk.

24. "Musicians Share Their Wildest Fan Stories," *Rolling Stone*, September
9, 2013, https://www.rollingstone.com/music/music-lists/musicians-
share-their-wildest-fan-stories-14796/karmin-20893/.

25. "Little Book of a Big Year: Bono's A to Z of 2014," U2, January 1,
2015, https://www.u2.com/news/title/little-book-of-a-big-year/#.

26. Chris Stokel-Walker, "What the Murder of Christina Grimmie by
a Fan Tells Us About YouTube Influencer Culture," TIME, May 3,
2019, https://time.com/5581981/YouTube-christina-grimmie-
influencer/.

27. From Matthew 10:16.

28. Jordan Runtagh, "Heal the World: 20 Songs for a Good Cause," *Rolling Stone*, November 22, 2018, https://www.rollingstone.com/music/
music-lists/benefit-concerts-songs-good-cause-geldof-live-aid-720175/
dont-drive-drunk-by-stevie-wonder-1984-722465/.

CHAPTER FIVE

29. Martin Lewis, "No Brian Epstein? No Beatles!," *Huffpost*, April 15,
2014, https://www.huffpost.com/entry/no-brian-epstein-no-beat-
l_1_b_5155998.

30. "fiduciary relationship," Merriam-Webster, https://www.merriam-
webster.com/legal/fiduciary%20relationship.

31. "Scooter Braun Projects," Scooter Braun, https://scooterbraun.com/
music.

32. Patrick Cremona, "Elvis True Story: Who Was Col. Tom Parker?"

RadioTimes.com, June 24, 2022, https://www.radiotimes.com/
movies/elvis-true-story-col-tom-parker/.

CHAPTER SIX

33. Michael Jackson, *Moonwalk* (New York: Crown Archetype 2009),
    181.
34. Ryan Mikeala Nguyen, "What Taylor Swift's Re-recordings
    Symbolize for Music Ownership," New University, April 12, 2121,
    https://www.newuniversity.org/2021/04/12/what-taylor-swifts-re-
    recordings-symbolize-for-music-ownership/.
35. Katie Sharp, "The Story of How Lorde Became Famous Will Make
    You Appreciate Her Success Even More," MIC, December 2, 2014,
    https://www.mic.com/articles/105476/lorde-may-be-the-last-true-
    rock-star#.XjVCIJP3f.
36. James Patric Herman, "Fostering Michael Bublé's Star Power: A
    Retired Super-Producer Steps Back In," *Variety*, November 16, 2018,
    https://variety.com/2018/music/news/david-foster-interview-
    michael-buble-1203030392/.
37. "Frequently Asked Questions (FAQ)," Chart Data, https://chartdata.
    org/faq/.

CHAPTER SEVEN

38. "101 Wonderful Paul McCartney Quotes to Inspire You to Great
    Heights," The Famous People, https://quotes.thefamouspeople.com/
    paul-mccartney-2531.php.
39. Leah Scarpelli, "Goodbye, Music Tuesday: Starting Today, Albums
    Come Out on Friday," NPR, July 10, 2015, https://www.npr.org/
    sections/therecord/2015/07/10/421483599/goodbye-music-tuesday-
    starting-today-albums-come-out-on-friday.
40. Felix Richter, "The Vinyl Comeback Continues," Statista, January 12,
    2022, https://www.statista.com/chart/7699/lp-sales-in-the-united-
    states/.
41. "The Basics," DistroKid, https://distrokid.zendesk.com/hc/en-us/cate-
    gories/360001223113-The-Basics.
42. "Luminate Data," Wikipedia, https://en.wikipedia.org/wiki/MRC_
    Data.
43. "List of best-selling albums in the United States of the Nielsen
    SoundScan era," https://en.wikipedia.org/wiki/List_of_best-selling_
    albums_in_the_United_States_of_the_Nielsen_SoundScan_era.
44. Erin Carson, "Lindsey Stirling's sterling YouTube career," CNET,

September 23, 2016, https://www.cnet.com/news/lindsey-stir-ling-YouTube-singer-dancer-violinist/.

45. Kristen Philipkoski, "Why Not Winning America's Got Talent and Avoiding a Major Record Label Was Awesome for Lindsey Stirling," *Forbes,* August 31, 2015, https://www.forbes.com/sites/kristenphilip-koski/2015/08/31/why-not-winning-americas-got-talent-and-avoiding-a-major-record-label-was-awesome-for-lindsey-stirling/?sh=5f711f2873a5.

CHAPTER EIGHT

46. Casey Van Wensem, "7 Quotes from the World's Greatest Producers to Inspire You in the Studio," Sonicbids, September 16, 2016, https://blog.sonicbids.com/7-quotes-from-the-worlds-greatest-producers-to-inspire-you-in-the-studio.

47. Mr. Bonzai, "Bill Szymczyk and Joe Walsh: 'Hotel California,'" The Record Plant Diaries Project, https://www.recordplantdiaries.com/2019/03/08/bill-szymczyk-and-joe-walsh-hotel-california/.

48. Steve Harvey, "Finneas on Producing Billie Eilish's Hit Album in His Bedroom," Mix, January 28, 2020, https://www.prosoundnetwork.com/recording/finneas-on-producing-billie-eilishs-number-one-album-in-his-bedroom.

49. Annie Clements, "Everything You Need to Know about the Nashville Number System," *Premier Guitar,* April 11, 2020, https://www.premierguitar.com/nashville-number-system.

50. Emilee Lindner, "15 Weird Sound Effects Sampled in Pop, from Farts to Sneaker Squeaks & More," Billboard, August 23, 2017, https://www.billboard.com/articles/columns/pop/7940888/pop-sound-effects-samples-farts-nicki-minaj-calvin-harris.

51. Rudie Obias, "10 Hit Songs that Were Almost Never Released," Mental Floss, September 1, 2017, https://www.mentalfloss.com/article/502946/10-hit-songs-were-almost-never-released.

52. Robyn Vinter, "Spotify Hides Shuffle Button after Adele Says Albums Should 'Tell a Story,'" *The Guardian,* November 21, 2021, https://www.theguardian.com/music/2021/nov/21/spotify-hides-shuffle-button-adele-albums-should-tell-a-story.

CHAPTER NINE

53. "25 Motivational Quotes from Musicians for Musicians," MusicNotes Now, https://www.musicnotes.com/now/news/25-quotes-from-musicians-for-musicians/.

54. Rachel Grate, "4 Music Festival Statistics Defining the Industry," Eventbrite Blog, July 7, 2016, https://www.eventbrite.com/blog/4-statistics-defining-the-2016-music-festival-season-ds00/.

55. "Garth Brooks," Wikipedia, https://en.wikipedia.org/wiki/Garth_Brooks.

56. Julie Zeveloff, "There's a brilliant reason why Van Halen asked for a bowl of M&Ms with all the brown candies removed before every show," Insider, September 6, 2016, https://www.insider.com/van-halen-brown-m-ms-contract-2016-9.

CHAPTER TEN

57. "Booking Quotes," BrainyQuote, https://www.brainyquote.com/quotes/brett_young_826639?src=t_booking.

CHAPTER ELEVEN

58. "Chris Stapleton Quote," QuotesLyfe, https://www.quoteslyfe.com/quote/I-always-tell-people-The-music-s-311795.

59. "Chance the Rapper Quotes," BrainyQuote, https://www.brainyquote.com/quotes/chance_the_rapper_858341.

60. Lindsey Havens, "Chance the Rapper's 'Coloring Book' Is First Streaming-Only Album to Win a Grammy," Billboard, February 13, 2017, https://www.billboard.com/articles/news/grammys/7686341/chance-the-rapper-coloring-book-first-streaming-only-album-grammy.

61. "10 Celebs You Didn't Know Started Off as Buskers," Heart 96-107, https://www.heart.co.uk/showbiz/famous-musicians-started-as-street-artists-buskers/.

62. "Jason Isbell Quotes," BrainyQuote, https://www.brainyquote.com/quotes/jason_isbell_831868.

63. Johnny Black, "Buzzards, snakes, and a live buffalo: inside ZZ Top's World Wide Texas tour," May 15, 2014, https://www.loudersound.com/features/fly-on-the-wall-29-may-1976-zz-top-take-texas-on-the-road.

64. Ibid.

65. Ibid.

66. "George Strait Quotes," BrainyQuote, https://www.brainyquote.com/quotes/george_strait_455490.

67. "Pat Benatar Quotes," BrainyQuote, https://www.brainyquote.com/quotes/pat_benatar_439783.

NOTES

CHAPTER TWELVE

68. "Mary J. Blige Quotes," BrainyQuote, https://www.brainyquote.com/quotes/mary_j_blige_593846?src=t_music_business.

69. Hugh McIntyre, "The New Role Merchandise Plays When Creating a Musician's Brand," *Forbes*, August 17, 2017, https://www.forbes.com/sites/hughmcintyre/2017/04/17/the-new-role-merchandise-plays-when-creating-a-musicians-brand/?sh=1a3d888529e6.

70. Jim Allen, "How Artists Are Making the Most of Merch During the Pandemic, Spotify for Artists, August 13, 2020, https://artists.spotify.com/blog/how-artists-are-making-the-most-of-merch-during-the-pandemic.

CHAPTER THIRTEEN

71. "Simon Cowell Quote," AZ Quotes, https://www.azquotes.com/quote/66297.

72. Sydney Fiorentino, "Top 10 Artists that Blew Up on TikTok, Gen-Zine, January 25, 2022, https://www.gen-zine.com/the-gen/post/top-10-artists-that-blew-up-on-tik-tok.

73. Cate, "8 Things You Didn't Know About Shawn Mendes," Fame10, January 17, 2017, https://www.fame10.com/entertainment/10-popular-singers-who-were-discovered-through-social-media/.

74. "How Halsey Got Discovered—Troubled Past, Fame and Present," GemTracks, April 4, 2022, https://www.gemtracks.com/guides/view.php?title=how-did-halsey-get-discovered&id=197.

75. Lydia Sweatt, "YouTube Monetization: 5 Smart Ways to Make Money from Videos," VidIQ, April 20, 2022, https://vidiq.com/blog/post/how-to-monetize-youtube-channel-beginners-guide/.

CHAPTER FOURTEEN

76. "Quotes by Elvis," Graceland Official Website, https://www.graceland.com/quotes-by-elvis.

77. From James 4:2.

CHAPTER FIFTEEN

78. "63 Insightful Quotes by Bono that Will Prod You to Dare," The Famous People, https://quotes.thefamouspeople.com/bono-3427.php.

79. Nestor Gilbert, "10 Celebrities Who Got Scammed for Huge Money: Billy Joel & Robert de Niro Lost Millions," FinancesOnline, November 28, 2022, https://financesonline.com/10-celebrities-who-got-scammed-for-huge-money-billy-joel-robert-de-niro-lost-millions/.

80. Paul Grein, "Billy Joel Sues Former Manager for $90 Million," *Los Angeles Times,* September 26, 1989, https://www.latimes.com/archives/la-xpm-1989-09-26-ca-257-story.html.

81. Brett Milano, "Oldest Bands in Music: Acts that Defy the Laws of Age and Time," DiscoverMusic, August 10, 2021, https://www.udiscovermusic.com/stories/oldest-bands-in-music-history/.

82. Mike Stallard, "How U2's Extraordinary Team Culture Helps the Band Thrive," Connection Culture Group, November 27, 2017, https://www.connectionculture.com/post/how-u2s-extraordinary-team-culture-helps-the-band-thrive.

83. Ken Sweeney, "B-OH NO! Bono reveals that Adam Clayton tried to take a bullet for him at a US gig," *The Irish Sun,* February 23, 2017, https://www.thesun.ie/tvandshowbiz/music/622085/bono-reveals-that-adam-clayton-tried-to-take-a-bullet-for-him-at-a-us-gig/.

84. Brett Milano, "Oldest Bands in Music: Acts that Defy the Laws of Age and Time."

85. "25 Motivational Quotes from Musicians for Musicians," MusicNotes Now, https://www.musicnotes.com/now/news/25-quotes-from-musicians-for-musicians/.

THANK-YOUS

I WOULD LIKE TO THANK all of those who helped make this book possible, including, but not limited to, Robert Noland, thank you for taking all of this knowledge combined with your authenticity and experience and making into a resource for all, Dr. Stacy Brickell, Jake and Emily Brickell, Sara Brickell, Mary-Clair Brickell, Ruthie Brickell, Geri Evans, Kim Davis, Chase Swayze, Kelsey Smith, Caleb Gauntt, Callie Lutche-Argent, Donna Ecton, Brian and Toni Becker, and the BrickHouse team of assistants and artists, MercyMe, Micah Tyler, Phil Wickham, Trace Adkins, Moriah Smallbone, David Nasser, Mark Stuart, TobyMac and the Mac is back, no slack; also Mark Nicholas, Jeff Moseley, Brown Bannister, Mike Snider, Jacob Reiser, and Velvet Kelm.

When I think about all the work that has gone into the thirty-plus years I have been doing this, it makes me want to take a nap. Between the buses, the planes, the venues, the churches, the arenas, the theaters, the festivals, the label meetings, the booking agency meetings, the promoter phone calls, the sponsorship negotiations, the routing discussions, the album releases, the marketing plans, the budget meetings, the board meetings, the executive committee meetings, the chair meetings, and any other business-related endeavor, it reminds me that if you are not called to do what you are doing, then there is no way you can do it and stay sane. I always told my kids, "Figure out what you love to do, find a job where you can do that, and live within the means to which that job provides." To me that is the only way to truly live.